America in Fiction

America in Fiction

An Annotated List of Novels That Interpret Aspects of Life in the United States

Fourth Edition

OTIS W. COAN
Los Angeles City College

RICHARD G. LILLARD
Los Angeles City College

STANFORD UNIVERSITY PRESS
Stanford, California

STANFORD UNIVERSITY PRESS
STANFORD, CALIFORNIA

© 1941, 1945, 1949, AND 1956 BY THE BOARD OF TRUSTEES
OF THE LELAND STANFORD JUNIOR UNIVERSITY

PRINTED AND BOUND IN THE UNITED STATES
OF AMERICA BY STANFORD UNIVERSITY PRESS

Fourth edition, May 1956
Reprinted twice
Fourth printing, August 1957

Library of Congress Catalog Card Number: 56-7269

PREFACE

America in Fiction is designed to aid students of American civilization—adults using the facilities of public libraries, college under-
graduates, and young people in the eleventh and twelfth grades. As the
title indicates, it lists fiction only—novels, whole volumes of short
stories, or collections of digested folklore. It aims to help readers understand their country better through imaginative writings which present specific human beings in realizable situations.

The book titles are arranged in lists to correspond to the phases
and aspects of American life that have been most generously treated
by writers of fiction. The first three main lists and their subdivisions
indicate the major integrated patterns of culture through which America has passed. They are the frontier (forest, plain, and Far West),
farm and village (in five regions), and the Machine Age (industry,
labor, business and finance, the city, high society). The remaining
three lists both overlap the foregoing and stand alone as elements in
America that merit special attention; they are: politics, religion, and
ethnic minorities (especially the Indian, the Negro, and the European
immigrant). Since the subjects and issues that these six lists cover
also appear in novels with plots laid to the north and the south of the
United States, a few of the books inventoried deal with Canada or
Mexico.

Several subjects that the reader might expect to receive separate
treatment will seem to be missing until he sees that they have become
minor parts in the general scheme. The Colonial Period, for example,
does not appear as such. Books laid in pre-Revolutionary days are
distributed among several categories such as "Pioneering" and "Religion." And war, which has certainly been a topic much favored by
writers, appears under other topics. The novels of the Revolution and
the Civil War are under "Politics," and those of the World Wars
under "Industrial America." Novels of several other wars appear in
a subdivision of "Pioneering."

Many novels important in literary history are absent because they
are of interest only to specialists. A number of big names in standard
American literature are missing; either they do not fit into the scheme
of the book list or they never wrote anything that could be classified,
however loosely, as prose fiction. The lists are representative rather
than exhaustive. In general, popular but unenduring writers like G. A.
Henty, F. Marion Crawford, Joseph Altsheler, and Harold Bell Wright
do not appear; but a number of writers popular or propagandistic to

v

the point of being pulpish are included because they are the only writers to deal with certain important subjects or because they illustrate characteristic approaches to given material—Zane Grey and his *U. P. Trail,* for example, and certain proletarian novelists. By and large, novels in the list possess at least a minimum of excellence in both form and content.

We have listed the books alphabetically by author under the various topics, giving the author's dates (when available), the date of first publication, and the publisher's name if the book was first published after 1919. We have briefly annotated all titles so as to suggest the subject matter and the treatment given it. Often a title appears in two or three lists, since a solid novel may give a good picture of more than one phase of American life. Stars indicate our recommendations. We have tended to favor the substantial, realistic books over those that are romantic or sentimental or melodramatic or that merely first broke ground.

Otis W. Coan
Richard G. Lillard

Los Angeles City College

CONTENTS

AMERICA IN FICTION

PIONEERING

Pioneering has long been considered one of the major molding influences of American life. Noteworthy books make the claim that it has been the most important single influence in American history and literature. We divide novels dealing with the frontier into three sections in accordance with the type or types of pioneering activity carried on. There was a type of life, mainly in the East, in which the forest was dominant. In another era, and particularly in the great plains, grassland and the absence of trees determined the way of life. In the Far West, from the eastern foothills of the Rockies to the Pacific, the mountains and the deserts caused ways of living different from anything that had occurred farther east.

Since recent historians have shown that the Indian wars, the War of 1812, and the Mexican War all grew out of the movement westward, we have made these wars a fourth topic under pioneering.

1. TREES (THE FOREST PRIMEVAL)

Novels about the wooded frontier, from Maine to Oregon, have been numerous ever since Cooper first gave the tradition a popular start. This fiction has shown a way of life that involves log architecture, long rifles, wild meat, domestic industries, picturesque character, and Indian warfare. In general the treatment has been romantic. It has stressed young love, the ruggedness and the perils of the terrain, lucky coincidence, Arcadian homesteads, the bravado and virtuosity of the scout and trapper and settler, and the noble and feral extremes of Indian character. For a genuine understanding of an almost extinct way of living, the best presentations are careful realistic novels such as James Boyd's *The Long Hunt,* Esther Forbes' *Paradise,* and Vilhelm Moberg's *Unto a Good Land.*

ADAMS, SAMUEL HOPKINS, 1871–

Canal Town (Random, 1944). A robust tale of vigorous, colorful folk in a semi-frontier community in upstate New York during boom days on the Erie Canal.

ALLEN, HERVEY, 1899–1949

The Forest and the Fort (Farrar, 1943). First written of a series of six projected novels (to be called *The Disinherited*), this tells of frontier life among Indians and colonists in the Shawnee country of western

1

Pennsylvania. Romantic, picaresque, the book gives an epic-like treatment to the interplay of early Americans and their forest environment. **Bedford Village** (Farrar, 1944). The second volume of *The Disinherited,* set in a small village east of the present Pittsburgh, in 1763–1764.

ALLIS, MARGUERITE, 1886–

Not Without Peril (Putnam, 1941). This shows the customs, language, excitement, and hardship of pioneers in Vermont.

Now We Are Free (Putnam, 1952). The story follows Moses Cleaveland, General Rufus Putnam, and a variety of fictional persons who emigrate from Connecticut to lands of the Ohio Company in order to seize material opportunities and to realize freedom of conscience in religion and politics.

To Keep Us Free (Putnam, 1953). Continues *Now We Are Free* from 1797 to 1815, in Marietta, Chillicothe, and the settlement spelled Cleveland. Attention to the problems of changing from a territory to a state. The Blennerhassets appear, on their island, and William Henry Harrison helps during the war with Britain. Some of the research shows through.

ALTROCCHI, JULIA, 1893–

Wolves against the Moon (Macmillan, 1940). America of the Great Lakes region and Mississippi Valley, 1794–1834. The hero is a fur trader who marries a French-Indian girl and builds up a fortune.

BEST, HERBERT, 1894–

Young'un (Macmillan, 1944.) A portrait of a pioneer girl, schooled in the life of forest and field, developing from childhood to maturity. Shows a New York community on Lake Champlain changing from woods to farms in the late eighteenth century. Recreates the ways of thought and action of the common people.

BOYD, JAMES, 1888–1944

***The Long Hunt** (Scribner, 1931). One of the best stories of the frontier. A realistic story of a trapper who could not adjust himself to permanent settlement of the country. A rich background of land speculators, squatters, Indians, and frontier individualists. The main character goes on the "long hunt" from North Carolina into Tennessee.

CANNON, LeGRAND, 1899–

Look to the Mountain (Holt, 1942). A fresh, detailed story of homemaking in the New England forest between the Saco River and Lake Winnipesaukee. Shows frontier individualism gradually emerging into socialized communities. A sincere, clear transcript from the American past.

CARMER, CARL, 1893–

Genesee Fever (Farrar, 1941). Depicts land promotion and town building in the Genesee Valley, New York, in the 1790's, and the consequent moving in of settlers.

CARUTHERS, WILLIAM ALEXANDER, 1800–1846

The Cavaliers of Virginia (1834–35). About Bacon's Rebellion and about Indian fights. The author shows sympathy for the more democratic elements.

CHENEY, BRAINARD

River Rogue (Houghton, 1942). A picture of logging and rafting in the East Georgia back country. An illegitimate child whose past catches up with him struggles to adjust himself to a hard, turbulent world of raftsmen, squatters, and small farmers.

CHURCHILL, WINSTON, 1871–1947

The Crossing (1904). Of the conquest of the Northwest Territory by George Rogers Clark and his band. An epic story of the French in frontiering and "our manifest destiny" in extending our borders westward. The hero is a boy of fourteen, the plot old-fashioned.

COLBY, MERLE ESTES, 1902–

All Ye People (Viking, 1931). Presents the panorama of settlers crossing from Vermont to the Northwest Territory.

COOPER, JAMES FENIMORE, 1789–1851

The Pioneers (1823). Pictures the "Deerslayer" as an old man in New York, feeling cramped by civilization.

*Deerslayer (1841). A classic story of the woodsman of the dense Eastern forests. Forerunner of hundreds of stories.

The Oak Openings (1848). Of Michigan about 1812. A story of the flight from Indians of a family led by a bee hunter. Cooper's last frontier story.

DERLETH, AUGUST, 1909–

Bright Journey (Scribner, 1940). Growth of the small villages near the Mississippi River. Of the subjection of the Wisconsin Indians and the retirement of the French-Canadian trapper.

DONOVAN, JOSEPHINE

Black Soil (Stratford, 1930). Of Irish immigrants to Illinois, their struggles with drought, insects, and cold.

DOWNES, ANNE MILLER

The Pilgrim Soul (Lippincott, 1952). A fictionalized biography of Hayes and Dolly Copp, who pioneered around 1830 at the foot of Mount Madison, New Hampshire. A quiet, detailed, charming picture of self-subsistence and of social change over a fifty-year period.

EGGLESTON, EDWARD, 1837–1902

The Hoosier Schoolmaster (1871). An account of the life and love of a Hoosier schoolmaster in the backwoods of Indiana. Presents a "spelling bee," children's pranks, etc. Describes the activities of both schoolteacher and pupils. An American classic. Sentimental.

*The Circuit Rider (1874). A story showing the great part played by "Methodism" and other evangelical religions in the early days. Setting in Ohio in the first quarter of the nineteenth century.

The Graysons (1887). Of Illinois about 1850, with realistic portraiture of the habits of people, including the shiftless, unprogressive poor whites.

ELLIS, WILLIAM DONOHUE

The Bounty Lands (World, 1952). A careful historical novel with an antiquarian twist, laid in Ohio before and after 1800. The author faces basic matters such as land surveying, land titles, land values and money values, and legal and Indian problems.

Jonathan Blair: Bounty Lands Lawyer (World, 1954). Stimulating, with ample action, on how a frontier lawyer helped put a big tract of Ohio lands on a sound financial basis. Fresh and vigorous on land and money problems, banking hazards, and the settlers' struggle against the United States Bank.

FELTON, HAROLD W. (ed.), 1902–

Legends of Paul Bunyan (Knopf, 1947). An important collection containing more than one hundred collected tales and a bibliography.

FORBES, ESTHER, 1894?–

***Paradise** (Harcourt, 1937). A kaleidoscopic view of the seventeenth-century English Puritans being modified by the Massachusetts frontier. The characters are hardened and democratized by the frontier.

FRIERMOOD, ELISABETH HAMILTON

Hoosier Heritage (Doubleday, 1954). A local color and love story, designed for older girls, about a pioneer Indiana girl who becomes a schoolma'am in the Missouri Ozarks.

GARTH, DAVID

Fire on the Wind (Putnam, 1951). See below, p. 83.

GEBLER, ERNEST, 1915–

The Plymouth Adventure: A Chronicle Novel of the Voyage of the Mayflower (Doubleday, 1950). Inventing dialog and sensuous detail, the the author has carefully and conscientiously reconstructed the ocean voyage and the first winter in Massachusetts.

GORDON, CAROLINE, 1895–

Green Centuries (Scribner, 1941). Laid on the southern frontier just before the American revolution, this gives an account of Cherokee life and of a group of settlers who moved across the mountains into Tennessee.

HAVIGHURST, WALTER, 1901–

The Winds of Spring (Macmillan, 1940). Of pioneer days in Wisconsin from the early 1840's to about 1870. The main character is a naturalist-pioneer.

HAYCOX, ERNEST, 1899–1950

The Earthbreakers (Little, 1952). Full of credible details of settlement, work, community building, and the rise of leaders—in a coastal Oregon valley in 1845.

HÉMON, LOUIS, 1880–1913

Maria Chapdelaine: A Tale of the Lake St. John Country (translated by W. H. Blake; Macmillan, 1921). A tender, moving story of French Catholic pioneers on the Canadian forest frontier. Dramatizes the role of church and family mores.

JOHNSTON, MARY, 1870–1936

The Great Valley (Little, 1926). Set in the Shenandoah Valley in 1735.

Deals with the strong faith of the daughter of a Scotch-Presbyterian minister who endured the hardships of the French and Indian War. Gives a version of Braddock's defeat.

KROLL, HARRY H., 1888–

Rogue's Companion: A Novel of John Murrell (Bobbs, 1943). A romantic historical tale, based on research, of the dangerous and debonair ruffian of the area near Natchez, Mississippi. A fast-moving yarn of a horse stealer and slave snatcher, the founder of Murrell's Mystic Clan.

Fury in the Earth (Bobbs, 1945). An account of the effect of the earthquake of 1811–12 on various inhabitants of New Madrid, Missouri Territory. Lively, humorous, and satisfying.

KROLL, HARRY H., 1888–   , AND SUBLETTE, C. M., 1887–1939

Perilous Journey (Bobbs, 1943). A lusty, lurid novel of the Natchez Trace and the Mississippi River, this dramatizes life in the days of flatboats and pirogues, backwoods cutthroats, boastful keelboatmen, and Hoosier railsplitters. Much social history is worked in.

LAIRD, CHARLTON, 1901–

West of the River (Little, 1953). Pictures events in 1837, when the fur trade was declining, in the region around the junction of the Mississippi and the Wisconsin. Concerned with the relations of whites and Indians, of the fur company and the government. Written with historical integrity.

LANCASTER, BRUCE, 1896–

For Us the Living (Stokes, 1940). A story of pioneer days in Indiana and Kentucky. Deals with a worth-while settler's son, and also with the adolescence of Abe Lincoln.

LONGSTREET, AUGUSTUS BALDWIN, 1790–1870

*****Georgia Scenes** (1835). Many humorous and realistic sketches of backwoods types on the Southern frontier.

MATSCHAT, CECILE (HULSE)

Preacher on Horseback (Farrar, 1940). A novel of the struggle for existence on the Michigan frontier after the close of the Civil War. The main characters are a Hungarian immigrant, who later became a minister, and his wife.

MEINE, FRANKLIN JULIUS, 1896–

*****Tall Tales of the Southwest** (Knopf, 1930). Realistic stories of a varied assortment of forest and river frontiersmen, including bear hunters, levee woodcutters, county politicians, horse traders, backwoods doctors, homespun lovers, and hard-shell preachers. The tales exploit the humor in the lives and speech of non-slave-holding common men. They give an enjoyable and yet revealing picture of certain aspects of Alabama, Mississippi, Arkansas, and neighboring states when they were the Western frontier rather than the South.

MEINE, FRANKLIN JULIUS, 1896–   , AND BLAIR, WALTER, 1900–

Mike Fink, King of Mississippi Keelboatmen (Holt, 1933). A biography based on legends and folklore, this is a full account of the man who became a symbol of the prowess of the rivermen.

MILLER, CAROLINE, 1903–

*Lamb in His Bosom (Harper, 1933). A vivid, realistic account of pioneers in Georgia in the early nineteenth century. One of our finest novels. Shows the traits developed by frontier life.

MOBERG, VILHELM, 1898–

*Unto a Good Land (translated by Gustaf Lannestock; Simon, 1954). This details the experiences of a party of Swedish immigrants as they travel from New York City to forested land in Minnesota Territory, where they establish homes and spend the first winter. A substantial novel, documentary in flavor.

MOORE, IDA L.

Like a River Flowing (Doubleday, 1941). Of pioneer life in one community in North Carolina from the earliest settlement up to the coming of industrialism. Author evidences a solid knowledge of her background.

MYERS, JOHN, 1906–

The Wild Yazoo (Dutton, 1947). A humorously romantic book about the settlement of southerners in the lower Mississippi country in the early nineteenth century. A style just short of burlesque.

NORTH, JESSICA NELSON, 1906–

Morning in the Land (The Greystone Press, 1941). A novel of English immigrants who settle in Milwaukee in 1840. Gives a good picture of the times—the forcing of the Indian out of the Wisconsin Territory, the 1857 depression, the coming of better highways and railways, etc. A picture of the many Norwegians, Indians, and British who lived in the territory.

O'MEARA, WALTER

The Trees Went Forth (Crown, 1947). A quiet, convincing story of life in a logging camp as seen by a young college student working as a clerk. Good detail about Americans of Irish, French, and Finnish descent.

PAGE, ELIZABETH, 1889–

Wilderness Adventure (Rinehart, 1946). Story of an expedition from western Virginia to New Orleans, led by Captain Howard of the Virginia Rangers, in the early eighteenth century.

PAUL, CHARLOTTE, 1916–

Gold Mountain (McGraw, 1953). The author sets her story in a "mountain-enclosed area of big trees and cold rivers"—the Snoqualmie Valley in Washington Territory in the 1880's. She builds her plot around a young woman's experiences in love and schoolteaching.

PAULDING, JAMES KIRKE, 1779–1860

The Dutchman's Fireside (1831). A leisurely romantic novel, with several dramatic episodes, laid in and around Albany in the early 1750's. Introduces Dutch, Negro, Indian, urban, military, and frontier types. Gives interesting portraits of Indians as drunkards and woods fighters.

PINCKNEY, JOSEPHINE, 1895–

Hilton Head (Farrar, 1941). Based on the actual adventures of a young surgeon who went to Carolina from England by way of Barbados. Time, 1665–1686.

POUND, ARTHUR, 1884–

Hawk of Detroit (Reynal, 1939). Story of the founding of Detroit by the French under the leadership of Sieur Antoine de la Mothe Cadillac. Gives a good picture of the political and social background of French expansion in America.

RAWLINGS, MARJORIE K., 1896–1953

South Moon Under (Scribner, 1933). Unusual story of backwoodsmen of the swamp regions of Florida. Emphasizes the development of the animal senses of man. Vivid.

The Yearling (Scribner, 1938). Sentimental but effective portrayal of a family living in the Florida scrublands under pioneer conditions requiring constant struggle.

RICHTER, CONRAD, 1890–

The Trees (Knopf, 1940). Tells the story of the transition of American pioneers from the ways of the wilderness to the ways of civilization. Pictures a normal frontier family and their life from one day to the next. Shows the daily struggle for security.

The Fields (Knopf, 1946). Continues story of the family in *The Trees*. The settlement grows into a town.

Light in the Forest (Knopf, 1953). Briefly and adroitly this tale sets forth the points of view of settlers and Indians in Pennsylvania and Ohio, at the time of Bouquet's expedition in 1765 to free the captives of Indians. Excellent style.

ROBERTS, ELIZABETH MADOX, 1886–1941

The Great Meadow (Viking, 1930). Combination of poetry and prose in the setting of the heroic life of early pioneers. A significant portrayal of the mental and spiritual reactions of these settlers to their environment. Also a dramatic presentation of a love triangle.

ROBERTS, KENNETH LEWIS, 1885–

*Northwest Passage (Doubleday, 1937). A stirring re-creation of events in the life of Robert Rogers. Details of the expedition of Rogers' rangers against the St. Francis Indian village and of the fur business in the Great Lakes region. Gives detailed accounts of the life of an Indian scout and of the politics of fur trading. Deservedly popular.

ROURKE, CONSTANCE M., 1885–1942

Davy Crockett (Harcourt, 1934). One of the most delightful retellings of a choice bit of American folklore. A biography not afraid to make use of legend.

SCHLYTTER, LESLIE, 1896–

Tall Brothers (Appleton, 1941). Of lumbering in Wisconsin. Contrasts the attitudes of loggers and a Swedish couple who have come to Wisconsin to make a permanent home.

SEIFERT, SHIRLEY, 1889–

Land of Tomorrow (M. S. Mill Company, 1937). Virginians carrying on pioneering activities in central Kentucky. The story chronicles three generations of one family.

SINGMASTER, ELSIE, 1879–

A High Wind Rising (Houghton, 1942). Dealing with the relationships of Mohawks and whites, this novel depicts German immigrants in Pennsylvania and the "high wind" of Indian discontent, 1728–1755.

STEVENS, JAMES, 1892–

Paul Bunyan (Knopf, 1925). A literary and somewhat sophisticated rendering of the Bunyan legend. Racy enough to be in line with the tradition.

SWANSON, NEIL H., 1896–

The Phantom Emperor (Putnam, 1934). The fictional re-creation of an obscure incident in history concerning one James Dickson, who in the 1830's attempted to form, with Indian backing from the Great Lakes area, a vast empire in the Southwest.

The Forbidden Ground (Farrar, 1938). Old-fashioned swashbuckler of early Detroit and its environs in Revolutionary days. A romance of the fur trade.

VACZEK, LOUIS

River and Empty Sea (Houghton, 1950). Canada in 1671–78 during uneasy co-operation of royal officials, the fur company, and the Jesuits. Good on the hardships of over-winter journeys as to Hudson's Bay, on political problems raised by the traffic in brandy, and on men caught between civilizations.

WILSON, WILLIAM EDWARD, 1906–

Abe Lincoln of Pigeon Creek (Whittlesey, 1949). Based on Lincoln's life from 1816 to 1830, from the arrival of his Kentucky stepmother to his return from his trip to New Orleans. A credible, detailed, and sometimes amusing account.

ZARA, LOUIS, 1910–

This Land Is Ours (Houghton, 1940). From Braddock's defeat in 1775 to the withdrawal of the Indians across the Mississippi in 1835. A historic novel of the Northwest Territory.

2. GRASS (ALSO GRASSHOPPERS AND SOD HOUSES)

Novels depicting pioneer life on the grassy prairies and plains have been abundant since about 1890, when first-generation pioneers began to look back reminiscently. These novels narrate hard and difficult lives. They tell a grim epic, of blizzards, droughts, grasshoppers, loneliness, inevitable disasters, and bleak homesteads, although often strong characters win through. They show pioneers used to forests and ample wood painfully adjusting themselves to a woodless, semiarid region which called for dry farming, windmills, and barbed wire. The very fact that pioneering was so difficult in the region west of "the great bend of the Missouri" contributed to the development of a more realistic treatment of the frontier.

ADAMS, ANDY, 1859–

*Log of a Cowboy (Houghton, 1903). A classic account of a cattle drive from Texas north to the railroad. Realistic, rich in detail.

ALDRICH, BESS STREETER, 1881–1954

A Lantern in Her Hand (Appleton, 1928). Intimate story of the life of a pioneer woman in Nebraska who brought up her family with true courage and faith. Sentimental, but skillful enough to move the reader. Makes the farmer heroic and important.

Song of Years (Appleton, 1939). Sentimental story of pioneer hardships and of love in eastern Iowa, 1854–1865.

The Lieutenant's Lady (Appleton, 1942). Of the frontier of the 1860's. The story of an army wife, based on an actual diary.

AYDELOTTE, DORA, 1878–

Trumpets Calling (Appleton, 1938). A story of the land rush in Oklahoma, followed by detail about life on an Oklahoma homestead. Sentimental, but fairly good in detail, as are her other books.

BENSON, RAMSEY, 1866–

Hill Country (Stokes, 1928). About the building of a railroad by J. J. Hill through the Northwest, Minnesota, etc.

BOATWRIGHT, MODY COGGIN, 1896–

Tall Tales from Texas (Southwest Press, 1934). A collection of wild yarns about many matters, especially Pecos Bill.

BOJER, JOHAN, 1872–

*The Emigrants (Century, 1924). A solid, informative account of Norwegians under a medieval land system who come to North Dakota to get good soil and greater wealth.

BUSCH, NIVEN, 1903–

Duel in the Sun (Morrow, 1944). Superior to the standard Texas ranch-and-border novel. An exciting tale of ranch and town on the Staked Plains after the Civil War.

CATHER, WILLA SIBERT, 1876–1947

*My Antonia (Houghton, 1918). Story of the life of a young Bohemian girl on the prairie of Nebraska and her adjustment to its conditions. She works in the fields with the men and does not attend school. She works as a hired girl in town but gains her greatest happiness as a farm wife, mother of many children.

O Pioneers! (1913). A somewhat realistic story of a Norwegian girl running a large farm in Nebraska. It contains melodramatic incidents of the life of what may be termed "the younger set" among the pioneers.

COOPER, COURTNEY RILEY, 1886–1940

Oklahoma (Little, 1926). A romance about the homesteading rush of Oklahoma.

COOPER, JAMES FENIMORE, 1789–1851

The Prairie (1826). Describes the last days of "Leatherstocking" on the Great Plains. (The other four novels about this famous character will be found under "Trees" and "Wars of the Westward Movement.")

CUNNINGHAM, EUGENE, 1896–
Texas Sheriff (Houghton, 1934). A sample "Western story" full of excitement, thrills, and murders.

DAVIS, CLYDE BRION, 1894–
Nebraska Coast (Farrar, 1939). Story of a "York state" farmer who went West to a Nebraska frontier town with his family because he found his antiwar sentiments making him unpopular at the outbreak of the Civil War.

DRAGO, HARRY SINCLAIR, 1888–
Montana Road (Morrow, 1935). A story of hectic years in the Dakota Territory. Brings in the activities of General George Custer, the rush to the Black Hills, and the great wrong done to the Indians of the Dakota country. Shows the part played by the railroad magnates in this wrong.

ERDMAN, LOULA GRACE
The Edge of Time (Dodd, 1950). A quiet tale of sodbusters with their "sort of stubborn courage"—the women particularly—in the Texas Panhandle wheat country of the 1880's.

FERBER, EDNA, 1887–
***Cimarron** (Doubleday, 1930). A romantic story of the Oklahoma land rush and the gradual establishment of permanent civilization. The main character is a sort of superman.

FISHER, VARDIS, 1895–
***Toilers of the Hills** (Houghton, 1928). A well-rounded picture of dry farmers on the benchland of southeastern Idaho a generation ago. The husband fights the locusts, the drought, and the heat; his wife is dissatisfied. The fictional counterpart of Annie Pike Greenwood's *We Sagebrush Folks*.

GARLAND, HAMLIN, 1861–1940
Rose of Dutcher's Coolly (Harper, 1896). Of a country girl who goes to the city. The thesis is that the hard life of the farm destroys the finer things of life.

HARRIS, JOHN, 1911–   , and HARRIS, MARGARET, 1912–
Arrow in the Moon (Morrow, 1954). A good, carefully researched Western and love story that tells of a man's building up a cattle ranch in Nebraska and facing the moral problem of displacing the Cheyennes under Dull Knife.

HAVILL, EDWARD, 1907–
Big Ember (Harper, 1947). Story of daily life in southern Minnesota from 1863 on. Emphasizes the hardihood of the pioneers and their will to go on even after a terrible Indian massacre.

HOUGH, EMERSON, 1857–1923
The Covered Wagon (Appleton, 1922). Popular fiction, treating the Westward emigration. Melodrama and heroic action.

JAMES, WILL, 1892–1942
Smoky (Scribner, 1926). The horse Smoky fills an important place in the life of the cowboy, Clint. Sentimental, but entertaining.

KIRKLAND, JOSEPH, 1830–1894

Zury, the Meanest Man in Spring County (1887). An unsparing picture of an Illinois pioneer greedily acquiring property. Shows what the struggle against natural environment and fellow profit-makers does to a potentially fine man.

LANE, ROSE WILDER, 1887–

Free Land (Longmans, 1938). Deals with the struggles of a young couple homesteading in South Dakota. Describes the cold, hunger, and crop failures. These did not discourage the couple, because they were independent, heroic pioneers.

LANHAM, EDWIN M., 1904–

The Wind Blew West (Longmans, 1935). Of the booming of a new town west of Fort Worth by advertising the adventures of its settlers, hardships, Indian fights, etc. Realistic.

LEA, TOM, 1907–

The Wonderful Country (Little, 1952). A lively, well-written adventure story with a pro-Army, pro-Ranger slant, of a man who grows up in Chihuahua in post–Civil War times and later becomes a Texas Ranger.

MANFRED, FREDERICK FEIKEMA (originally FEIKE FEIKEMA), 1912–

Lord Grizzly (McGraw, 1954). A vigorous retelling of the story of Hugh Glass. Built around his wrestle with a grizzly bear, his long crawl, and his vengeful chase—during the period 1822–33.

O'MEARA, WALTER

The Grand Portage (Bobbs, 1951). A carefully documented novel, free of clichés but also slim on story, based on the life of Daniel Harmon of the North West Company during the great days of the fur business in central Canada. Readable history for the period 1800–1819.

OSKISON, JOHN M., 1874–

Black Jack Davy (Appleton, 1926). Life among Indian Territory pioneers and the Oklahoma land rush of 1889. A quarrelsome neighbor makes trouble for the settlement Indians and for Black Jack Davy's foster parents, who are newcomers.

PORTER, WILLIAM SYDNEY (O. HENRY, pseud.) 1867–1910

The Heart of the West (1907). Stories of Texas cow country, in O. Henry style.

QUICK, HERBERT, 1861–1925

Vandemark's Folly (Bobbs, 1922). A well-rounded picture of immigrants to Iowa and their establishment of permanent homes. Some realistic details; a romantic plot reminiscent of *Lorna Doone*.

Hawkeye (Bobbs, 1923). Sequel to *Vandemark's Folly;* same community, but not the same main characters.

REID, MAYNE, 1818–1883

Boy Hunters of the Mississippi (1852). Of boys who go west from Louisiana to hunt for a white buffalo. Their adventures over what is now Texas. Much data about flora and fauna. Adventures in hunting various animals.

RHODES, EUGENE MANLOVE, 1869–1940

Good Men and True (1910). A tale of cowboy ingenuity. Debunks some of the cowboy legend.

RICHTER, CONRAD, 1890–

The Sea of Grass (Knopf, 1937). Story of the struggles of the nesters to till the dry country. Shows the cattleman as knowing the uses to which the country could be put, also the waste involved in plowing this land. Pictures the contrast of a courageous husband, who wishes to grow wheat, and his wife, who longs for the city of theaters.

ROLLINS, PHILIP A., 1869–

Jinglebob (Scribner, 1927). Based on the story of a real cowboy, comparable to Adams' *Log of a Cowboy*.

ROLVAAG, OLE E., 1876–1931

*Giants in the Earth (Harper, 1927). Our finest novel of pioneering on the Great Plains. Realistic. Per Hansa, strong and resourceful, Beret, his homesick and neurotic wife, and other Norwegian immigrants open up new lands in Dakota territory. Emphasizes psychological effects of their struggle.

SANDOZ, MARI, 1899–

Slogum House (Little, 1937). A story of rip-roaring days in the sand hills of Nebraska. Slogum House is a country inn (also bawdy house) for teamsters, cowhands, etc. The Slogums, who run the house, are a gang of thieves and lawbreakers. Emphasis on the crude and hard.

SANTEE, ROSS, 1889–

The Bubbling Spring (Scribner, 1949). A yarn—idiomatic, fresh, comprehensive, flavorsome, richly anecdotal—of the cowboy's West from Montana and Dakota to Texas and New Mexico. Excellent on buffalo, cattle trailing, *remudas,* bronco busting, on the people of ranches, board towns, and the vast plains.

SCARBOROUGH, DOROTHY, 1858?–1935

The Wind (Harper, 1925). Settlers in Western Texas and their struggle against wind and drought. Melodramatic.

TAYLOR, ROSS, 1909–

Brazos (Bobbs, 1938). Tells the adventures of a Texas cattleman during the 'seventies and 'eighties. Depicts Indian fights, cattle stealing, the drives to Kansas. Realistic.

WELLMAN, PAUL ISELIN, 1898–

*Jubal Troop (Carrick, 1939). A lively tale of a man who begins as a sheepherder-cowboy, becomes a cattle baron of Texas and Oklahoma. Vivid.

The Bowl of Brass (Lippincott, 1944). Of an entrepreneur who staked out a town in western Kansas and dealt in land mortgages. "An unlovely world, people . . . primitive . . . , beastly . . . stupid."

The Iron Mistress (Doubleday, 1951). Episodes fictionalized around the life of James Bowie in Louisiana, Mississippi, and especially Texas, including the final fracas at the Alamo. Weak in characterization but good for history of the Old Southwest in the period 1817–36

WILSON, MARGARET, 1882–

The Able McLaughlins (Harper, 1923). The story of the establishment of a home in Iowa by Scotch immigrants. The struggle with nature is dominant.

WINTHER, SOPHUS, 1895–

Take All to Nebraska (Macmillan, 1936). Of a Dane who sold all his possessions, came to Massachusetts, then to Nebraska in 1898. Details the family's hardships from 1898 to 1908. Especially good in presenting the psychology of the farm boy.

WISE, EVELYN VOSE

Long Tomorrow (Appleton, 1938). In Minnesota in the 1880's, a Catholic priest becomes the leader of the community, starting co-operative undertakings.

3. MOUNTAIN AND DESERT
(ALSO PAY DIRT, COVERED WAGONS, AND ALKALI DUST)

Stories of pioneer days in the eleven western states deal with a greater variety of experiences and situations than those of the grasslands. Some matters represented in many books are the overland trips of the Spanish moving northward into California and of the easterners moving westward across the mountains and deserts; the life of the "mountain men," especially in the Rockies; the earliest Mormon settlements; the wild mining towns; the growth of settlements and farming communities, especially near the west coast; and the ever-present rancher and cowboy. A new matter for discussion and treatment was the necessary adjustment between the cultures of the Mexican-Spanish settlers and the "Yanqui" from all points east.

BAILEY, PHILIP A.

Golden Mirages (Macmillan, 1940). Tells of "lost" mines of the desert and mountain country of far Southwest. Much use is made of legends and anecdotes.

BINNS, ARCHIE, 1899–

*The Land Is Bright** (Scribner, 1939). A wagon party, in the face of many hardships, makes the trip from Independence to The Dalles, over the Oregon trail. A realistic and dramatic presentation.

You Rolling River (Scribner, 1947). Of Astoria 60–70 years ago. Vivid and interesting.

BOYD, JAMES, 1888–1944

Bitter Creek (Scribner, 1939). A boy runs away to the West and becomes a cowboy. Realistic. Revitalized version of the cowboy story because of a subtle psychological subtheme. The West of the 'eighties and 'nineties.

BRINIG, MYRON, 1900–
Wide-Open Town (Farrar, 1931). Of a wild Montana copper-mining town before the Civil War. The love story of a young Irishman and the prostitute, Zola.

BRISTOW, GWEN, 1903–
Jubilee Trail (Crowell, 1950). A big, formula-written romance laid along the route of the Spanish Trail between Santa Fe and Los Angeles in the 1840's. Overplotted. Best for social history, as of low life in Los Angeles at the time of the war with Mexico.

CANIFIELD, CHAUNCEY L., 1843–1909
The Diary of a Forty-Niner (third edition; James Ladd Delkin, 1947). A lively description of life in the diggings. Written in 1906. Combines storybook romance and the reminiscences of an old miner named Lewis Hanchett.

CATHER, WILLA SIBERT, 1876–1947
Death Comes for the Archbishop (Knopf, 1927). See below, p. 148.

CLARK, WALTER VAN TILBURG, 1909–
*The Ox-Bow Incident (Random, 1940). A searching analysis of members of a lynching party in a western Nevada town in 1885. Shows them getting into the mood to go beyond the law and reacting later to what they have done. Highly competent realism.

CLEMENS, SAMUEL LANGHORNE (MARK TWAIN, pseud.), 1835–1910
*Roughing It (1872). Amusing, exciting, and informative personal account of the silver-rush days in early Nevada. Contains vivid accounts of an overland stage trip, prospecting in the Great Basin, speculating in Virginia City, and the picturesque population of a mineral stampede.

COOLIDGE, DANE, 1873–1940
Horse-Ketchum (Dutton, 1929). A romantic tale of Death Valley and the surrounding territory, involving Indian fights, etc.
Snake Bit Jones (Dutton, 1936). Of a clever Death Valley prospector who finds much gold and outwits his opponents. A formula "Western."
The Trail of Gold (Dutton, 1937). A wild tale of a gold rush in southern Nevada, resembling the historical excitement at Tonopah and Rhyolite. A representative subliterary "Western."
Gringo Gold (Dutton, 1939). A romance of the Gold Rush to California in 'forty-nine and the adventures of Joaquín Murieta, the Mexican bandit.

CORLE, EDWIN, 1906–
Coarse Gold (Dutton, 1942). Tale of a present-day tungsten strike in a Nevada ghost town. Contrasts nineteenth-century mining camps with the contemporary ones.

CRONYN, GEORGE W., 1888–
'49, a Novel of Gold (Dorrance, 1925). A novel of the Gold Rush. An interesting tale with good local color.

DAVIS, HAROLD L., 1896–
*Honey in the Horn (Harper, 1935). Mr. Davis depicts all the types

of old-timers and homesteaders to be found in Oregon in 1906–1908. The hero, mixed up in a "jail delivery," has contacts with Indians, half-breeds, herders, horse traders, and others. Records the manners, dress, speech, and morals of the early settlers. Realistic and racy.

Team Bells Woke Me, and Other Stories (Morrow, 1953). Tales and sketches of early days in eastern Oregon. Vivid, authentic.

DE LA RHUE, TREVINO, 1894–

Spanish Trails to California (Caxton, 1937). The epic of the Spanish pioneers who traveled in covered wagons to the Pacific Coast.

DOBIE, JAMES FRANK, 1888–

Coronado's Children (Southwest Press, 1931). A collection and (in part) a retelling of many tales of "lost" mines and treasures in the desert Southwest. Richly detailed and accurate reportage on highly romantic material.

Apache Gold and Yaqui Silver (Little, 1939). Similar to *Coronado's Children*.

DODGE, LOUIS, 1870–

The American (Messner, 1934). Of a New Englander who leaves his family on a farm and joins the Gold Rush, later engaging in other frontier activities, such as homesteading.

EDGERTON, LUCILE SELK

Pillars of Gold (Knopf, 1941). Standard Western characters in a freshly presented background—the gold rushes and hazardous travel in pioneer Arizona in Civil War days.

FERGUSSON, HARVEY, 1890–

Followers of the Sun (Knopf, 1936). Shows the migration to the West of all sorts of disappointed people. Depicts the struggles of the migratory pioneer. Shows degenerate elements of frontier life—prostitution, abundance of liquor, and so on.

The Conquest of Don Pedro (Morrow, 1954). Of an immigrant from New York to New Mexico soon after the Civil War; of how he adapts himself to Mexican customs and builds up a business. Quiet, well-written.

FISHER, VARDIS, 1895–

Dark Bridwell (Houghton, 1931). A realistic story of an Idaho frontiersman who is unbelievably brutal to both human beings and beasts. A debunking of the romantic frontier.

*In Tragic Life (Caxton, 1932). A sensitive boy grows up amid brutalities in Idaho. A powerful study of a boy's reactions to the unpleasant things in a pioneer community.

City of Illusion (Harper, 1941). A melodramatic, oversexed picture of flush days in Virginia City, Nevada. Built around the rise to wealth of Sandy and Eilley Bowers. Suggests the background of life in a metropolitan mining camp.

The Mothers (Vanguard, 1943). A retelling in fictional form of the adventures and misfortunes of the Donner Party. Told from the point of view of the courageous mothers of the party.

FOOTE, MARY HALLOCK, 1847–1938

The Led-Horse Claim (1882). A trite love story with a substantial background of actual life in a mining camp. A story of illegal mining near Leadville, Colorado, in the 1870's.

FURNAS, MARTHEDITH (MRS. S. E. STAUFFER), 1904–

The Far Country (Harper, 1947). A story of the overland trip to California, told in the form of a diary, and full of details of daily existence.

GABRIEL, GILBERT WOLF, 1890–

I, James Lewis (Doubleday, 1932). Tale of James Lewis, clerk on the ship *Tonquin,* who became a hero by his tragic death. He died in blowing up the ship after a massacre by the Indians. Story of a fur-trading expedition sponsored by John Jacob Astor to Oregon in 1811.

GARLAND, HAMLIN, 1861–1940

Cavanaugh, Forest Ranger (1910). A romantic tale of an early government forest ranger, of his conflicts with the cattlemen who resist regulation, and of his outmaneuvering of the villain.

GREY, ZANE, 1875–1940

The U. P. Trail (1918). Melodramatic tale, but a sincere attempt to capture some of the epic importance of the building of the first transcontinental railroad.

GUTHRIE, ALFRED BERTRAM, 1901–

*The Big Sky (Sloane, 1947). Story of a boy who fled from the brutality of his home in Kentucky, and then became a "mountain man" of the 1840's, living ruthlessly and violently. The story shows that the violence of the early West brought neither peace nor a solution of personal problems.

The Way West (Sloane, 1949). Of an emigrant party crossing from Independence to Fort Hall and on to Fort Vancouver, Oregon, in the 1840's. Excellent for dialog, characterization, the contrast between agricultural pioneers and the earlier mountain men, and for the social history of parties on the Oregon Trail.

HARTE, FRANCIS BRET, 1839–1902

The Luck of Roaring Camp: and Other Sketches (1870). The book which first exploited local color of the early mining camps in California. Skillful in form, sentimental in selection and treatment of material.

Gabriel Conroy (1876). Harte's longest novel. Weak in construction but contains interesting character portrayals and dramatic incidents.

HAYCOX, ERNEST, 1899–1950

Deep West (Little, 1937). Of the jealousies and suspicions of neighboring ranchers in Wyoming. The old theme of cattle rustling and attempts to find the guilty party. Staccato talk and good suspense. Wyoming in 1884.

Sundown Jim (Little, 1938). About fifteen years after the Civil War in a Western territory. Ranchers are both Southerners and Yankees. Tells of their conflicts and how a U.S. deputy, "Sundown Jim," brought order.

HERSCH, VIRGINIA DAVIS, 1896–
   The Seven Cities of Gold (Duell, 1946). A story of early Spanish explorers and settlers and of the hero, Carlos, who joins Coronado's expedition in search of the seven cities of Cibola. Good romance about explorations antedating those of the Yankees.

HULBERT, ARCHER, 1873–1933
   Forty Niners (Little, 1931). A party crosses from the Missouri to Placerville, California, on the Overland Trail. A clumsy patchwork of quotations and diaries, but realistic and satisfying to read.

IRVING, WASHINGTON, 1783–1859
   Astoria (1853). A plain narrative of hardships and the endurance of the men taking part in the earliest settlements in the Northwest. Not as dramatic as the real events seem to warrant.
   The Adventures of Captain Bonneville (1856). Continues the subject matter of *Astoria*.

IRWIN, WILL, 1873–1948
   Youth Rides West; A Story of the Seventies (Knopf, 1925). A tenderfoot meets adventure in a Colorado mining camp.

JANVIER, THOMAS ALLIBONE, 1849–1913
   The Aztec Treasure-House (1890). Americans discover an Aztec city. An old-fashioned adventure story.

JONES, IDWAL, 1890–
   Vermilion (Prentice, 1947). A story of three generations in California from the early 1800's to the twentieth century. Mining, ranching, and finally grape-growing are parts of the story. Old-time romance plus a few modern touches.

JONES, NARD, 1904–
   The Petlands (Harcourt, 1931). Story of the Petland family, whose lives through three generations reflect the growth of Seattle and its back country.
   Swift Flows the River (Dodd, 1940). Beginning with the Indian massacre at The Cascades, 1856, this novel pictures early steamboating and town-building on the Columbia and Snake rivers and the gold rush to the Clearwater in Idaho.
   Scarlet Petticoat (Dodd, 1941). A popular adventure set against the background of the fur trade on the lower Columbia in the early nineteenth century.

KNIBBS, HENRY HERBERT, 1874–
   The Tonto Kid (Houghton, 1936). A lively, dry-humored story of the cowboy West. Full of action.

LAUGHLIN, RUTH, 1889–
   The Wind Leaves No Shadow (Whittlesey House, 1948; "enlarged edition," Caxton, 1952). Laid in Santa Fe and elsewhere in the Rio Grande Valley in 1821–46, and based on the life of the locally famous gambler, Doña Tules, who was for a time mistress to Armijo. Good for regional

flavor, ethnic contrasts, and political and military tensions. The second edition adds thirty pages and six years to the story and supplies a nine-page glossary.

LAURITZEN, JONREED, 1902–

The Rose and the Flame (Doubleday, 1951). A swashbuckling romance about a Spanish journey to New Mexico at the time of the Pueblo Revolt, 1680.

LEWIS, ALFRED HENRY, 1842–1914

Wolfville (1897). Stories of frontier days in Arizona as told in dialect by an old cattleman. Entertaining but conventional anecdotes.

LOTT, MILTON

The Last Hunt (Houghton, 1954). This depicts buffalo hunters in 1882, giving their reactions and those of ranchers and Indians as the buffalo go, forever: "A piece of a continent would be gone, and with it a people and the life they lived."

McNEILLY, MILDRED M., 1910–

Each Bright River: A Novel of the Oregon Country (Morrow, 1950). A period romance, laid when "54-40" was an issue, based on careful research into Indian relations, the effect of the California gold rush, the growth of settlements, and the political rise of Oregon and Washington territories.

MASON, VAN WYCK, 1897–

End of Track (Reynal, 1943). Wild days in Julesburg, Colorado, when the Union Pacific was being put through.

MEIGS, CORNELIA LYNDE, 1884–

Railroad West (Little, 1937). Deals with the laying of the Northern Pacific railroad from Minnesota to the Yellowstone and the hardships of the undertaking. The love element is between a young engineer and the sister of another engineer.

MILLER, MAY MERRILL

First the Blade (Knopf, 1938). Missouri of Civil War times and California (the San Joaquin Valley) of the 'sixties and 'seventies. The struggle with nature and predatory capitalism.

NORDHOFF, WALTER (ANTONIO DE FIERRO BLANCO, pseud.) 1858–1947

Journey of the Flame (Houghton, 1933). Deals with one of the earlier expeditions to California. Good detail of hardships of the trail.

O'CONNOR, JACK, 1902–

Boom Town (Knopf, 1938). Details life in a representative mining camp of the old days. A biography of a boom town from the accidental discovery of the lode to the advent of ghosthood. Much action and adventure, also vice and character degeneration. A "hard-boiled" novel that overstresses sex and violence but is worth while nevertheless. Laid in Arizona in the 'nineties.

O'DELL, SCOTT, 1903–

Hill of the Hawk (Bobbs, 1947). Historical novel of California in 1846 and '47, leading up to the march on Los Angeles of the Army of the West.

O'MEARA, WALTER

The Spanish Bride (Putnam, 1954). Of a Castilian girl who became mistress of a governor of New Mexico in the early 1700's. A close-up of a Spanish colony and a dramatic romance that includes fighting on the Great Plains against French from La Luisiana.

PETTIBONE, ANITA

Light Down, Stranger (Farrar, 1942). An unretouched picture of a boy growing up in a bustling frontier community in Washington Territory.

RENNIE, YSABEL, 1918–

The Blue Chip (Harper, 1954). Of boyhood in Arizona Territory copper camps. A non-formula story of mining town life and of mine profits and losses.

RHODES, EUGENE MANLOVE, 1869–1940

Copper Streak Trail (Grosset, 1922). Story of two incredibly astute Westerners who outwit their enemies and succeed in their copper-mining venture. Gunplay, and cowboy humor.

RICHTER, CONRAD, 1890–

Tacey Cromwell (Knopf, 1942). Set in an Arizona mining town about 1890. The title character is a sporting-house madam. Written in a "cold, stereopticon-slide" style.

ROSS, LILLIAN B.

The Stranger. A Novel of the Big Sur (Morrow, 1942). Of a Californian who married a Kansas spinster in the decade following the Civil War. A story of ranch life.

RUXTON, GEORGE F., 1820–1848

*Life in the Far West (1848). (Reprinted in part as **In the Old West . . .** , Macmillan, 1920). An enthusiastic Englishman's description of the delights of wide-open spaces and the mountains. Fictionalized.

SANTEE, ROSS, 1889–

Cowboy (Cosmopolitan Book Co., 1928). Story of a man going out West (Arizona) and becoming a cowboy. Delicate, but realistic.

SEIFERT, SHIRLEY, 1889–

Those Who Go against the Current (Lippincott, 1943). An adventurous, romantic fiction based on the life and times of Manuel de Lisa, fur trader on the Missouri River frontier.

SNELL, GEORGE D.

And If Man Triumphs (Caxton, 1939). Of adventure going down the Green River, of rescue by Indians, of attempts to cross Death Valley. Based on Lewis Manly's book, *Death Valley in '49*.

STEVENS, JAMES, 1892–

Homer in the Sagebrush (Knopf, 1927). Stories of jerkline teamsters, powder monkeys, and reclamation-project laborers during sprees in town, gamblers, ranch boys. Heroic evocation of the Old West in tales that are somewhat tall.

STEWART, GEORGE R., 1895–
East of the Giants (Holt, 1938). An interesting account of Yankee-Mexican relationship in the area south and east of San Francisco, after the Mexican war. A good realistic tone.

SUBLETTE, CLIFFORD M., 1887–1939
The Golden Chimney (Little, 1931). A romance of a rich Colorado silver mine.

TERRELL, JOHN UPTON, 1900–
Plume Rouge (Viking, 1942). A story of the McKenzie expedition to Oregon along the trail of Lewis and Clark. Capable realism.

WHITE, HELEN CONSTANCE, 1896–
Dust on the King's Highway (Macmillan, 1947). The story of the effort to found an inland route from Sonora to the upper California missions. The central character is a Franciscan priest, Fray Francisco Garces (1738–1781).

WHITE, STEWART EDWARD, 1873–1946
Gold: A Tale of the Forty-niners (1913). The lives of men during the Gold Rush and how many became permanent settlers.
Long Rifle (Doubleday, 1932). Historical novel about the life of a young man who inherited a long rifle from his grandfather's friend, Daniel Boone. He became a "mountain man" of the Rockies in the 1820's. Here he was captured by the Blackfeet Indians and was adopted into their tribe. Full of details about the trappers.

WISTER, OWEN, 1860–1938
The Virginian 1902). A Wyoming cowboy from Virginia wins a prim schoolma'am from Vermont. Romantic treatment of the conflict between Western and Eastern ideas. The "classic" Western story of cowboys and rustlers.

4. WARS OF THE WESTWARD MOVEMENT
(ALSO INJUNS AND GREASERS)

The pioneers didn't move forward in a vacuum. Not only did they meet the hardships described in the three lists of novels preceding this but they engaged in many wars with the Indians who disputed their progress. Also the "tide of empire" met other nationalities who had established claims to various parts of western North America. Aside from Indian wars, the most dramatic struggle was that with the Mexicans (by the Texans in 1836, and by the United States in 1848).

ARNOLD, ELLIOTT, 1912–
Blood Brother (Duell, 1947). A careful historical novel packed with action about conflict between the Army and the Chiricahua Apaches from 1856 to 1872. A clear account of certain historical events, such as the Camp Grant Massacre.

The Time of the Gringo (Knopf, 1953). Of Manuel Armijo, who became Mexican governor of New Mexico after a revolution staged by New Mexicans and Indians. Also of the repercussions set off in New Mexico by events in Texas and by the arrival of General Kearny. Sympathetic to Indians, New Mexicans, and the United States nationals. Excellent.

BAKER, KARLE (CHARLOTTE WILSON, pseud.), 1878–

Star of the Wilderness (Coward, 1942). Of Texas in the 1830's and the uprising against Mexico. Center of action, Nacogdoches.

BARRETT, MONTE

Tempered Blade (Bobbs, 1946). A well-told fictionized biography of James Bowie, using most that is known about his life in the Southwest from 1815 to 1836.

BINNS, ARCHIE, 1899–

Mighty Mountain (Scribner, 1940). A picture of the Northwest frontier. A New Englander settles in Washington Territory. The relationship of Indians and whites. Appreciation of both points of view. Indian fighting.

BIRD, ROBERT M., 1803–1854

*Nick o' the Woods (1837). A bloodthirsty story, one that helped to give Kentucky the name "dark and bloody ground." Most Indians involved are savage and uncontrollable.

BLAKE, FORRESTER

Johnny Christmas (Morrow, 1948). A serious and adventurous tale of fights against Mexicans and Indians in the Southwest between 1836 and 1846. Based on research and travel, and inspired by the sweep and history and beauty of the land.

BOYD, THOMAS, 1898–

*Shadow of the Long Knives (Scribner, 1928). Pioneers from Kentucky fight British and Indians for the old Northwest Territory.
Simon Girty (Minton, 1928). A fictional reconstruction of the life of the "white renegade" of the Revolution.

BURNETT, WILLIAM RILEY, 1899–

Adobe Walls: A Novel of the Last Apache Uprising (Knopf, 1953). A fictionalized version of Al Sieber's successful pursuit of Chief Victorio, in spite of Army incompetence, amid the savage Southwestern desert country, in 1886. A lively, graphic narrative.

CAMPBELL, WALTER S. (STANLEY VESTAL, pseud.), 1887–

Revolt on the Border (Houghton, 1938). A romance laid in and about Santa Fe in 1846. Includes scenes of General Kearny's annexation of the New Mexico territory.

CHURCHILL, WINSTON, 1871–1947

The Crossing (1904). See above, p. 3.

COMFORT, WILL L., 1878–1932

Mangus Colorado (Stein, 1931). A fictional biography of a famous Apache chieftain. Tells of his fighting a losing battle to drive the whites from Santa Rita and reunite the Indians. Shows the real Indian—his greatness and his weakness.

Apache (Dutton, 1931). The story of an uprising led by Mangus Colorado. The usual story of white double-crossing and desperate Indian fighting, ending in disaster for the Indian. New Mexico and Arizona.

COOLIDGE, DANE, 1873–1940

Comanche Chaser (Dutton, 1938). The U.S. Army, guided by scouts, pursues Indians in the Southwest. Melodramatic.

COOPER, JAMES FENIMORE, 1789–1851

*The Last of the Mohicans (1826). Perhaps the most popular of Cooper's works. Uncas, the last of the Mohicans, is a leading character. Of fights against the French and their allies in upper New York.

Wept-of-the-Wish-Ton-Wish (1827). An episode in King Philip's War, 1675–76.

The Pathfinder (1840). The father of Uncas ("the last of the Mohicans") is a leading character. Uncas and his father are notable examples of Cooper's "good Indians."

Wyandotte (1843). Wyandotte is a more realistic Indian than Cooper's usual portrait. Set in upper New York at the beginning of the Revolution.

DAVIS, JAMES F., 1870–

*The Road to San Jacinto (Bobbs, 1936). Romantic story of heroism as far as the main character is concerned, but good feeling for the plight of the Mexicans and a realistic account of the massacre at San Jacinto. Upholds Houston in the Houston *vs.* Austin strife.

DERLETH, AUGUST, 1909–

Wind over Wisconsin (Scribner, 1938). A careful novel centering around Black Hawk and his "war" in Illinois, Wisconsin, and Washington, D.C., for the lands promised the Indian.

DUFFUS, ROBERT L., 1888–

Journada (Covici, 1935). Set in the Mexican War, deals with lovers who have to make La Journada alone after being separated from their wagon train. Describes a Comanche attack. Much background material, Spanish dancing, frontier life, homicide. By the author of the nonfiction *Santa Fe Trail*.

EDMONDS, WALTER DUMAUX, 1903–

*Drums along the Mohawk (Little, 1936). A pro-settler novel of the Revolution, which includes scenes of Indian raids in the Mohawk, especially those led by Walter Butler.

In the Hands of the Senecas (Little, 1947). A brief novel about captivity among eighteenth-century Indians. The characters are believable and the story full of suspense.

FAST, HOWARD MELVIN, 1914–

*The Last Frontier (Duell, 1941). A novelized history of the flight of the Northern Cheyennes from Oklahoma to Montana, of the series of whippings they gave the United States Army, of the cold, slow cruelty with which the whites retaliated. A deeply moving picture of a simple people fighting for their homeland.

FOREMAN, LEONARD LONDON, 1901–

The Road to San Jacinto (Dutton, 1943). A romantic tale of the Texas War of Independence. Contains more down-to-earth detail than does the book by James F. Davis.

FREY, RUBY FRAZIER PARSONS

Red Morning (Putnam, 1946). A vivid story of pioneering on the Monongahela about the time of the French and Indian War, with a Scotswoman as the protagonist.

FULLER, IOLA

The Shining Trail (Duell, 1943). Emphasizes the tragedy of the Indians' position in the Black Hawk War.

GORMAN, HERBERT SHERMAN, 1893–

The Wine of San Lorenzo (Farrar, 1945). This romance of the Mexican War presents well-studied social and military history. It contrasts Anglo-Saxon and Latin cultures, and portrays General Santa Anna, old-style hacienda life, and the battles fought by Winfield Scott and Zachary Taylor.

KREY, LAURA (SMITH)

On the Long Tide (Houghton, 1940). Historical novel of the fight for the independence of Texas.

LAIRD, CHARLTON, 1901–

Thunder on the River (Little, 1949). Realistic, strong-flavored, and concerned with the struggles between settlers and Indians at the time of the Black Hawk War and the decline of the Sauk Indians. Interesting for its social history of whites and Sauks.

LEA, TOM, 1907–

The Wonderful Country (Little, 1952). See above, p. 11.

MIERS, EARL SCHENCK, 1910–

Valley in Arms (Westminster Press, 1943). Of early settlement in Connecticut and Indian fighting.

O'CONNOR, JACK, 1902–

Conquest: A Novel of the Old Southwest (Harper, 1930). Of Anglo-American domination in Arizona and of a brave villain, killer of many Indians and a conqueror of his environment.

PARKHILL, FORBES, 1892–

Troopers West (Farrar, 1945). Story of violence and of individual character reactions to unusual situations. Critical of the type of person selected for the Indian service. Time, 1879.

REMINGTON, FREDERIC, 1861–1909

John Ermine of the Yellowstone (1902). Popular fiction of a young scout for United States troops sent to subdue the Sioux Indians. Illustrated by the author.

ROBERTS, RICHARD EMERY, 1903–

The Gilded Rooster (Putnam, 1947). Of physical and spiritual conflicts among four persons confined by hostile Sioux in Wyoming during the Civil War. Creates a vigorous mountain man, a cruel captain, and other characters.

SABIN, EDWIN L., 1870–

On the Plains with Custer (Lippincott, 1913). Tells of a youth who is captured by the Indians and is rescued by Custer. He then serves in the "fighting seventh cavalry" as bugler. Facile romance.

SCHUMANN, MARY

*Strife before Dawn (Dial Press, 1939). A conscientious, adventurous account of the struggle for the old Northwest Territory. Of Pontiac's War, Dunmore's War, and the Revolution. Introduces several historical characters, including Simon Girty, Henry Hamilton the hairbuyer, George R. Clark, and the famous half-breed, Logan. Imaginative use of much source material.

SEARS, CLARA ENDICOTT, 1863–

The Great Powwow (Houghton, 1934). King Philip's War in early Massachusetts, 1675–76. Considered historically accurate.

SHEPARD, ODELL, 1884–   and SHEPARD, WILLARD O.

Holdfast Gaines (Macmillan, 1946). A novel of American expansion westward, 1780–1815. Holdfast Gaines, a Mohegan adopted by a white family, is the central character. A twentieth-century "Cooper" story.

SIMMS, WILLIAM GILMORE, 1806–1870

*The Yemassee (1835). War between the English and the Yemassee. Notable Indian characters.

STONE, GRACE Z., 1896–

The Cold Journey (Morrow, 1934). A realistically told history that deals with the attack on a Massachusetts village by the French and Indians in 1704 and of the journey through the snow to Quebec by the inhabitants and captors of the village. Deals with the fortunes of the captives when they reached Canada.

STOVER, HERBERT E.

Song of the Susquehanna (Dodd, 1949). Good for a picture of Lancaster, Pennsylvania, as a trading post and on campaigns and battles during the French and Indian War. Colonel Bouquet, John Bartram, and other personages appear.

SWANSON, NEIL H., 1896–

Judas Tree (Putnam, 1933). A historical novel about the siege of Fort Pitt by the Indians and the dauntless Swiss commandant who saved the fort. Details of the Indian tortures of the time.

TURNBULL, AGNES SLIGH, 1888–

The Day Must Dawn (Macmillan, 1942). Western Pennsylvania during the Revolution. Good detail on pioneer life and Indian fighting.

WARREN, CHARLES MARQUIS, 1912–

Only the Valiant (Macmillan, 1943). A psychological, dramatic story of a small army detail fighting hopelessly against the Apaches.

WHITE, STEWART EDWARD, 1873–1946

Westerners (Doubleday, 1901). Wars with the Sioux on the Great Plains.

WILDER, ROBERT, 1901–

Bright Feather (Putnam, 1948). A story of the bloody fights between settlers and Seminoles on the Florida frontier. Authentic military and social history compounded with the gusty romance now standard in historical novels.

FARM AND VILLAGE LIFE

In each section of the country after the early stages of exploration and settlement the pioneer way of life was succeeded by "farm and village life." This stage, which still exists everywhere except in cities and in their immediate environs, naturally came to each section at a different time. Our division, then, is not chronological exactly but in accordance with how people lived. If a novel represents a settled way of life on the farm or in the village, rather than early hardships, it belongs in this section rather than under pioneering. Such a settled way of life was established in the Northeast throughout most of the nineteenth century, in the Middle West approximately from the Civil War onward. Since in the regions farther west the pioneering stage was passed at divers times, some pioneering books may have their settings in the twentieth century; other books may represent a settled stage which certain sections reached much earlier. The South, of course, reached one "settled" way of life before the Civil War and an entirely different one after the "Reconstruction."

The story of American life in the village or small town or on the American farm became a major theme in letters when a country-raised generation found itself in crowded cities after the Civil War. From the beginning the treatment varied from the starkly realistic to the romantically optimistic. The later farm books have been heavily sociological, taking up tenant farming, disease, decay, and the farm laborer, who isn't a farmer in the older sense at all. The books about the village or town have followed much the same development, with much satire and debunking during the 1920's and since then a good deal of fresh psychological re-evaluation.

1. THE NORTHEAST (ALSO YANKEES AND VILLAGE GREENS)

The "recorders of the New England decline" (Pattee: *History of American Literature Since 1870*) first made daily life in New England a popular subject for fiction in the 1870's and 1880's. There has been a great variety of treatments, with a general trend of development from the sentimental toward the more matter-of-fact picture of actuality. This section is characterized by small, diversified farms and old-fashioned villages. Stories of New York, New Jersey, Pennsylvania, and New England are included in this section.

ALCOTT, LOUISA M., 1832–1888

*Little Women (1868). A story of childhood and home life in a New

England village. Immensely popular. Shows the integrity and virtues of the American villager.

Work (1873). Tells of a girl who works as a housemaid, a governess, and an actress.

ALDRICH, THOMAS B., 1836–1907

The Story of a Bad Boy (1869). Tells a boy's experiences in a New England seaport town. A wholesome account of a normal life.

ALLIS, MARGUERITE, 1886–

Charity Strong (Putnam, 1945). Against the opposition of her Puritan father a Connecticut girl of the 1820's struggles to become an opera singer.

Water Over the Dam (Putnam, 1947). Fair-to-middling story of the building of a dam across the Connecticut River in the early 1800's. Triangle story of two sisters and the man who married one of them.

ASCH, NATHAN, 1902–

The Valley (Macmillan, 1935). A group of sketches and short stories of life in a small decadent place in the Berkshires as told by a native of Warsaw, Poland. Shows the essentials of Yankee rural life with all its simple delights.

BEALS, HELEN RAYMOND, 1888–

The River Rises (Macmillan, 1941). Through the eyes of a minister and his wife and a construction engineer the reader sees a cross section of life in a Massachusetts village which is to be flooded for a reservoir.

BEER, THOMAS, 1889–1940

Collected Stories of Thomas Beer: Mrs. Egg and Other Americans (Knopf, 1947). Adroit and entertaining stories of rural, village, and small-city people in New England, New York, and Ohio. Discerning presentations of American behavior and mentality, in several series that were popular in the *Saturday Evening Post.*

BENÉT, LAURA

Come Slowly, Eden: The Story of Emily Dickinson (Dodd, 1942). Biographical novel of the gentle, whimsical New England poet. Some material on customs and attitudes.

BROWN, ALICE, 1857–1948

Meadow Grass (1895). Short tales of New England village life.

Tiverton Tales (1899). Full details of New England village life and the peculiarities of its folk. Discusses an old maid and an annual village fair.

The Country Road (1906). Thirteen stories of New England folk, their love affairs and domestic difficulties. Little of the shadows of life; plenty of its comedy.

Country Neighbors (1910). Short stories emphasizing the romance of humble lives.

BUCK, PEARL SYDENSTRICKER, 1892–

Portrait of a Marriage (John Day, 1945). An interesting study of the effect of the land and farm life on a sensitive artist who married a Pennsylvania farm woman and spent his life in the country. Interesting speculations, a rather unbelievable plot, and live characters.

BUCKLER, ERNEST

The Mountain and the Valley (Holt, 1952). A detailed picture of daily and seasonal work and social life on a Nova Scotia farm. "In the country the day is the determinant. The work, the thoughts, the feelings, to match it, follow." Much attention to the emotional needs and outlets of adolescents and young men and women.

CANNON, LEGRAND, 1899–

A Mighty Fortress (Farrar, 1937). Story of a boy farmer who grew up to become a minister at the time of the abolition movement during the middle of the nineteenth century. New Hampshire setting.

CARROLL, GLADYS H., 1904–

As the Earth Turns (Macmillan, 1933). A story of the events of one year in the life of a Maine farmer of the present day.

Neighbor to the Sky (Macmillan, 1937). Of a girl who escaped the farm, fell in love with a Maine farmer, and tried to remake him but decided in the end not to do so.

CHASE, MARY ELLEN, 1887–

Mary Peters (Macmillan, 1934). Mary Peters spent her childhood on her father's sailing ship. In her teens she went to live with her family in a Maine village. Her anxiety, sorrow, loneliness, and final serenity. An amiable recollection.

Silas Crockett (Macmillan, 1935). Chronicle of four generations of a New England family. Depicts seafaring people of Maine from Silas, captain of a clipper, to his great-grandson Silas, who could not follow the ways of his seafaring family but was forced to leave college to work in a herring factory.

COATSWORTH, ELIZABETH, 1893–

Here I Stay (Farrar, 1940). Story of a woman who lived alone and liked it. She lived on a New England farm, her nearest neighbor being thirty miles away. She is contrasted with other New Englanders who wish to escape their environment.

COFFIN, ROBERT PETER TRISTAM, 1892–1955

Lost Paradise; a Boyhood on a Maine Coast Farm (Macmillan, 1934). Childhood on a Maine coast farm of the late 1890's, with its pleasurable toil and sheer delights.

COOKE, ROSE TERRY, 1827–1892

Rootbound and Other Sketches (1885). Perhaps the best collection of short stories by this author. Gives the authentic flavor of New England.

Huckleberries Gathered from New England Hills (1891). Vernacular tales of plain, hardy characters.

COZZENS, JAMES GOULD, 1903–

The Last Adam (Harcourt, 1933). Presents the seamy side of a New England village.

The Just and the Unjust (Harcourt, 1942). "A presentation and an analysis of the American way of discipline" in a small Connecticut village.

CRANE, STEPHEN, 1871–1900

Twenty Stories (Knopf, 1940). Contains five stories of a New England town, including "The Monster," one of Crane's finest tales.

CUDDEBAK, JANE, 1891–

Unquiet Seed (Pellegrini, 1947). Good detail about life on a tobacco farm in New York, mostly from the viewpoint of a child.

D'AGOSTINO, GUIDO, 1910–

The Barking of a Lonely Fox (McGraw, 1952). A rounded picture of the struggle for existence and love on a dairy farm in Pennsylvania. Although the book admits flaws in the environment, especially in the towns, it is essentially optimistic; it is *pro* country living.

DUFFUS, ROBERT L., 1888–

West Hill (Macmillan, 1942). Excellent character studies centering about a ninety-five-year-old man and his doctor. Vermont from the Revolution to the present.

FERBER, EDNA, 1887–

American Beauty (Doubleday, 1931). Tells the story of a family mansion in Connecticut from 1700 to 1900. Shows Polish peasants replacing the "old-stock" Yankees.

FIELD, BEN, 1901–

The Last Freshet (Doubleday, 1948). A wholesome and honest regional novel, laid in a town on the upper Delaware River and the surrounding farms and woods. The main interest is a love story, but the area and its people come alive—though in no deeply significant way.

FISHER, DOROTHY CANFIELD, 1879–

Hillsboro People (Holt, 1915). Centered around the lives of simple village folk in Vermont. Their lives may not be eventful, but the people are real and smart in the ways of life itself.

The Brimming Cup (Holt, 1916). Family life in a little Vermont community.

Rough Hewn (Harcourt, 1922). A picture of family life in the ideal American home. Deals with a couple who return from Paris to live a contented life in a small Vermont village.

FLINT, MARGARET, 1891–

Enduring Riches (Dodd, 1942). Appealing story of Maine country people. The building of a happy family life by two people who marry in their thirties.

FORBES, ESTHER, 1894?–

The Running of the Tide (Houghton, 1948). A long novel, better realized as history than as literature, that gives a period picture of people in Salem, Massachusetts, in its great days as a seaport for the China trade, before its period of decline after 1812.

*Rainbow on the Road (Houghton, 1954). About an itinerant peddler and portrait painter. An episodic re-creation of New England life, speech, and scenery in the 1830's. Entertaining as social history and interesting as a parallel to Hawthorne's *American Notebooks*.

FREDERIC, HAROLD, 1856–1898

*Seth's Brother's Wife (1887). A drab, bitter tale of farm life in upper New York State. Pictures country journalism and politics and rural frustration. A good companion for *Main-Travelled Roads* by Garland, published in 1891.

FREEMAN, MARY E. WILKINS, 1862–1930

A Humble Romance (1887). Twenty-eight realistic stories and sketches of a Massachusetts village. All deal with unhappiness.

*A New England Nun; and Other Stories (1891). The title story is the author's most famous, and a true portrayal of New England character.

Pembroke (1894). A loosely constructed novel, strong in its episodes, portraying New England life.

GREBENC, LUCILE, 1893–

The Time of Change (Doubleday, 1938). A story of a Connecticut woman in the early nineteenth century, centering on details of farm life.

HALL, LELAND, 1883–

They Seldom Speak (Harcourt, 1936). Full of detailed daily events of average American farm life. Deals with a family from the 'eighties until the close of the war of 1914–1918, showing the changing ideas during this time.

HAWTHORNE, NATHANIEL, 1804–1864

The House of the Seven Gables (1851). Shows the descendants of a Puritan family about 1850, involved in the consequences of past mistakes and misdeeds. Throws light on New England moralistic notions.

HOWARD, ELIZABETH METZGER

Before the Sun Goes Down (Doubleday, 1946). The year 1880–81 in the town of Willowspring, Pennsylvania. Fine treatment of social classes and problems of the time.

HUMMEL, GEORGE F., 1882–

Subsoil (Liveright, 1924). One of the better early forerunners of the down-to-earth stories published in the 1930's. Separate stories of various people, all connected with each other by residence in or near Norwold, Long Island.

Heritage (Stokes, 1935). Set in Norwold, Long Island, this is a chronicle of village life from the time the railroad came in 1846, bringing with it a sturdy German immigrant family. Concerned with domestic problems.

IRVING, WASHINGTON, 1783–1859

Knickerbocker's History of New York (1809). A humorous, kindly re-creation of events in early New York. Irving pretends to be presenting a firsthand account written by one Diedrich Knickerbocker, who lived in the Dutch period.

The Sketch Book (1819). The best-known volume by Irving. Contains such famous stories of early New York as "The Legend of Sleepy Hollow," "Rip Van Winkle," and "The Devil and Tom Walker."

JANEWAY, ELIZABETH, 1913–

The Walsh Girls (Doubleday, 1943). Psychological novel of two New England sisters, one married, one a spinster, and their attitudes.

JEWETT, SARAH ORNE, 1849–1909

A Country Doctor (1884). Based on the life of Miss Jewett's father. Realistic. Intimate.

A White Heron (1886). Stories of rural New England. Humble people and Puritan character.

A Native of Winby and Other Tales (1893). Of deserted farms, occasional returns of those who went West, and of summer boarders.

*The Country of the Pointed Firs (1896). Portraits and scenes of a seaside village in Maine. Homely and old-fashioned characters.

LAING, DILYS B.

The Great Year (Duell, 1948). This tells of three generations of Vermont farming folk. Catches the flavor of rural New England, in appealing poetical fashion.

MacLENNAN, HUGH, 1907–

The Precipice (Duell, 1948). The love story of an Ontario village girl and a New Yorker. A thoughtful novel that studies the differences between Canadians and Americans and between their civilizations.

McINTIRE, MARGUERITE

Free and Clear (Farrar, 1939). A novel of Maine farm life. Good in details of country life.

Heaven's Dooryard (Farrar, 1940). The story of the building of a farm and the establishment of a family in New England. Setting: New Hampshire, Maine, and Vermont.

MARQUAND, JOHN PHILLIPS, 1893–

Point of No Return (Little, 1949). There is much here on a small town in Massachusetts up to 1930, when the central character moves away to become a suburbanite working in a Manhattan bank. Most of the book is his recollections—in backflashes—of the environment that basically molded him.

MAYO, ELEANOR R., 1920–

Turn Home (Morrow, 1945). Of the town bad boy who returned after five years' absence to make good in his home town. Emphasis on small-town narrowness.

Loom of the Land (Morrow, 1946). The portrait of a self-made man in Maine—a dictator, Yankee model—who caused unhappiness to his children but kept the respect of the townspeople.

MERRICK, ELLIOT, 1905–

From This Hill Look Down (Daye, 1934). A series of sketches interpreting life in Vermont in the present day.

Ever the Winds Blow (Scribner, 1936). Story of a sensitive lad on a Vermont farm during the pre-depression years.

MUIR, EMILY

Small Potatoes (Scribner, 1940). An authentic portrait of country life in the Penobscot Bay region of Maine.

NATHAN, ROBERT, 1894–

Barly Fields (Knopf, 1938). A collection of five short novels. Of these *Fiddler in Barly* is an excellent phantasy of life in a small village, with neighborly gossip carried on by the poultry, the birds, etc.

OGILVIE, ELISABETH, 1917–

Storm Tide (Crowell, 1945). An appealing story of a lack of understanding between husband and wife in a carefully drawn portrait of a small island community off the coast of Maine.

*The Ebbing Tide (Crowell, 1947). A well-told psychological novel of a woman whose husband is away from home in World War II. Bennett's Island, the locale, and the people represent an authentic northeastern community. Continues *Storm Tide*.

PARMENTER, CHRISTINE (WHITING), 1877–

Swift Waters (Crowell, 1937). A love story in which a few descendants of the foreign-born commence associating with older members of New England society.

PARTRIDGE, BELLAMY, 1878–

January Thaw (McGraw, 1945). A city couple buy a Connecticut farm which has a flaw in the title. A country couple with a claim on the place move in with them. The struggle between the two couples serves to bring out various New England attitudes and customs.

PETRY, ANN, 1911–

The Narrows (Houghton, 1953). A perceptive story of a disastrous love affair between a rich white girl and a Negro. The principal setting is the Negro section of a small industrial town in Connecticut.

ROBINSON, ROWLAND EVANS, 1833–1900

Uncle Lisha's Shop (1887). One of the more satisfactory "local color" stories; township life centering about a shoemaker's shop.

Sam Lovell's Camps (1889). Stories of the fishing and hunting expeditions of Samuel Lovell, a neighbor of Uncle Lisha. Sequel to *Uncle Lisha's Shop*. A French-Canadian is an important character.

Danvis Folks (1894). Satisfactory presentation of details of country happenings and folkways of Danvis township, Charlotte County, Vermont.

SCHRAG, OTTO, 1907–

Sons of the Morning (Doubleday, 1945). Two veterans returned to a New England village find themselves alien to the townspeople (although their friendship with the town's conscientious objector remains unbroken).

SETTLE, MARY LEE

The Love Eaters (Harper, 1955). An acidulous report on the upper class in a coal town in the Alleghenies.

STOWE, HARRIET B., 1812–1896

*The Minister's Wooing (1859). A valuable picture of villagers in the undiluted Puritan tradition. Full of authentic detail.

The Pearl of Orr's Island (1861). Faithful portraits of New England village life. A pioneer book in portraying this section.

Old Town Folks (1869). A Massachusetts village, similar to The Pearl of Orr's Island.

Sam Lawson's Oldtown Fireside Stories (1872). A Massachusetts village about 1800. Indians, Hibernians, English, Puritans, ghosts. Good old-style humor.

WALKER, MILDRED, 1905–

The Quarry (Harcourt, 1947). Life in a Vermont village from 1857 to 1914, emphasizing the New Englander's sense of duty.

WATKIN, LAWRENCE E., 1901–

Geese in the Forum (Knopf, 1940). Realistic picture of professors and townsfolk in a village.

WESTCOTT, EDWARD N., 1847–1898

David Harum (1898). A rural "Yankee" of New York. Considered an excellent portrayal of a shrewd country banker who is also a good horse trader and a rustic humorist. A very popular novel about 1900.

WHARTON, EDITH NEWBOLD (JONES), 1862–1937

*Ethan Frome (1911). A realistic story of the restricted moral atmosphere of a bleak New England farm. The hero is compelled by circumstances to stay on his farm—to deny himself the chance to practice his chosen profession or to enjoy a normal life. One of the best books for this section.

WILDER, ISABEL

Let Winter Go (Coward, 1937). A story of life in a New England university town. Shows the havoc one selfish woman is able to create and its effect on the four intelligent people around whom the story is centered.

WINSTON, CLARA, 1921–

The Closest Kin There Is (Harcourt, 1952). A vigorous story of the bitter lives of an emotionally trapped family on a New England farm in the 1940's. Catches many aspects of isolated farm life.

WYLIE, IDA ALEXA ROSS, 1885–

Ho, the Fair Wind (Random, 1945). Romantic story of Martha's Vineyard after the Civil War. A rough man of Portuguese descent and a lay preacher of the island compete for the love of a woman. Interesting primitive religious practices.

2. THE MIDDLE WEST (ALSO MAIN STREETS AND MAIN-TRAVELED ROADS)

The states of the Middle West contain the most productive farm land of the country. The farms have been slightly larger than those of New England. They have been characterized mainly by the raising of corn and hay and their subsidiary livestock—hogs, dairy cattle, mules, horses, and poultry. The writers have concentrated to a great extent on the frankly realistic or even naturalistic presentation of farm life. Writers of this region waged most intensively the "battle of the village."

ADE, GEORGE, 1866–1944
   *Fables in Slang (1900). Short, humorous, and satirical sketches of small-town life at the end of the nineteenth century. Sharp portraits of social climbers, drummers, bashful boys, mandolin players, merchants, Spanish War heroes. A convenient collection of Ade stories is *Thirty Fables in Slang* (Arrow Editions, 1933).

ANDERSON, SHERWOOD, 1876–1941
   *Winesburg, Ohio (1919). A famous book of short stories dealing with the frustrations and inhibitions of many sorts of people in a small Ohio village. Sentimental, bitter. Attacks the hypocrisies and the pharisaic code of villagers.
   Triumph of the Egg (Viking, 1921). A collection of short stories, told very simply in the style of *Spoon River Anthology,* about the ugliness, emptiness, and misery of some futile lives of people with repressed emotions, petty desires, and thwarted instincts.

AYDELOTTE, DORA, 1878–
   Long Furrows (Appleton, 1935). Midwestern farm life, centering on homely activities, such as threshing, quilting, skating, and picnicking.
   Full Harvest (Appleton, 1939). Shows the disasters that follow after an ambitious farmer's wife has succeeded in moving the family to town for the sake of the children.

BABCOCK, FREDERIC, 1896–
   Hang Up the Fiddle (Doubleday, 1954). Of a minister's son growing up in Nebraska in the early 1900's.

BAHR, JEROME
   All Good Americans (Scribner, 1937). See below, p. 183.

BELLAMANN, HENRY, 1882–1945
   Kings Row (Simon, 1940). A sardonic picture of village life in the tradition of *Winesburg, Ohio.* The rottenness and corruption that follow in the wake of economic stagnation.

BELLAMANN, HENRY, 1882–1945, and BELLAMANN, KATHERINE J.
   Parris Mitchell of Kings Row (Simon, 1948). Story of a well-edu-

cated doctor fighting the cause of simple people against political bigotry, especially during the war of 1914–1918. Sheds light on a town in the St. Louis area.

BLAKE, ELEANOR, 1899–

Seedtime and Harvest (Putnam, 1935). Pictures a young, eager Norwegian immigrant girl forced by marriage into a lifetime of drudgery and work on a Michigan farm a generation or so ago.

BLUMENTHAL, ALBERT, 1902–

Small Town Stuff (University of Chicago, 1932). A sociological study of a small town of about 1,400 inhabitants, showing the activity of the town, its agencies of social control, its social life, and changes which take place.

BOYD, THOMAS, 1898–

Samuel Drummond (Scribner, 1925). Story of a family's struggle to make their farm in Ohio prosper. The advent of the Civil War destroys all their work and they are forced during middle age to start anew in town.

BROMFIELD, LOUIS, 1896–1956

*The Farm (Harper, 1933). Contrasts the purposes of the two types of early Ohio settler—the one rich and well educated, the other the "no-account." Details of the settling of the Ohio Valley, the religion of these people, their work on the farm, etc. Really the biography of the farm told in terms of the people who worked it.

BUSEY, GARRETA HELEN, 1893–

The Windbreak (Funk, 1938). Realistic story, coming up to present times. Illinois.

CLEMENS, SAMUEL LANGHORNE (MARK TWAIN, pseud.), 1835–1910

The Adventures of Tom Sawyer (1876). Missouri village life. A famous story giving much detail of life around 1850.

*The Adventures of Huckleberry Finn (1885). Some presentation of village life and much of the customs and ideas of the mid-century in Missouri. The American classic of boy life on the river.

Pudd'nhead Wilson (1894). A small Missouri town looks with disfavor upon the intellectual lawyer, Wilson, who later proves his superiority. Clever, cynical, but thin.

COREY, PAUL, 1903–

*Three Miles Square (Bobbs, 1939). Struggle of a widow to keep her farm and educate her four children in Iowa. Develops the life of a family against this rural community background. Realistic.

The Road Returns (Bobbs, 1940). Continues story begun in *Three Miles Square*. Covers the period immediately after the war of 1914–1918.

County Seat (Bobbs, 1941). A many-threaded story of life in an Iowa county in the late 1920's. Third of the trilogy.

Acres of Antaeus (Holt, 1946). A story of the depression years in Iowa and of the development of a corporation farm by those who were foreclosing mortgages on the land of small farmers. A realistic story, ending with an argument for farm co-operatives.

CROY, HOMER, 1883–
  *West of the Water Tower (Harper, 1923). Excellent picture of a Missouri village.

DELL, FLOYD, 1887–
  *Moon Calf (Doran, 1920). Of a dreamy youth fighting against poverty and the conventions of a small factory town on the Mississippi. The two bondages of American youth of 1920: "his environment and his sentimental heritage."

DERLETH, AUGUST, 1909–
  Still Is the Summer Night (Scribner, 1937). A love story set in a small town in Wisconsin in the 1880's. Good pictures of the everyday town and prairie life of the time.
  Restless Is the River (Scribner, 1939). A Wisconsin farm from 1839 to 1850.
  Country Growth (Scribner, 1940). Stories of life in and about Sac Prairie, Wisconsin.
  Village Year (Coward, 1941). An unforced chronicle of life for three years in Sac Prairie, Wisconsin. Sensitive and mellow.
  Sweet Genevieve (Scribner, 1942). Of a girl who hated her life in the small town of Sac Prairie and finally had a chance to go on a showboat.

DOWNING, J. HYATT, 1888–
  Sioux City (Putnam, 1940). Life in Sioux City in the gaudy boom period of the middle 'eighties.

DUNCAN, THOMAS WILLIAM, 1905–
  Gus, the Great (Lippincott, 1947). Of a circus man in the Midwest. Long and rambling. Varies from burlesque to straight realism in style and characterization—but seems to recapture some of the spirit of 1890 nevertheless.

ELLISON, JAMES WHITFIELD
  I'm Owen Harrison Harding (Doubleday, 1955). The social, academic, and "romantic" problems of a sixteen-year-old high-school boy in a Michigan town. A conversational report on adolescence.

ENGSTRAND, SOPHIA, 1908–
  Miss Munday (Dial Press, 1940). This shows the limited but secure life of a schoolma'am in a Wisconsin village. Miss Munday chooses easy security rather than romance with a poor fisherman.

ERDMAN, LOULA GRACE
  Years of the Locust (Dodd, 1947). Story of a successful Missouri farmer and his community, emphasizing neighborliness and commonsense customs.

FREEMAN, MARTIN JOSEPH, 1899–

Bitter Honey (Macmillan, 1942). An amusing sketch of a small Ohio town in 1908. Filled with a myriad of details of ordinary people and their lives.

GALE, ZONA, 1874–1938

Friendship Village (Macmillan, 1908). An old-fashioned story of "neighborly friendships and quiet lives."

Birth (Macmillan, 1918). A faithfully realistic picture of life in a Wisconsin small town.

Miss Lulu Bett (Appleton, 1920). A story of the restrictions of small village life. Miss Lulu Bett revolts.

GARLAND, HAMLIN, 1861–1940

*Main-Travelled Roads (Harper, 1891). Renowned as the first truly realistic picture of the Middle Western farm. A collection of short stories of the drab, debt-ridden lives of farmers in Wisconsin and neighboring states. An epoch-making book.

Prairie Folks (Harper, 1892). Continues the style of *Main-Travelled Roads*.

Rose of Dutcher's Coolly (Harper, 1896). See above, p. 10.

GLASPELL, SUSAN, 1882–

Judd Rankin's Daughter (Lippincott, 1945). Story of Midwestern mores in 1944. Shows that not all Midwesterners are isolationist and provincial.

HOWELLS, WILLIAM D., 1837–1920

The Leatherwood God (1916). Story of a man who claimed to be God, causing excitement in a small community.

JOHNSON, JOSEPHINE, 1910–

*Now in November (Simon, 1934). Beautifully written, tragic story of life on a run-down farm in Missouri during a terrible drought.

Jordanstown (Simon, 1937). One year in the life of a little city on a Midwest river.

KITCH, KENNETH HAUN (VICTOR HOLMES, pseud.), 1907–

Salt of the Earth (Macmillan, 1941). An understanding and sympathetic account of ordinary people in an ordinary town. Good-natured realism.

KRAUSE, HERBERT ARTHUR, 1905–

The Thresher (Bobbs, 1946). A realistic picture of rural life in Minnesota. The hardening effect of brutal toil and brutal competition is a major theme.

LANE, ROSE WILDER, 1887–

Old Home Town (Longmans, 1935). Short stories of small-town life during the first decade of the century, with its neighborly intimacy, conventional morality, gossip, and isolation from the world.

LARDNER, RING, 1885–1933

Round Up (Scribner, 1924). A collection of thirty-five of Lardner's stories. He excels in portraying the life of the Midwest village. Exact dialect.

How to Write Short Stories (Scribner, 1924). Contains some of Lardner's best stories, with a few interspersed remarks.

LEWIS, SINCLAIR, 1885–1951

*Main Street (Harcourt, 1920). A book centering on life in a small Midwestern town, "Gopher Prairie." The heroine tries to make the town over, but in the end becomes one of the people (almost). Emphasis on the pettiness and deadly dullness of the townfolk. An important satire.

LOCKRIDGE, ROSS FRANKLIN, 1914–1948

Raintree County (Houghton, 1948). A long novel of Indiana life from 1844 to 1892, with particular emphasis on the life of an introspective, idealistic character who becomes the village schoolmaster, a man who never seems quite to belong among his daily associates. Many glimpses of village mores and ways of thinking prevalent in the period. A book which debunks some of the myth about the good old days, and succeeds in presenting some phases of the horse-and-buggy days quite realistically.

LUTES, DELLA THOMPSON, 1872?–1942

Millbrook (Little, 1938). A charming reminiscence of farm life in Michigan a generation ago.

MACLEOD, LEROY, 1893–

Three Steeples (Covici, 1931). A farm community of Indiana. The life of the town is revealed through a story telling of the building of the community church.

Years of Peace (Century, 1932). Of the everyday life of farming folk in the Wabash Valley after the Civil War.

Crowded Hill (Reynal, 1934). Indiana. A sequel to *Years of Peace*. Covers the years 1876 to 1878. Of the conflicts between two families under one roof.

MANFRED, FREDERICK FEIKEMA (originally FEIKE FEIKEMA), 1912–

*This Is the Year (Doubleday, 1947). Excellent account of a farmer's life in northwestern Iowa. In the tradition of showing the hardening effect of harsh conditions on character. The major characters are Frisian, and there is considerable about their European customs and folkways.

MARQUIS, DON, 1878–1937

Sons of the Puritans (Doubleday, 1939). Illinois in the latter nineteenth century, emphasizing changing conventions and the results of suppression and frustration.

MARQUISS, WALTER

Brutus Was an Honorable Man (Scribner, 1946). The development of a community from 1899 to 1941, showing that the business leaders do things for a community through coercion or to salve conscience.

MASTERS, EDGAR LEE, 1869–1950

The Tide of Time (Farrar, 1937). Follows the development of Ferrisburg, Illinois, from the time of its first land grants in 1812 to the end of the century. The conventions of the village defeat a natural Jeffersonian aristocrat.

MAXWELL, WILLIAM, 1908–

Time Will Darken It (Harper, 1948). An entertaining and sympathetic chronicle of events in an Illinois town in 1912. Probes into the psychological elements in human relationships but presents sweeter matters than those in the Henry Bellamann novels. Written in a poetic, thought-bearing style.

MORRIS, WRIGHT, 1910–

*The Home Place (Scribner, 1948). An off-beat documentary novel, illustrated with fine photographs of a Nebraska farm and town that typify "folk depletion." Strong in dialog and in details of farm life.

POUND, ARTHUR, 1884–

Once a Wilderness (Reynal, 1934). A family chronicle having for its background a large Michigan farm. Many of the farming activities, especially cattle breeding, described in detail.

PRICE, EMERSON

Inn of That Journey (Caxton, 1939). A dreary, small Ohio town. A realistic portrayal of boyhood therein.

REES, GILBERT, 1923–

Respectable Women (Random, 1954). A chatty, homespun story of Kansas in the 1890's. Built around some of the decent women of the post-frontier middle border and a mother's legitimate drive for social status.

REYHER, FERDINAND, 1891–

I Heard Them Sing (Little, 1946). A short novel glorifying the virtue of a Middle Western town, beginning before the Spanish-American War and ending in 1918.

RICHTER, CONRAD, 1890–

The Town (Knopf, 1950). Follows the rise of a town on the site of the cabin of *The Trees*. A recognizable, credible story of physical and social changes, including the coming of the first railroad locomotive and individual reactions to altering circumstances. The author has fully digested his research, he writes in an easy style, and he imaginatively communicates a feeling for past times.

ROBERTS, DOROTHY JAMES, 1903–

A Man of Malice Landing (Macmillan, 1943). Of a small town in Ohio, with emphasis on the theme of narrow-mindedness.

SANDOZ, MARI, 1899–

The Tom-Walker (Dial, 1947). A study of three postwar periods in the Middle West (after Civil War, World War I, and World War II), and leading up to the period when a dictator takes over in Washington. The "tom-walker" or man on stilts is a symbol of giantism and irresponsibility.

SEAGER, ALLAN, 1906–

Inheritance (Simon, 1948). An attack, using graphic characterizations and incidents, on the stultifying effect of life in a small Michigan town upon its inhabitants. Exposes the double standard, the snobbery, the unvarying cultural patterns that pass from father to son.

SHEEAN, VINCENT, 1899–

Bird of the Wilderness (Random, 1941). Curious tangle of psychological elements in an Illinois town in the spring of 1917. Midwestern village "Morbidia" in Sheean's seemingly light vein. Shows attitudes toward the coming war.

SINCLAIR, HAROLD, 1907–

American Years (Doubleday, 1938). Story of the development of an Illinois small town for thirty years, following the stories of its first settlers until Lincoln's election and the fall of Fort Sumter.

The Years of Growth (Doubleday, 1940). Continues *American Years*. Everton, Illinois, from 1861 to 1893. Careful re-creation of nineteenth-century life.

Years of Illusion (Doubleday, 1941). Third of the trilogy. Period, 1900–1914.

SMITH, LABAN C., 1911–

No Better Land (Macmillan, 1946). Vigorous novel about a Wisconsin farmer, with authentic detail about the life of one family.

SMITH, MADELINE BABCOCK, 1887?–1952

Lemon Jelly Cake (Little, 1952). A sweet, pleasant vignette of domestic life in a small Illinois town in 1900.

STEGNER, WALLACE, 1909–

Remembering Laughter (Little, 1937). A novelette of farm life in Iowa, reminiscent of Mrs. Wharton's *Ethan Frome*.

STREET, JAMES HOWELL, 1903–1954

The Gauntlet (Doubleday, 1945). A young Baptist minister and his wife meet new responsibilities in their first pastorate in a Missouri village. He finds that preaching is more than a profession.

SUCKOW, RUTH, 1892–

Country People (Knopf, 1924). Chronicle of three generations of German-American Iowa farmers. Tells of the early hardships of pioneers and their way of living until they became prosperous farmers.

*****Iowa Interiors** (Knopf, 1926). A group of sixteen sketches of the drabness of existence on farms and in small Midwestern towns of the corn country.

The Bonney Family (Knopf, 1928). Twenty years of life in a minister's family in a small Iowa town.

*****The Folks** (Farrar, 1934). Lengthy, detailed novel of the folks in a small Iowa town during the last twenty years. Two parents found security and happiness but could not transfer their sense of well-being to their children.

TARKINGTON, BOOTH, 1869–1946

The Gentleman from Indiana (1899). A popular novel of the romantic type. Pictures the Midwest village as the home of democracy. Things turn out right for the hero and his sweetheart.

The Conquest of Canaan (1905). Of a small town and an idealized young lawyer of the lower class who became its mayor. Progressive Era political novel.

Penrod (1914). A popular story of a boy. Good details of life in a small Indiana town, the folk habits, moral codes, etc., of fifty years ago.

THOMAS, DOROTHY, 1899–

The Home Place (Knopf, 1936). A Nebraska farm after the depression. The sons and their families all return to the old farm. A year of turmoil ensues. Realistic.

TROYER, HOWARD W., 1901–

The Salt and the Savor (Wyn, 1950). A folksy, leisurely, aphoristic, scrapbook-like picture of pioneer and rural Indiana from 1840 to 1865. "Every incident . . . has historical authenticity. . . ."

TULLY, JIM, 1888–1947

Biddy Brogan's Boy (Scribner, 1942). Of a ne'er-do-well in an Ohio town, told in the strong, simple style of Tully.

WALKER, MILDRED, 1905–

Fireweed (Harcourt, 1934). A quiet, natural story of a young couple in a Michigan lumber-mill town.

WESCOTT, GLENWAY, 1901–

The Apple of the Eye (Dial Press, 1924). Interesting story of Wisconsin country life, showing accurate knowledge of the people and their mores.

Good-Bye Wisconsin (Harper, 1928). A group of short stories emphasizing the landscape of Wisconsin. Unemotional. By an expatriate who spent many years in Paris.

WEST, JESSAMYN

*The Friendly Persuasion (Harcourt, 1945). Contains fourteen tales about a Quaker farm family in southern Indiana in the Civil War period. Quiet characterizations and antiquarian charm.

The Witch Diggers (Harcourt, 1951). Indiana in 1899–1900. Rural life and life on a county "poor farm" with its "sheltered" existence.

WHITLOCK, BRAND, 1869–1934

J. Hardin and Son (Appleton, 1923). Of small-town life in Ohio. The story centers around Hardin, Junior, who doesn't share his father's religious and moral enthusiasms but leads a colorless, unexciting life of duty.

3. THE PLAINS AND THE NORTHWEST
(ALSO DROUGHT AND WHEAT)

The Northwest, from the great bend in the Missouri northwestward, is a land characterized by large farms and ranches, raising wheat, cattle, and sheep. In the Plains are included major portions of Kansas and Nebraska. The general themes used by writers are much the same as for the Middle West, with an extra tendency toward grimness. See the discussion under "Pioneering—Grass."

ALDRICH, BESS STREETER, 1881–1954
A Lantern in Her Hand (Appleton, 1928). See above, p. 9.

BOLSTER, EVELYN, 1909–
Come Gently Spring (Vanguard, 1942). Story of an Idaho farming community. A pastoral view of people who blend naturally into the landscape.

CANNON, CORNELIA JAMES, 1876–
Red Rust (Little, 1928). Story of Swedish immigrants in the farm lands of Minnesota. Discusses their hardships, mostly economic; the search for a rust-resisting wheat is a central theme.

CASTLE, MARIAN (JOHNSON), 1898–
Deborah (Morrow, 1946). A story of three generations, beginning on a Dakota farm in the early 'nineties and ending in the same place during the depression. Indicates the changes that took place in the attitudes and cultural ambitions of America during that period.

CATHER, WILLA SIBERT, 1876–1947
*Youth and the Bright Medusa (Knopf, 1920). Various stories showing the restrictions on expressive living in towns and on ranches.
One of Ours (Knopf, 1922). The story of a young man so oppressed by the frustrations and restrictions of Nebraska farm life that he preferred the life of a soldier in France.

COMSTOCK, SARAH
Speak to the Earth (Doubleday, 1927). Shows an ex-service man trying to make a living from an arid sheep ranch in the Dakota Bad Lands.

DAVIS, HAROLD L., 1896–
*Honey in the Horn (Harper, 1935). A novel collecting much of the folklore about early settlers in Oregon. Realistic detail about ranches, hop-pickers, dry-farmers, etc., shortly after 1900. In the main realistic. Written in a brisk style.
Winds of Morning (Morrow, 1952). Laid in rural Oregon in the 1920's. A strong story, free of clichés and notable for its contrast of petty people and noble natural settings. Good characterizations, exciting incidents, and a direct style that is rich in idiom.

DOWNING, J. HYATT, 1888–
*A Prayer for Tomorrow (Putnam, 1938). A story of the coming of wheat farmers, the ruin of grazing land, a boom during war years, and the letdown afterward. Comprehensive treatment of an era in South Dakota (approximately 1890–1930). Good details concerning small-town life.
Hope of Living (Putnam, 1939). Of a woman farmer and her ambitionless husband on a South Dakota farm.

DRISCOLL, CHARLES B., 1885–
Kansas Irish (Macmillan, 1943). An understanding account of an intemperate Irish immigrant who settled in Wichita. Much rich anecdote and a record of pioneer life. Can be taken as either humorous or thoroughly unhappy.

EUNSON, DALE

Homestead (Farrar, 1935). Homesteading in Montana. Written in the matter-of-fact style popular in Western action stories. Cattleman versus farmer theme.

FISHER, VARDIS, 1895–

Toilers of the Hills (Houghton, 1928). See above, page 10.

In Tragic Life (Caxton, 1932). Picture of a sensitive boy amid harsh conditions along the Snake River in Idaho. The family has a desperate economic struggle.

HALDEMAN-JULIUS, EMANUEL, 1889–1951, and HALDEMAN-JULIUS, A. M., 1888–

Dust (Brentano's, 1921). Pictures the drudgery of farm life on the Kansas plains. Story of the unsuccessful marriage of a coarse farmer and a sacrificing wife.

HART, ALAN, 1892–

Doctor Mallory (Norton, 1935). A general practitioner in a bleak little Oregon town battles against dishonest competition, ignorance, poverty, and disease.

HAYES, CHARLES EDWARD, 1912–

The Four Winds (Macmillan, 1942). A swift and merciless account of a tenant-farm family in Kansas that is wrecked and scattered by economic misfortunes in the mid-1930's. A pessimistic picture of rural life, told with some humor and tenderness.

HOWE, EDGAR W., 1854–1937

*The Story of a Country Town (1883). One of the better early village stories. Realistic. Pictures farm life, especially the life of apprenticed farmhands. The piety of the community is a point for satire.

HUGHES, LANGSTON, 1902–

Not Without Laughter (Knopf, 1930). Negro life in a Kansas town. Pathetic and realistic.

JOHNSON, ALVIN SAUNDERS, 1874–

Spring Storm (Knopf, 1936). The record of a few years of a boy's life on a Nebraska farm in the early 1900's.

JONES, NARD, 1904–

Oregon Detour (Harcourt, 1930). A good picture of a small town in eastern Oregon, also of farm life in the same community.

Wheat Women (Duffield, 1933). Set in wheat lands of Washington, a story of three generations of wheat growers and their families.

Still to the West (Dodd, 1946). Live, real account of people living in the area to be affected by the building of the Grand Coulee.

KRAMER, HORACE

Marginal Land (Lippincott, 1939). About farmers and ranchers on the high plains, where farming is not very successful. A textbook on soil conservation in the form of a novel.

KRAUSE, HERBERT, 1905–
*Wind without Rain (Bobbs, 1939). An intense picture of emotionally hardened farmers in Minnesota.

McKAY, ALLIS
They Came to a River (Macmillan, 1941). Farm life in the apple-growing region of Washington from 1900 to 1920. A richly colored study of a countryside and its people.

MACLEOD, NORMAN, 1906–
The Bitter Roots (Smith and Durrell, 1941). Thirty-eight episodes from a Montana boyhood during the war of 1914–1918.

NELSON, IRA S., 1912–
On Sarpy Creek (Little, 1938). A good realistic novel of Montana in the 1920's and '30's, with emphasis upon the homely goodness and reliability of the folk when faced by adversity.

OSTENSO, MARTHA, 1900–
*Wild Geese (Dodd, 1925). Shows a greedy and heartless farmer dominating his household so that his children get no chance for self-realization. Scandinavians on a Minnesota farm.
The Dark Dawn (Dodd, 1926). A drama of grim psychological conflict, resulting from an ill-advised and disastrous marriage. Laid against a background of farm life.
There's Always Another Year (Dodd, 1933). Story of present-day life on a Dakota farm. Concerned mostly with a farm-loving young man, his selfish wife, and the young girl on whose farm he worked.

ROE, WELLINGTON
The Tree Falls South (Putnam, 1937). A tragic story of dust storms and drouth in Kansas, and of grim farmers who staged a riot.

ROLVAAG, OLE E., 1876–1931
*Peder Victorious (Harper, 1929). See below, p. 187.
*Their Father's God (Harper, 1931). See below, p. 151.

SANDOZ, MARI, 1899–
Slogum House (Little, 1937). See above, p. 12.
The Tom-Walker (Dial, 1947). See above, p. 39.

SNELL, GEORGE D.
The Great Adam (Caxton, 1934). An uncensored presentation of the slow disintegration of the influential banker in a small Idaho town.

STEGNER, WALLACE, 1909–
The Big Rock Candy Mountain (Duell, 1943). A long biography of a trapshooter, gambler, bootlegger, and real-estate man in the post-pioneer West. The book reveals life in the contemporary West; its theme is the frontiersman's dreams and frustrations.

STEWART, GEORGE, 1892–
Reluctant Soil (Caxton, 1936). Story of a widow and her two small children who struggle to make a living on the desert soil of the southwestern part of Idaho between 1900 and 1920.

THORPE, BERENICE, 1900–
Reunion on Strawberry Hill (Knopf, 1944). A warm, understanding novel of life and love on a small berry ranch in Washington.

WALKER, MILDRED, 1905–
Winter Wheat (Harcourt, 1944). A strong, simple story of the wheat country of Montana, with emphasis on place and character rather than plot. Shows the inexorability of nature, its influence on human lives.
The Curlew's Cry (Harcourt, 1955). Pictures a Montana town in a cattle region during a period of change, 1905–41, as a woman lives through the main events of her life.

WELLMAN, PAUL ISELIN, 1898–
The Walls of Jericho (Lippincott, 1947). See below, p. 142.

WHITE, WILLIAM ALLEN, 1868–1944
In Our Town (Century, 1904). A chatty story of a small town in Kansas. Emphasizes the neighborliness and moral uprightness of the people.
In the Heart of a Fool (Macmillan, 1918). Of three generations from the Civil War to 1914. Plays up the idealism of the pioneer, decries the attitudes of later generations. Looks forward to the war of 1914–1918 reawakening our idealism.
A Certain Rich Man (Macmillan, 1926). Pictures the growth of a Kansas town from the Civil War to the war of 1914–1918.

WHITE, W. L., 1900–
What People Said (Viking, 1938). About life in a small plains city, telling of people's manners, clothes, food, and ideas. The chief interest is in the struggle between "liberals" and "conservatives." Neither group is pictured as being very intelligent.

WINTHER, SOPHUS K., 1895–
Take All to Nebraska (Macmillan, 1936). See above, p. 13.
Mortgage Your Heart (Macmillan, 1937). Continuation of *Take All to Nebraska*. About this family's experiences on the Nebraska farm as rent farmers. Showing the differences between the father and his Americanized sons. Time of the story about 1906–1917.
This Passion Never Dies (Macmillan, 1938). Continuation of *Mortgage Your Heart*. Speaks of the family's struggle after their father's death, and of the personal conflicts of these Americanized Danish immigrants.
Beyond the Garden Gate (Macmillan, 1946). Story of an Oregon college boy who partially solves some difficult personal problems by taking the advice of a doctor friend. Throws some light on changing mores in regard to sex and family life.

4. THE SOUTH

4a. The Old South (The Plantation and Slavery)

No pattern of life in America has been more completely detailed by novelists than life in the Old South between 1800 and 1860. Ever since the 1830's, fiction has treated plantation life from varied view-points. Novels have been pro-South, anti-South, pro-Negro, anti-Negro, pro-abolition, anti-North—but whatever their point of view, they have all attributed glamour to the vanished plantation civilization, and they have always taken up, at least by implication, the problem of human freedom.

Writing about the plantation has consisted of two major streams, the sentimentalists of the 1880's and 1890's—Allen, Page, Harris, and F. H. Smith—followed by the realists of the twentieth century—Stribling, Bristow, Bontemps, and others. Aside from this, of course, there have been lesser streams: Harriet Beecher Stowe and her followers; a comparable group of propagandists for the South; flamboyantly romantic writers like John E. Cooke and Stark Young; old-fashioned realists like Ellen Glasgow; and historical romanticists, such as Mary Johnston and Margaret Mitchell.

ALLEN, JAMES LANE, 1849–1925

A Kentucky Cardinal (1895). Lyrical and sentimental, but famous for its descriptions of the Kentucky of about 1850.

BARKER, ROLAND, 1905–   , and DOERFLINGER, WILLIAM

The Middle Passage (Macmillan, 1939). Pedestrian fiction based on much research. An informative picture of the slave trade from the purchase of slave captives in the island cities of the Gold Coast to delivery to smugglers off South Carolina.

BONTEMPS, ARNA, 1902–

Black Thunder (Macmillan, 1936). About an attempted slave insurrection in the early nineteenth century. Good on realistic detail.

BRADFORD, ROARK, 1896–1948

Kingdom Coming (Harper, 1933). Plantation life. Some pictures of voodoo and of the Underground Railway and of unhappy "free" Negroes.

BRISTOW, GWEN, 1903–

Deep Summer (Crowell, 1937). Deals with the establishment of a plantation in Louisiana around 1800.

CARUTHERS, WILLIAM ALEXANDER, 1800–1846

Kentuckian in New York, or, the Adventures of Three Southerns (1834). "A contribution to the cause of intersectional good-will." In a series of letters, several Southerners make charming, intelligent comment on Yankees, slavery, poverty in Virginia, and so on.

CATHER, WILLA SIBERT, 1876–1947

Sapphira and the Slave Girl (Knopf, 1940). Beginning in the South in 1856, the story deals with Sapphira Dodderedge Colbert, a Virginia lady, whose husband ran a mill on the frontier. There is great conflict between the Colberts over the beautiful slave girl, Nancy, and the plot centers around Sapphira's unfounded jealousy. Artistic but lifeless writing.

CLEMENS, SAMUEL LANGHORNE (MARK TWAIN, pseud.), 1835–1910
*Life on the Mississippi (1883). An autobiographical narrative, mostly about Twain's experiences as a river pilot. Perceptibly but entertainingly fictionized. The classic account of steamboating on Old Man River.

COOKE, JOHN E., 1830–1886
The Virginia Comedians (1854). A romantic and fairly expert picture of the social life of colonial Virginia, with its charm, irresponsibility, and aristocratic code of love. One of the early fixers of the romantic interpretation of old plantation days.

CRABB, ALFRED LELAND, 1884–
Dinner at Belmont (Bobbs, 1942). An effective, romantic picture of the Old South and its fine first families.
Home to the Hermitage: A Novel of Andrew and Rachel Jackson (Bobbs, 1948). Laid in the Nashville area. A story of Jackson's marriage and his fights against slanderers who accused his wife of bigamy.

CROY, HOMER, 1883–
River Girl (Harper, 1931). A realistic romance of the high days of Mississippi steamboating.

DORRANCE, WARD, 1904–
The Sundowners (Scribner, 1942). Of a Missouri plantation in the early 1800's. Good portraiture of rural scene and people.

DOWDEY, CLIFFORD, 1904–
Gamble's Hundred (Little, 1939). Historical novel of Gamble's Hundred, a plantation in tidewater Virginia in the early eighteenth century. The hero is the surveyor employed by the owner of the plantation. Gives good historical information about the South of this period.

ENDORE, GUY, 1901–
Babouk (Vanguard, 1934). A revolutionary Marxist novel, opposed to slavery and imperialism, which presents in ghastly detail the horrors of the African slave trade.

FAULKNER, WILLIAM, 1897–
Absalom, Absalom! (Random, 1936). An involved and complicated novel of the old South and of an ambitious planter who settled near Jefferson, Mississippi, in 1833.

GAITHER, FRANCES O., 1889–1955
*Follow the Drinking Gourd (Macmillan, 1940). A beautifully written novel of pre-Civil War days in Georgia and Alabama. Presents the economic wastefulness of slavery and the social effect of such an institution on all concerned.
The Red Cock Crows (Macmillan, 1944). Shows how even the best plantation life was a failure because of its unreconcilable combination of human values. Of a slave revolt on a model plantation in Mississippi.
Double Muscadine (Macmillan, 1949). A story of love and slavery on a Mississippi plantation. The plot centers in a murder trial, and the trial, which is dramatic, crosscuts existence in a Southern community.

GORDON, CAROLINE, 1895–

The Forest of the South (Scribner, 1945). Sixteen well-told stories of the South, ranging in time from pioneer days to the present.

GRUBB, DAVIS, 1919–

A Dream of Kings (Scribner, 1955). A love story laid in western Virginia (West Virginia) during the period 1855–64. Details of American life are implied or given tangentially, for the author is lyrical, connotative, and emotional rather than informative.

HARRIS, JOEL CHANDLER, 1848–1908

Nights with Uncle Remus (1883). Humorous and charming folklore created by the slave. Pictures a pleasant relationship between white and black.

HERGESHEIMER, JOSEPH, 1880–1954

The Limestone Tree (Knopf, 1931). A Kentucky family chronicle covering part of the eighteenth and most of the nineteenth century.

JOHNSTON, MARY, 1870–1936

Lewis Rand (1908). Lively portrait of interaction between the various classes of people in Virginia in Jefferson's time.

The Slave Ship (Little, 1924). A well-told novel about the slave trade in the eighteenth century, giving one man's reaction to the buying and selling of human flesh.

Miss Delicia Allen (Little, 1933). The cultured and gracious life on Indian Leap plantation in Virginia before and during the Civil War.

JOHNSTON, RICHARD M., 1822–1898

Dukesborough Tales (1871). Stories of yeomen and nobodies during plantation days in Georgia. Some sharp characterizations in the "local-color" manner.

KANE, HARNETT T., 1910–

Bride of Fortune (Doubleday, 1948). A true account, adorned by fictional scenes and conversations, of Mrs. Jefferson Davis. Rich details on wealthy Mississippi planting society, Washington City in the 1850's, and also the Confederate period. A clear portrait of a remarkable woman.

KENNEDY, JOHN P., 1795–1870

*Swallow Barn (1832). This is a mellow, well-rounded, Southern account of a plantation in the Old Dominion. Slow but satisfying reading.

KING, GRACE, 1852–1932

The Pleasant Ways of St. Médard (Holt, 1916). Reminiscent, nostalgic sketches of the old régime in New Orleans during and right after the Civil War. Much on the folkways of French, "Americans," and Negroes and on the role of the father in a patriarchal society.

LEWIS, BESSIE

To Save Their Souls (Christopher, 1939). Running from 1810 to about 1870, this story shows that the Negroes gained a great deal in being brought to America. Satirizes Northerners who tried to "save their souls," and implies that Southerners know best.

MARGULIES, LEO, 1900–   , and MERWIN, SAMUEL

The Flags Were Three (Curl, 1945). Novel of New Orleans and its development from a wilderness outpost in 1732 to the sophisticated city of the early nineteenth century. The romance of the old city is preserved. Three generations of believable characters.

MARQUAND, JOHN PHILLIPS, 1893–

The Black Cargo (Scribner, 1925). An adventure story of illicit slave trade in the New England clipper-ship era, with the interest centered on the black deeds and tormented conscience of an elderly slaver and "pirate" who has come home from the sea.

MITCHELL, MARGARET, 1900?–1949

*****Gone with the Wind** (Macmillan, 1936). Full-length portrait of a Georgia plantation before and after the Civil War. A conventional plot combined with lively social history and interesting human psychology. Shows how war wiped out an integrated way of life.

ODUM, HOWARD WASHINGTON, 1884–

Cold Blue Moon (Bobbs, 1931). An old Negro tells things he remembers of plantation days.

PAGE, THOMAS NELSON, 1853–1922

In Ole Virginia (1887). Stories of plantations, slaves, and masters, containing much Negro dialect. A sentimental, nostalgic treatment of the Old South which did much to "set up" the plantation tradition.

PARRISH, ANNE (MRS. CHARLES A. CORLISS), 1888–

A Clouded Star (Harper, 1948). Of Harriet Tubman, the notable Negro who helped lead the Underground Railroad. A fictional account of one of her trips north from Maryland toward Canada, in 1860.

SASS, HERBERT RAVENAL, 1884–

*****Look Back to Glory** (Bobbs, 1933). The story is weak, but the background of South Carolina aristocracy is fully depicted, especially the Secessionists' rationalizations.

SCOTT, EVELYN, 1893–

Migrations (Boni, 1927). A record of unpleasant and tragic aspects of slavery.

SMITH, F. HOPKINSON, 1838–1915

Colonel Carter of Cartersville (1891). Comic-sentimental treatment of the traditional Southern colonel.

STEWARD, DAVENPORT, 1913–

Rainbow Road (Tupper and Love, 1953). A romantic tale with an authentic background of the gold rush in the Georgia hills in the 1820's. This rush had, the author says, "its tide of blatant greed, its seething undercurrent of animal ferocity."

STOWE, HARRIET B., 1812–1896

*****Uncle Tom's Cabin** (1852). One of the greatest of our propaganda novels. A sentimentalized and also sensationalized version of ante-bellum plantation life. Kentucky and Louisiana.

Dred, A Tale of the Dismal Swamp (1856). Rich in background material of the ordinary life on the plantation. A study of the economic problems of Negro emancipation.

STRIBLING, THOMAS SIGISMUND, 1881–

*The Forge (Doubleday, 1931). Good realistic treatment of a middle-class family at the time of the Civil War, a family ranking between the plantation owner and the poor white or hillbilly. All the traditional classes are represented but with a better feeling of actuality than is usual.

TATE, ALLEN, 1899–

The Fathers (Putnam, 1938). A dramatization of the plantation code in Virginia in the decade before the Civil War, when social forces were rapidly hatching a national crisis.

THACKERAY, WILLIAM M., 1811–1863

The Virginians (1858–59). Story of an English family divided by our Revolutionary War. Good on the manners of the time.

TOURGEE, ALBION W., 1838–1905

A Royal Gentleman (1874). A melodramatic story of a Southern gentleman who made a mistress of his slave girl. Presents forcibly the effect of the slave system on the white owner as well as the effect on the slave.

WARREN, LELLA, 1899–

Foundation Stone (Knopf, 1940). Novel of Alabama in the last century. A chronicle of a family of planters who came to Alabama from South Carolina. Follows their lives from the 1820's to the end of the Civil War. Shows their economic struggles and their relations with Negroes.

WELD, JOHN, 1905–

Sabbath Has No End (Scribner, 1942). A South Carolina cotton plantation in 1815. Good portrayal of Negro character.

WELLMAN, PAUL ISELIN, 1898–

Angel with Spurs (Lippincott, 1942). A spirited narrative of unconquerable Confederates who crossed the Rio Grande, going south, after Appomattox.

YOUNG, STARK, 1881–

Heaven Trees (Scribner, 1926). A picture of a Mississippi plantation before the Civil War. Contrasts the spacious, lazy, easy life with that which the young kinswoman from Vermont knew.

4b. The South Today (Also Sharecroppers and Country Squires)

Since about 1880 the South has become the land of the sharecropper and is dominated, as it was before our Civil War, by the raising of cotton, tobacco, and cane. The people engaged in farming have been divided into a new set of classes: owners, tenants, croppers, and hands. There has been much realistic and naturalistic writing, particularly since 1920, but also a persistent, perennial reappearance of the old-fashioned romantic story. During the past twenty-five years there has appeared a new school of Southern writers, William Faulkner, Eudora Welty, and Robert Penn Warren among them, that place a great value on immediacy, symbolism, thematic variation, myth, subtleties in point of view, and other aesthetic matters praised by the "new criticism." Many of these new Southern authors make heavy use of the hypotheses of twentieth-century psychology. But whether the approach emphasizes contents or artistic presentation, the unavoidable problem of Negro-white adjustment runs through most of these books.

ALEXANDER, LILLIE (McMAKIN)

Candy (Dodd, 1934). A very frank novel, "realistic" after the newest style, of South Carolina Negro characters.

ALLEN, JAMES LANE, 1849–1925

Flute and Violin; and Other Kentucky Tales (Macmillan, 1891). Of the Blue Grass region. Old-fashioned and sentimental.

ARMFIELD, EUGENE MOREHEAD

Where the Weak Grow Strong (Covici, 1936). The picture of Tuttle, North Carolina, in the autumn of 1912. A cross-section view of all the types of people in the town.

BASSO, HAMILTON, 1904–

Cinnamon Seed (Scribner, 1934). Of life on a twentieth-century plantation near New Orleans, as given perspective by the memories of a veteran of the Civil War.

The View from Pompey's Head (Doubleday, 1954). A discursive study of the hold his Southern background has on a man who has achieved a career in Manhattan. Deals with the psychological complications and the sociological castes in a Southern town and throws an angular light on New York literary life.

BELL, VEREEN, 1911–

Swamp Water (Little, 1941). A melodrama set in the deep South. Simple, direct treatment.

BETHEA, JACK, 1892–1928

Cotton (Houghton, 1928). Larry Maynard returns to Alabama to try to raise cotton by the scientific methods he has learned in school. After many failures, he succeeds in convincing his fellow planters.

BURMAN, BEN LUCIEN, 1895–

Steamboat Round the Bend (Farrar, 1933). A gently humorous story of an old shanty-boat dweller who always longed to own a steamboat.
*Blow for a Landing (Day, 1938). Self-respecting shanty-boat people strive to establish a little farm on the land. Realistic yet charming.
The Four Lives of Mundy Tolliver (Messner, 1953). See below, p. 73.

BYRD, SIGMAN

Tall Grew the Pines (Appleton, 1936). Short stories told by the young son of a school superintendent about life in a small Texas town at the beginning of this century.

CALDWELL, ERSKINE C., 1903–

*Tobacco Road (Duell, 1932). The story of a sharecropper shelved by the plantation owner, allowed to live in a tumble-down shack but not allowed to raise a crop. Pictures a family unbelievably degraded and destitute—the end result of a bad system. Contains grim farcical humor.

God's Little Acre (Viking, 1933). Story of a dirt farmer who for fifteen years dug holes in his Georgian soil, hoping to find gold. The only other occupation indulged in by him and his two sons was sex. Outrageous details given in a casually humorous manner. A social and economic study of the poor white.

We Are the Living (Duell, 1933). A collection of twenty stories ranging in setting from North to South, mostly concerned with the sex impulses of the characters.

*Kneel to the Rising Sun (Viking, 1935). A book of short stories of which the title story is an unusual presentation of the relationships between a poor white, a Negro, and the plantation owner. A classic story of "the system" and its effect on the people.

CAMPBELL, WILLIAM E. MARCH, 1894–1954

Come in at the Door (Smith, 1934). Story of the childhood of a white boy in Alabama and the lasting impression that the hanging of his Negro comrade, following his childish betrayal, has upon his later life.

The Looking Glass (Little, 1943). A psychoanalytic picture of Reedyville, Alabama, about 1917. Sardonic writing in the tradition of *Spoon River Anthology*.

CARTER, HODDING, 1907–

The Winds of Fear (Farrar, 1944). A study of a small Southern town during World War II. Built around the civil struggle over Negro rights.

Floodcrest (Rinehart, 1947). Of a great flood and how a corrupt Southern senator tried to make the people believe he was doing all he could for them.

CHAMBERLAIN, WILLIAM WOODROW, 1914–

Leaf Gold (Bobbs, 1941). Of tobacco growing in Kentucky. Realistic detail.

CHEVALIER, ELIZABETH PICKETT, 1896–

Drivin' Woman (Macmillan, 1942). From the time of the Civil War to 1911. A mingling of sentimentality with a good story of the tobacco war between Kentucky planters and New York financiers.

CHILDERS, JAMES SAXON, 1899–

Novel about a White Man and a Black Man: In the Deep South (Farrar, 1936). Discusses the entire Negro problem. Explains the Negro's desire to be treated like other people and how his rights are ignored. Shows how by irrational reasoning and for their own advantage the whites find justification for their treatment of the Negro. Introduces the problem of the Negro's retarded cultural development.

CLAYTON, JOHN BELL, 1906–1955

Six Angels at My Back (Macmillan, 1952). An intimate view of have-nots in Florida—their essential decency, their uneducated groping for a home and a good life, and their attitudes toward tourists and flashy resorts. Told in the words of a nineteen-year-old boy who becomes involved in crime. Dramatic, suspenseful, excellent in style.

COAN, OTIS W., 1895–

Rocktown, Arkansas: An Ozark Novel (Exposition, 1953). A series of brief episodes that dramatize simply and directly most facets of life in a small community. Sympathetic and tender.

COCHRAN, EDWARD LEWIS

Son of Haman (Caxton, 1937). Of the delta land of Mississippi in late 'eighties and early 'nineties. Effective local color written in the style of the "stark realism" school.

Boss Man (Caxton, 1939). Continues the story of *Son of Haman*. A fair, sympathetic analysis of miserable sharecroppers and the Southern economic system that causes their troubles.

COLEMAN, WILLIAM LAURENCE, 1920–

Clara (Dutton, 1952). A character study of a selfish Southern white woman who drives her husband to drink and to an affair with a Negro woman. Stresses human characterization rather than sociology but is a protest against intolerance.

COOK, FANNIE, 1893–

Boot-Heel Doctor (Dodd, 1941). Of a doctor's work in southeast Missouri during a Mississippi flood and a sit-down strike of destitute sharecroppers. A story of human beings trapped by an economic system.

COOPER, MADISON ALEXANDER, 1894?–

Sironia, Texas (Houghton, 1952). This two-volume, 1,731-page novel tells a great deal about a town during the period 1900–1925, as mores disintegrate. Good reportage.

CRUMP, LOUISE ESHRIGGE

Helen Templeton's Daughter (Longmans, 1952). A young girl has to manage a plantation on the Mississippi Delta in 1910. A favorable picture of Delta life—of whites, Negroes, and agriculture.

CUNNINGHAM, WILLIAM, 1901–

The Green Corn Rebellion (Vanguard, 1935). Good on Oklahoma folkways of the present. The rebels didn't want to be drafted in 1917–1918.

Pretty Boy; a Novel (Vanguard, 1936). Story of the career of Pretty Boy Floyd, who left his rural home and became a gangster. Tells something of the life among the pellagra-ridden poor of Oklahoma.

DOUGHTY, LEGARDE S.

Music Is Gone (Duell, 1945). Story of a country doctor and his struggle to bring health and some happiness to his patients, in a Southern village. Good, simple, realistic picture.

DOUGLAS, MARJORY STONEMAN, 1890–

Road to the Sun (Rinehart, 1952). The locale is the Miami district in the 1910's and 1920's. A picture of rapid development of farm and city areas and a drama of conflicts between the old established inhabitants—crackers—and the new exploiters and boomers—rice farmers, canal builders, and real estate men included.

FAHERTY, ROBERT, 1900–

Big Old Sun (Putnam, 1941). A *Tobacco Road* of the Florida keys, with local color.

FAULKNER, JOHN, 1901–

Men Working (Harcourt, 1941). A comic folk epic in the manner of *Tobacco Road*. Matter-of-fact presentation of a Mississippi tenant-farmer family that moves to town and makes a meager living on checks from "the WP and A."

Dollar Cotton (Harcourt, 1942). A vigorous tale of a Mississippian who leaves the hills and founds a cotton plantation in the rich delta country. A case-study of the poor white.

FAULKNER, WILLIAM, 1897–

*The Sound and the Fury (Cape, 1929). Of the decay of a Southern family of gentle blood and of its members, who became drunkards, suicides, idiots, pathological perverts, etc. Comparable to works of Dostoevsky and James Joyce in its picture of insanity and futility.

Sartoris (Harcourt, 1929). Story of life in the hills of northern Mississippi. About Bayard Sartoris, whose brother's death during the war of 1914–1918 makes him on his return from war more reckless than even the traditional Sartorises.

As I Lay Dying (Smith, 1930). An unusual book about a moronic Mississippi family and their trek across the state with the corpse of their dead mother on a wagon. A morbid social and psychological study.

Sanctuary (Smith, 1931). A rather nauseating picture of the downfall of a flighty college-age girl and the sadistic pervert who has her in his control as she becomes a prostitute in Memphis. The author makes complicated use of the stream of consciousness.

Light in August (Smith, 1932). A story in which four major characters lead frustrated lives: a part-Negro who passes for white and finally ends the victom of a mob; a preacher whose religion doesn't meet reality; a lonely woman; a migratory worker. Clearer, better writing than some of Faulkner.

Knight's Gambit (Random, 1949). Six stories, all of violence. A recurrent Faulkner character, Gavin Stephens, a county attorney, appears in all of them.

Big Woods (Random, 1955). Contains four hunting stories, including a new version of the splendid and important "The Bear" with its evocation of Mississippi forests, an almost mythical bear, and a boy's growing up.

FERBER, EDNA, 1887–

Show Boat (Doubleday, 1926). Ultraromantic and rather popular, but nevertheless a robust treatment of a colorful aspect of river life.

FLANNAGAN, ROY C., 1897–1952

County Court (Doubleday, 1937). Story of some of the unlovely aspects of a Southern town, dealing mostly with a murder trial.

FLEMING, BERRY, 1899–

Colonel Effingham's Raid (Duell, 1943). Good-natured satire on Dixie politics in 1940. Probes the dry rot of local corruption.

Lightwood Tree (Lippincott, 1947). Of a Georgia community in 1943, and the fight of an academy history teacher to get the people to uphold civil rights.

The Fortune Tellers (Lippincott, 1951). Centers on the attempt of the leading citizen of a Southern town to keep hidden a family secret: a murder for which a Negro was unjustly condemned. Catches aspects of present-day mores.

FRENCH, ALICE (OCTAVE THANET, pseud.), 1850–1934

Knitters in the Sun (1887). Stories that describe social conditions in Arkansas. Discerning but somewhat sentimental.

GIBBONS, ROBERT, 1915–

Bright Is the Morning (Knopf, 1943). A first novel, full of warmth and humor, which portrays the life and emotions of ordinary Alabamans "who live neither behind the great white columns nor beneath the leaking roof."

GILES, BARBARA

The Gentle Bush (Harcourt, 1947). See below, p. 178.

GIVENS, CHARLES G.

All Cats Are Gray (Bobbs, 1937). Lively portraits of Tennessee villagers in a community "where ignorance and bigotry stalk the land."

GLASGOW, ELLEN, 1874–1945

*Barren Ground (Doubleday, 1925). An American *Far from the Madding Crowd*. A story of the worn-out land of Virginia and its rehabilitation by the use of scientific methods.

*They Stooped to Folly: A Comedy of Morals (Doubleday, 1929). Delightfully ironic treatment of changing attitudes toward feminine conduct.

The Sheltered Life (Doubleday, 1932). Of a young girl "sheltered" from a knowledge of life in true Southern fashion.

Vein of Iron (Harcourt, 1935). The fifth generation of a Virginia family of Scotch Presbyterians.

In This Our Life (Harcourt, 1941). A story of family relationships in Queensborough, Virginia. Shows philosophic understanding of Southern ways.

GORDON, CAROLINE, 1895–

Penhally (Scribner, 1931). Story of a Kentucky estate, Penhally, and of the one-hundred-year struggle to keep it within the family. Story starts in 1826.

Aleck Maury (Scribner, 1931). Biographical novel about Aleck Maury, whose predominant interest is his love for hunting and fishing. He finally satisfies his desire at the age of seventy in a Virginia valley, after all his family cares are in order.

The Garden of Adonis (Scribner, 1937). Shows the Southern sharecropper, the plantation owner, and the industrialist in conflict.

GREEN, PAUL, 1894–

This Body the Earth (Harper, 1935). A study of the Southern sharecropper who is condemned forever to the system no matter how industrious he may be.

Salvation on a String, and Other Tales of the South (Harper, 1946). Short stories about the Raleigh, North Carolina, back-country area, several of them about revivalism. Traditional treatment of hillbillies and Negroes, in the main.

HAMILL, KATHARINE

Swamp Shadow (Knopf, 1936). Of a strong, responsible woman who contrasts with the shiftless, fever-ridden poor whites in the swamp region of the Mississippi Coast. A picture of these backwoods people—their language, habits, and customs.

HARRIS, BERNICE K.

Purslane (University of North Carolina, 1939). An excellent presentation of the comfortable life of an independent Southern farmer about 1900. Slim in plot but abundant in sensuous descriptions of country food.

Sweet Beulah Land (Doubleday, 1943). An honest picture of life among landlords and tenants, good and bad alike—simple ordinary Americans who live on a neck of the Carolina coast. Rich in the everydayness of planting, harvesting, worshiping.

HAVRON, LAURIE

Hurricane Hush (Greystone, 1941). Vivid characterizations of poor whites in the Florida piney woods. Seemingly influenced by Faulkner.

HEARD, ANNETTE, 1888–

Return Not Again (Bobbs, 1937). The sickening conditions of poor whites of the Mississippi delta country.

HEATH, WILLIAM L., 1924–

Violent Saturday (Harper, 1955). A movie-like plot story with action and brutality, laid in an Alabama town in the midst of a regular but rainy week end and built around a bank robbery committed by outsiders.

HEDDEN, MRS. WORTH TUTTLE

*The Other Room (Crown, 1947). Tells of the daughter of an old Virginia family who becomes a teacher in a Negro college in New Orleans. Throws into relief the difficulties of young people, both black and white, south of Mason and Dixon's line.

HURSTON, ZORA NEALE, 1901–

Jonah's Gourd Vine (Lippincott, 1934). Story of Negro life in the Southern cotton lands told in authentic Negro dialect. Story is concerned with a Negro preacher and his irresistible attractiveness to women.

Seraph on the Suwanee (Scribner, 1948). A tender, simple story of life and love among Florida crackers in swamp and turpentine camps. Catches the literary flavor of "illiterate" Southern speech.

KELLEY, EDITH SUMMERS

*Weeds (Harcourt, 1923). Good presentation of life of renters on a tobacco farm. The heroine, Judy Pippinger, is said to be the first "poor-white" woman to become a leading character in a novel.

KEYES, FRANCES PARKINSON (WHEELER), 1885–

River Road (Messner, 1945). A long, romantically-told story of a family living along the river road between Baton Rouge and New Orleans, descendants of the earlier great plantation owners trying to live up to the great traditions of the past.

Steamboat Gothic (Messner, 1952). Deals with three generations on a Louisiana plantation from the Civil War to 1930. A carefully got-up, romantic period piece.

KIMBROUGH, EDWARD, 1918–

From Hell to Breakfast (Lippincott, 1941). A portrait of a demagogue in a Mississippi campaign for re-election as United States Senator. Reports on the traditional issues dealt with by Southern politicians and hints at the truths lying behind the campaign fronts. A sordid and apparently truthful picture.

Night Fire (Rinehart, 1946). Dramatic story of the rescue of a Negro boy from a lynching. The hero grows from a playboy into a responsible citizen.

KIRKBRIDE, RONALD DE LEVINGTON, 1912–

Winds, Blow Gently (Fell, 1945). See below, p. 158.

LANHAM, EDWIN M., 1904–

The Stricklands (Little, 1939). Of Oklahoma tenant farmers. One son organizes unions; another is an outlaw. Good arguments against "Jim Crow" and for unions.

LEE, CLARENCE P., 1913–

The Unwilling Journey (Macmillan, 1940). The story of a small boy in an Arkansas village. The story traces his life from the village to Pine Bluff and through one year of high school.

LUMPKIN, GRACE, 1898–

A Sign for Cain (Furman, 1935). Story of the organization of Negro and white workers of the South by a Negro Communist who has returned from the North, showing the deterioration of the former ruling families and the power of organized protest. A Marxist novel.

The Wedding (Furman, 1939). Story set in a small Georgia town in 1909. The lovers have a quarrel on the eve of their wedding, and the novel traces subsequent happenings. Shows the folkways of the Southern middle class.

MALLY, EMMA LOUISE, 1908–

The Mocking Bird Is Singing (Holt, 1944). A story of the changing South. Shows nineteenth-century business men engaged in blockade-running, railroad-building, and cotton- and cattle-dealing.

McCULLERS, CARSON, 1917–

*The Heart Is a Lonely Hunter (Houghton, 1940). A psychological study of the relationships of five lonesome people in a small city. Attests the seriousness of many Southern problems, such as the suppression of the intelligent Negro and the brutal slum environment of mill workers.

MEDEARIS, MARY, 1916–

Big Doc's Girl (Lippincott, 1942). Presents the dignified, virtuous, heroic side of village life. Set in the back country of Arkansas.

MELLINGER, MAY

Splint Road (Putnam, 1952). See below, p. 76.

MILBURN, GEORGE, 1906–

Oklahoma Town (Harcourt, 1931). Country and village life in Oklahoma. In part reminiscent of older Southern themes (Southern colonels, Southern attitudes toward Negroes, etc.)

No More Trumpets (Harcourt, 1933). A better collection than *Oklahoma Town*. Contains representative Southern humor, similar to that of Erskine C. Caldwell but mellower. More realistic than Caldwell, if not so pointedly satiric as Caldwell at his best.

The Catalogue (Harcourt, 1936). Shows the place of mail-order catalogues in the lives of farmers and small-town folk. Satisfying humor.

MILLEN, GILMORE, 1897–

Sweet Man (Viking, 1930). Story of John Henry, son of a mulatto and a white man, set on a Southern cotton plantation. His interest in women leads him into many adventures, climaxing in his job as chauffeur to a white woman in Los Angeles. A good description of Negro life on the plantation.

MILLS, CHARLES, 1914–

The Choice (Macmillan, 1943). Of a Southern boy who considered himself an aristocrat and his conflicts with the materialistic world of the small town.

The Alexandrians (Putnam, 1952). Covers a century of events, beginning in 1839, in an ordinary, normal small town in Georgia.

MUNZ, CHARLES CURTIS, 1905–

Land Without Moses (Urquhart, 1938). A strong picture of sharecroppers and their absolute dependence on the boss. Implies their need for leadership.

PALMER, FLORENCE G., 1895–

Spring Will Come Again (Bobbs, 1940). The story of a cotton planter and his family in Alabama from 1880 on, and his struggles to succeed.

PERRY, GEORGE SESSIONS, 1910–

Hold Autumn in Your Hand (Viking, 1941). A wholesome, well-rounded account of a good-natured, independent Texas tenant-farmer in a river bottom. A miniature *Grapes of Wrath* seen through rose-colored glasses.

Hackberry Cavalier (Viking, 1944). Short stories of backwoods Texas. Happy and romantic regionalism.

PINCKNEY, JOSEPHINE, 1895–

Three O'Clock Dinner (Viking, 1945). See below, p. 106.

PRATT, THEODORE, 1901–

The Big Blow (Little, 1936). Of a young couple who settle on a farm in Florida and have to face the hostility of their neighbors and the defeating forces of nature—insects, drought, sun, and hurricane.

ROBERTS, ELIZABETH MADOX, 1885–1941

*****The Time of Man** (Viking, 1926). Excellent portrayal of poor whites in Kentucky, their ambitions and daydreams, and the inescapability of their lot, generation to generation.

My Heart and My Flesh (Viking, 1927). Of half-sisters, one with a white mother, the other with a Negro mother.

He Sent Forth a Raven (Viking, 1935). With the death of his second wife a wealthy Kentucky farmer vowed he would never again leave the house. He directed his workers on the farm from the balcony. His news from the outside was related to him by his great-granddaughter.

RYLEE, ROBERT, 1908–

Deep, Dark River (Farrar, 1935). See below, p. 168.

St. George of Weldon (Farrar, 1937). Of a well-to-do family in a present-day village near Memphis. Emphasizes the dependence and lack of stamina of the younger generation.

SAXON, LYLE, 1891–1946

Children of Strangers (Houghton, 1937). An excellent story of the colored Creoles of Louisiana, a group entirely different in folkways from other Negroes of the United States.

SCARBOROUGH, DOROTHY, 1858?–1935

In the Land of Cotton (Macmillan, 1923). Presents the contrast of the rich, full life on the Texas cotton plantation and the meager, hard life of the poor tenant farmer.

Can't Get a Red Bird (Harper, 1929). Much on country customs, etc. Sentimental. Comes up to present day with its talk of farmer co-operatives.

SIMON, CHARLIE MAY, 1897–

The Share-Cropper (Dutton, 1937). Story of sharecroppers in Arkansas. A novel of social injustice. The main character takes part in union activities.

SIMS, MARIAN, 1899–

The City on the Hill (Lippincott, 1940). A realistic and dramatic account of a young lawyer's rebellion against the evil and corruption of a small North Carolina city.

SMITH, LILLIAN EUGENIA, 1897–

*****Strange Fruit** (Reynal, 1944). The story of a love affair between a white man and a Negro girl, a murder, and a lynching in a representative Georgia town. An informed and sensitive exploration of the effect of Southern ideas and customs on family and race relations.

SPENCER, ELIZABETH

This Crooked Way (Dodd, 1952). Of a religious man, both mean and tender, who gets what he wants. A Faulknerian version of psychic decay and physical violence, in the Mississippi hills and Delta. Several styles and points of view.

STEWARD, ANN, 1898–

Let the Earth Speak (Macmillan, 1940). A poetically written novel about a large estate in Kentucky. Love of the land is a theme.

STRAUSS, THEODORE, 1912–

Moonrise (Viking, 1946). Story of a boy's struggle to live in a small Southern town in which his father had been hanged for murder.

STREET, JAMES, 1903–1954

In My Father's House (Dial Press, 1941). Of a Mississippi farm family, as told by the fourteen-year-old son.

STRIBLING, THOMAS SIGISMUND, 1881–

*****Teeftallow** (Doubleday, 1926). Of poor whites, or mountain whites, of modern times in a Southern village.

*****Bright Metal** (Doubleday, 1928). The crudity of Tennessee farm life and the community class distinctions as seen by a girl of "tarnished metal" who married a Tennessee farmer.

Backwater (Doubleday, 1930). The love affair of the son of the local bootlegger of a small town in Arkansas and the daughter of an aristocratic family is halted because of their different social status. The breaking of the levee changes the situation.

*****The Store** (Doubleday, 1932). Gives the atmosphere of a small town in Alabama—the folkways, the class distinctions, the religions, the business practices. The ruthless, unethical main character becomes an important man in the town.

Unfinished Cathedral (Doubleday, 1934). Continues the story of *The Store*. In his nineties Colonel Miltiades Vaiden is the village patriarch, the chief donor toward a cathedral.

STYRON, WILLIAM, 1925–

Lie Down in Darkness (Bobbs, 1951). Skillful, immediate writing in the tradition of Joyce and Faulkner, about the minds and memories, the loneliness and love-searching of soul-sick members of an old Virginia family. Strong probing of alcoholism, Puritanism, and lostness. Notable for a 52-page paragraph that plumbs a girl's stream of consciousness.

SYLVESTER, HARRY, 1908–

Dearly Beloved (Duell, 1942). Of the attempts of a young Catholic layman to start a co-operative including Negroes in a Maryland community. Satirizes the church and Southern mores.

TAYLOR, PETER H., 1917–

A Long Fourth and Other Stories (Harcourt, 1948). Stories of middle-class life in Southern towns—the night's leave of a soldier, changes in a growing suburb, and so on. Concerned with growing boys, evolving social attitudes, and crises in moral understanding.

TILLERY, CARLYLE, 1904–

Red Bone Woman (Day, 1950). A touching story of the marriage of a poor Red Bone girl (a "Spanish white") and an elderly white man on a declining farm in southeastern Louisiana. Excellent for dialect, folkways, and social tensions.

VINES, HOWELL H., 1899–

This Green Thicket World (Little, 1934). Story of a large landowner of "the thicket" in Alabama. Some good details about daily life—socials, food, fishing, and hunting.

WARREN, ROBERT PENN, 1905–

Night Rider (Houghton, 1939). Deals with a Kentucky tobacco war in the early 1900's and with the men who resorted to terrorism in this fight between the manufacturers and growers.

At Heaven's Gate (Harcourt, 1943). A brutal melodramatic novel of shame and sin in the South. About the war hero, the religious seeker of salvation, the financier, and other types. Gives insight into morbid psychology.

Circus in the Attic, and Other Stories (Harcourt, 1948). In many of these stories of Tennessee, the author explores "the integral relation between a rural folk and the land." The title story diagrams the social relationships in a Tennessee town.

WELTY, EUDORA, 1909–

Delta Wedding (Harcourt, 1946). A week in the life of the Fairchilds of Shellmound Plantation, in the Mississippi Delta. A subtle and slow-moving story.

Golden Apples (Harcourt, 1949). A series of short stories that chronicle the passing of some forty years of a group of persons in a small Mississippi town. Artistic, perhaps even overwrought, with undertones and adroit immediacy. One remarkable tale deals with a Mississippian in San Francisco.

The Ponder Heart (Harcourt, 1954). An amusing brief comedy, appropriately written, of characters in a Mississippi village. A genre yarn with a tall-tale quality, told in the first person by a participant in a funny trial at the courthouse.

WERTENBAKER, GREEN PEYTON, 1907–

Rain on the Mountain (Little, 1934). A study of living in modern Virginia and of a romantic's search for "reality" in and around Charlottesville.

WILSON, JOHN W., 1920–

High John, the Conqueror (Macmillan, 1948). A touching short regional novel of cotton farmers in the Brazos River bottoms. Presents the feel of the land, the life and problems of Negro tenant farmers, and the economic conflict of small landholders with aggressive monopolists.

WOLFE, THOMAS, 1900–1938

*Look Homeward, Angel (Scribner, 1929). The story of Eugene Gant, a Southern boy. Much material on Southern mores and many unforgettable pictures. The boy breaks away from his pathetic family but is nevertheless caught in a web of futility and despair.

Of Time and the River (Scribner, 1935). Continues Eugene Gant's story.

WOOD, CHARLES B., 1906–
    First, the Fields (University of North Carolina, 1941). Of a South Carolina tobacco grower in his unsuccessful attempt to save his farm from bankruptcy.

YOUNG, STARK, 1881–
    River House (Scribner, 1929). Set in a little Mississippi town, *River House* tells of the conflict between the South of old and the modern South. Most of the characters are types rather than individuals, but the picture of the South is real.

YOUNGS, DELIGHT
    The Gladesman (Dodd, 1955). Of the marginal farmers who live in a frontier fashion in the sawgrass Everglades region. A story of inner and outer struggles brought on by human nature and social "progress."

4c. The Southern Highlands (Including the Hillbilly)

Unlike the planters and farm workers in the cotton-raising low-lands, the mountaineers were little affected by the Civil War, though they have been in time gradually influenced by industrialism and modernization in the South. Their way of life, unbroken for two centuries, is characterized by survivals of eighteenth-century customs and attitudes. Independent in spirit, picturesque in speech, increasingly antiquated in culture, the mountain folk have interested writers continuously since the local-colorists appeared in the 1870's.

No tradition has been more colorful and pleasing to the American public than the picture of the Southern hillbilly with a still in every other "holler" and with a disposition to carry on continuous feuds with his neighbors. The traditional story is best represented by the work of Charles Neville Buck and John Fox. While "proletarian" writers of the 1930's like Grace Lumpkin and Olive Dargan lean heavily on the old tradition for their portraits of the hill folk, others (seemingly more in touch with their materials), for example, Jesse Stuart, T. S. Stribling, and Harriette Arnow, create entire novels picturing what seem to be flesh-and-blood people living in the Southern Highlands in the twentieth century.

ARNOW, HARRIETTE LOUISA, 1908–
    *Hunter's Horn** (Macmillan, 1949). Excellent for many sides of life in the Kentucky hills during the 1930's—housework, fox hunting, molasses making, selling sheep and heifers at the yards, Federal farm relief, and so on. Excellences in style, including rendition of dialect.

BOONE, JACK, 1908–

Dossie Bell Is Dead (Stokes, 1939). A story of the hill people of West Tennessee in much the same style as *Tobacco Road*. Deals with the death of Dossie Bell, Luster Holder's woman, and of the confession of the minister at the funeral when he tells the part he played in the drama.

BUCK, CHARLES N., 1879–

The Call of the Cumberlands (1913). A story of the typical Kentucky mountain feud with all the expected local color and atmosphere.

Mountain Justice (Houghton, 1935). Story of a district attorney of Kentucky of the Cumberlands and how he served mountain justice on three men convicted of murder.

CHAPMAN, MARISTAN, 1895–

Happy Mountain (Viking, 1928). A simple and pungent story of Cumberland Mountain folk.

Homeplace (Viking, 1929). More about Tennessee hill people, with their fresh and charming vernacular.

The Weather Tree (Viking, 1932). Story of the conflict between a small conservative settlement in the Tennessee mountains and a man who tried to rebuild the town, only to meet with hate and resentment.

DARGAN, OLIVE T. (FIELDING BURKE, pseud.)

Highland Annals (Scribner, 1925). Chronicles of neighborly kindness on an upland farm, revealing the Southern mountaineer folk in all their contradictions of character. Sketchy short stories leaning heavily on the traditional treatment of mountain folk.

FOX, JOHN W., 1862–1919

The Little Shepherd of Kingdom Come (1903). See below, p. 126.

The Trail of the Lonesome Pine (1908). A very popular mountain story, with all the traditional trappings.

FURMAN, LUCY, 1869–

The Quare Women (Little, 1923). Of the Kentucky hills, with feuds, moonshine whisky, dialect, and quaint ways. Tells of the coming of a settlement school and of its work among the mountaineers as these "furrin" women tried to teach the women to cook, sew, play, and sing.

The Glass Window (Little, 1925). A story of Kentucky whites around 1910. Tells of workers in a settlement school.

GIVENS, CHARLES G.

The Doctor's Pills Are Stardust (Bobbs, 1938). Story of a country doctor in the Tennessee hills.

The Devil Takes a Hill Town (Bobbs, 1939). An easygoing tale of the Tennessee hillbillies. The Devil and God, in the persons of mountain men, are the chief characters. They speak in their native, colorful dialect and discuss the problems of capitalism and the class struggle together.

GOWEN, EMMETT, 1902–

Mountain Born (Bobbs, 1932). A tale of members of two rival families who fall in love. Gives insight into the lives of the mountain folk, their language, loves, and hates.

HANNUM, ALBERTA PIERSON, 1906–
  Thursday April (Harper, 1931). A story of West Virginia mountaineer life.
  The Hills Step Lightly (Morrow, 1934). Of a hill woman and her life from childhood to old age. Good detail of daily life in the late nineteenth century, but a romantic plot.
  The Gods and One (Duell, 1941). A simple, pleasant story of a North Carolina mountain girl.
  Roseanna McCoy (Holt, 1947). A satisfactory romance of the love of Roseanna McCoy for one of the Hatfields during the famous Hatfield-McCoy feud.

HARRIS, BERNICE (KELLY)
  Janey Jeems (Doubleday, 1946). A Blue Ridge Mountains story told in the vernacular. Seemingly true to the life of the people.

HARRIS, GEORGE WASHINGTON, 1814–1869
  *Sut Lovingood (1867; new edition, Grove, 1954). Twenty-two yarns that deal hilariously with many sides of life in the Great Smokies. Notable for vivid, often Rabelaisian details and for rich imagery. A masterpiece of American dialect humor.

HAUN, MILDRED, 1912–
  The Hawk's Done Gone (Bobbs, 1940). About the people of eastern Tennessee. Shows changes the motor roads, schools, and traveling libraries have made upon their lives.

KANTOR, MACKINLAY, 1904–
  The Voice of Bugle Ann (Coward, 1935). A long short story of a man and his fox hound, Bugle Ann, in the hills of Missouri. A glimpse into a long-settled community.

KROLL, HARRY HARRISON, 1888–
  Their Ancient Grudge (Bobbs, 1946). The story of the Hatfield-McCoy feud, which flared in the southern Appalachians during the nineteenth century, told from the standpoint of the six women most closely involved.
  Darker Grows the Valley (Bobbs, 1947). A story of the Clinch Valley in east Tennessee, covering five generations from 1778 to the coming of T.V.A. A satisfactory record of common experience.

LANE, ROSE WILDER, 1877–
  *Hill-Billy (Harper, 1926). Laid in the Ozarks of Missouri. A lively, authentic presentation of folkways and ideas, accompanied by the usual romantic plot.

LUMPKIN, GRACE, 1898–
  To Make My Bread (Macaulay, 1932). An important proletarian novel showing the old ways of the North Carolina mountaineers completely disintegrating under the impact of modern industry.

MACKAYE, PERCY, 1875–
  Tall Tales of the Kentucky Mountains (Doran, 1926). A group of

twelve tall tales supposedly by one Solomon Shell as he went from one cabin to another spinning them. Fantastic and with quaint description, each yarn gives a picture of the Kentucky mountain area.

MARSHALL, ROBERT K., 1901–

Little Squire Jim (Duell, 1949). A story of mountain folk in North Carolina, especially of a boy. Acceptable for style and for accounts of lore and ways of living.

MURFREE, MARY N., 1850–1922

In the Tennessee Mountains (1884). The book that "made" the tradition. Emphasizes the peculiarities of mountain folk.

*The Prophet of the Great Smoky Mountains (1885). A local-color story of religion and superstition in the Tennessee hills.

RANDOLPH, VANCE, 1892–

From an Ozark Holler; Stories of Ozark Mountain Folk (Vanguard, 1933). A collection of anecdotes about the Ozarks. Deals with homely melodramas and local superstitions, stories more imaginative than realistic.

SIMON, CHARLIE MAY (HOGUE), 1897–

Straw in the Sun (Dutton, 1945). A simple story, rich in detail, of kindly folk in the Ozark Mountains. Told as an autobiography of the author's experiences living in the Ozarks during the depression years.

SIMPSON, HARRIETTE, 1908–

Mountain Path (Covici, 1936). The experience of a young girl teacher in a rural school in the Kentucky hills who witnesses a mountaineer feud and its effect on the women and children.

SKIDMORE, HUBERT, 1911–1946

I Will Lift Up Mine Eyes (Doubleday, 1936). Pictures farmers of the Blue Ridge in a year of drought.

Heaven Came So Near (Doubleday, 1938). Continues the story of the preceding novel.

STILL, JAMES, 1906–

*River of Earth (Viking, 1940). A simple episodic novel of life in the hills and coal camps of Kentucky. Gives a vivid picture of the hard life of the hill people. Develops universal themes: man's search for security, man's bewilderment at the ways of destiny.

STUART, JESSE, 1907–

Head of W-Hollow (Dutton, 1936). A collection of poetically written short stories containing some beautiful descriptions of the Kentucky mountains and of the Kentucky people. Written by a native who loves his land, its trees, crops, streams, and storms.

Trees of Heaven (Dutton, 1940). An amusing, robust story of the Kentucky hills. Depicts the farmer's love of land, his agricultural activities the year around, his attitude toward squatters.

Taps for Private Tussie (Dutton, 1943). A warm-hearted story of a generous, ever-squabbling clan of mountaineers. More than a stereotyped hillbilly tale, more than a sociological case study; humorous, poetic, sympathetic.

The Good Spirit of Laurel Ridge (McGraw, 1953). An episodic folk tale that catches the natural setting, the lore, and the people of the Kentucky hills.

TENNESSEE WRITERS' PROJECT

God Bless the Devil (University of North Carolina, 1940). Twenty-five anecdotes of life from the Great Smokies to the Mississippi levees. Such themes as milk shakes, lady-killing, horse races, hunting dogs.

WILLIAMSON, THAMES ROSS, 1894–

Woods Colt (Harcourt, 1933). Arkansas and Missouri. Of an illegitimate boy and his young manhood in the Ozarks.

5. THE SOUTHWEST AND CALIFORNIA
(ALSO IRRIGATION DITCHES AND OKIES)

In this list "Southwest" means the agricultural valleys and the dry farming areas of western Texas and Oklahoma and of New Mexico, Arizona, Nevada, Colorado, and Utah. California, which is economically and culturally a region unto itself, appears in the same list because its agriculture is like that in the Southwestern states, characterized by large-scale operations, special crops, irrigation, and an army of migrant laborers. A large part of rural life in these eight states also centers around the raising of cattle and sheep, as in the Northwest. The stories range from those of early attempts to establish the small-farm, individualistic pattern, such as Norris' *The Octopus,* to stories of present-day "factories in the field," such as Steinbeck's masterpiece, *The Grapes of Wrath.*

ARMSTRONG, ARNOLD B., pseud.

Parched Earth (Macmillan, 1934). Set in Tontos Valley, California, the novel deals with the seamy side of California landlords and tricksters in exploiting the workers.

BAKER, HOWARD, 1905–

Orange Valley (Coward, 1931). A story of struggling orchardists of the San Joaquin Valley who finally succeed in making fruit country from the barren desert lands.

BEZZERIDES, A. I., 1908–

There Is a Happy Land (Holt, 1942). Of a family who come from the Great Plains to California and—in contrast to Steinbeck's Joad family—get along very well.

CLARK, WALTER VAN TILBURG, 1909–

The Track of the Cat (Random, 1949). Written in a good style and with much dialog, this takes place on a remote Nevada ranch and concerns itself symbolically with the struggle of good and evil.

FERBER, EDNA, 1887–

Giant (Doubleday, 1952). A plump job of journalistic research on present-day Texas. Casual in construction and repeatedly critical of Texans for "a mania for bigness" and the "littleness" of mind and culture that they hide. Points out maladjustments of Texans, their bigotry and hypocrisy and un-American treatment of Mexican-Americans. Centers on a vast cattle ranch.

FERGUSSON, HARVEY, 1890–

Grant of Kingdom (Morrow, 1950). A strong, skillful treatment of a private empire in New Mexico from the mid-nineteenth century to the present. Notable for characterizations of Indians, Spaniards, Mexicans, and American frontiersmen.

GILLMOR, FRANCES, 1903–

Fruit Out of Rock (Duell, 1940). A story of fruit-growing country in Arizona. Good local color.

HOBART, ALICE TISDALE (NOURSE), 1882–

*The Cup and the Sword (Bobbs, 1942). A family chronicle of Frenchmen who establish vineyards and wineries in California. Their enterprise is almost ruined by the Eighteenth Amendment but rises slowly again after 1934. A dramatic story told in terms of clearly realized characters.

The Cleft Rock (Bobbs, 1948). A thesis novel dealing with ownership and control of both land and irrigation water in the San Joaquin Valley. The problems set forth are made more important than the characters.

HORGAN, PAUL, 1903–

Main Line West (Harper, 1936). Picture of the restless spirit of Western United States in a tale of an orphan boy who at the age of thirteen set out alone on his wanderings. A portrait of a California town.

*The Return of the Weed (Harper, 1936). Six short stories showing man's inability to adjust himself to his environment. New Mexico. Each story deals with some ruin or destroyed Mission or abandoned habitation.

*Lamp on the Plains (Harper, 1937). Sequel to *Main Line West*. Story of a boy's life in a town on the plains of New Mexico. Good in detailed description of a small town and of the ranches. Typical plains people.

Far from Cibola (Harper, 1938). Excellent realistic sketches of life on the plains of eastern New Mexico. Good characterization.

KING, MARY PAULA, 1909–

Quincie Bolliver (Houghton, 1941). Of a Texas town in oil-boom times and a girl from the age of twelve to eighteen. A picture of social customs and of labor in the oil fields.

LAVENDER, DAVID SIEVERT

Andy Claybourne (Doubleday, 1946). A ranch story of modern Colorado.

MARION, FRANCES, 1890–
  Valley People (Reynal, 1935). Short stories of a small valley in northern California. Some are reminiscent of Sherwood Anderson in their emphasis on frustration. Others are light and happy in tone.

MARTIN, CURTIS, 1913–
  The Hills of Home (Houghton, 1944). Seventeen stories of a New Mexico town called Sangre de Cristo. Sincere, youthful, and simple in style.

NORRIS, FRANK, 1870–1902
  *The Octopus (1901). A California classic. The story of the struggle of the early wheat farmers of the San Joaquin to be independent, to establish the sort of neighborhoods of farmers that had long been the pattern in the Middle West. Shows what the monopolistic railroad, the "Octopus," did to their hope.

OSKISON, JOHN M., 1874–
  Brothers Three (Macmillan, 1935). Story of three brothers who owned an Oklahoma farm from 1873 to the present. The three are a town merchant, a cattleman, and a writer.

PERRY, GEORGE SESSIONS (editor), 1910–
  Roundup Time: A Collection of Southwestern Writing (McGraw, 1943). Stories, biographies, and essays. Stories by Atlee, Horgan, Thomason, Lanham, Richter, Porter, La Farge, Dobie, Steinbeck, and others. An introduction to the best of Southwestern literature.

SINCLAIR, JOHN L., 1902–
  In Time of Harvest (Macmillan, 1943). Of nesters from Oklahoma who settled in New Mexico. An earthy regional novel of the strengths and weaknesses of a bean rancher.

SORENSEN, VIRGINIA (EGGERTSEN), 1912–
  The Neighbors (Reynal, 1947). Beloved enemy plot laid in sheep country of Colorado highlands. Combines the open-air romance of a good Western with the realism of social and economic actualities such as water rights, stockmen's associations, and pressures of mores.
  The Evening and the Morning (Harcourt, 1949). Among Danish Mormons. Contrasts life in a Utah town as lived by children in the 1920's and decades before by their grandmother, but shows the essential continuity of pattern.
  Many Heavens (Harcourt, 1954). A love story containing much of life in a mountain-enclosed valley town in Utah in 1890, just after polygamy came to an end.

STEINBECK, JOHN, 1902–
  Pastures of Heaven (Viking, 1932). Describes farm life in California's central valley. Theme of the book is the people's failure to find happiness in these perfect surroundings. Supposes this failure to be caused by people's inability to look at neighbors with tolerance. Effective characterizations.

To a God Unknown (Viking, 1933). Story of a man who plants a tree on his California ranch to symbolize his father's spirit. The ranch prospers until his brother, not understanding his sacrifices to the tree, cuts it down. Years of famine and drouth follow. An almost mystical treatment of farming.

*In Dubious Battle (Viking, 1936). A story of attempts to organize migratory fruit pickers in California. In the fights between pickers, vigilantes, owners, etc., not only is the outcome "dubious" but even the motives and desires of the various elements are not clear to themselves or others. Incompletely convincing.

*Of Mice and Men (Viking, 1937). Discusses the problems of the migratory ranch workers who cherish the unrealized dream of some day owning their own land. Shows the physical and spiritual conditions of these laborers, who work for not much more than their food. A pathetic story of frustration.

*The Grapes of Wrath (Viking, 1939). An outstanding book describing the plight of the migratory farm worker in the 1930's. The Joad family travel from Oklahoma to California looking for work. In California they live in poverty and degradation. Shows the "factory in the field" system of farming. Realistic, and beautifully written.

*The Long Valley (Viking, 1938). Realistic short stories of people in the Salinas Valley. Shows how people live there, and their relationship to the migrants who are a constant part of the scene.

East of Eden (Viking, 1952). Contrasts two families over a fifty-year period on ranches and in towns of the Salinas Valley, California. A self-conscious reworking of the story of Cain and Abel. Effective in certain scenes but weak in key characterizations and naïve in philosophy.

STEWART, GEORGE R., 1895–

Storm (Random, 1941). About a low-pressure storm center that crosses the Pacific and brings disaster in California and the Sierra Nevada Range. The storm's "birth, growth, adventures, and final death," says Stewart, are the "main vortex of the story," with "the various little human beings . . . isolated here and there around the edges." No characterizations.

Fire (Random, 1948). A taut story of the birth, work, and death of a forest fire in a California national forest. Dramatizes mankind versus an element on the rampage. The nonfiction far surpasses the fiction.

STILWELL, HART, 1902–

Uncovered Wagon (Doubleday, 1947). A novel dealing with life in west Texas in the early 1900's.

SYKES, HOPE WILLIAMS, 1901–

Second Hoeing (Putnam, 1935). The beet fields of Colorado. A picture of unending toil.

TOTHEROH, DAN, 1898–

Wild Orchard (Doran, 1927). An outstanding novel of the California fruit country and of the daughter of an Italian prune picker. Tells of her coming maturity through a series of tragic love episodes and of the nomadic life of prune pickers.

VAN DER VEER, JUDY, 1912–
   November Grass (Longmans, 1940). Of a girl who belonged to the intellectual world of Eastern friends and also to the everyday world of her father's ranch in California.

WEST, JESSAMYN
   Cress Delahanty (Harcourt, 1954). Amusing episodes in the life of a bright girl growing up from her twelfth to sixteenth year on a southern California orange ranch and attending her first year in "Woolman" College.

WILDER, ROBERT, 1901–
   The Wine of Youth (Putnam, 1955). See below, p. 143.

INDUSTRIAL AMERICA

Just as pioneering was superseded in each part of the United States at some time during the nineteenth century by a more stable way of living, so the farm-and-village pattern has been superseded in many sections by urban-industrial life during the past fifty to seventy years. As the change took place it was reflected immediately by writers, who in this area made the United States the leading nation of the world in the production of fiction. The most noticeable effect of the industrial age on literature was the development of realism, with its twin facets of reform and naturalism and with the development of analytical, critical attitudes. Of course the romantic element is still in evidence, too, and amid all the realistic and critical treatments of labor, business, the city, modern society, and modern war there are hundreds of books creating a romantic picture of the same elements.

1. LABOR AND THE INDUSTRIAL MACHINE
(ALSO ROBOTS AND BUTTON PUSHERS)

The earliest and most persistent subject matter used in fiction in the industrial age has concerned, quite naturally, the laborer and his relation to the industrial machine. In general, writers have sympathized with the worker's plight. The "Depression" years produced a flood of the so-called proletarian novels. Mostly they were propagandistic, but there was much solid writing too. Books such as those of Thomas Bell, John Steinbeck, and John Dos Passos have combined excellent literary quality and insight into the social scene. There have been many interesting books giving the details of work in certain industries and the "leisure time" activities of the workers.

ADAMS, SAMUEL HOPKINS, 1871–
   *Sunrise to Sunset (Random, 1950). A dramatic novel of work, love, and mystery laid in the collar and cotton mills of Troy, New York, in the 1830's, at the time when labor was winning the 12-hour day. Interesting as an enlivened piece of history and as a contrast and parallel to Dreiser's *An American Tragedy*.

ALDRICH, THOMAS BAILEY, 1836–1907
   The Stillwater Tragedy (1880). Various aspects of life in a manufacturing village, including a love story, the detection of a murder, and the passions and calamities of a strike.

ALGREN, NELSON, 1909–
   Somebody in Boots (Vanguard, 1935). A story of jobless youth and

their disillusionment. Bitter indictment of a social system that condemns its younger generation to soup lines and a hobo existence.

ANDERSON, SHERWOOD, 1876–1941

Poor White (Huebsch, 1920). Of a poor country man who became an inventor. The story of how out-of-place he felt among industrialists.

ARNOW, HARRIETTE LOUISA, 1908–

The Dollmaker (Macmillan, 1954). A strong sociological presentation of Cumberland mountain people who migrate to Detroit to work during World War II and there endure shack housing in an impoverished environment. Centers on the wife and children and the impact on them of conditions in the industrial city.

ATTAWAY, WILLIAM, 1911–

Let Me Breathe Thunder (Doubleday, 1939). Strong novel of two migratory laborers and a small Mexican boy they pick up on the road. Their life as migrants forces them to be hard, but their feelings underneath show through the staccato language and harsh deeds.

BELL, THOMAS, 1903–

*Out of This Furnace (Little, 1941). A gripping story of Slovak immigrants in the steel mills of Pennsylvania.

There Comes a Time (Little, 1946). An urbane, realistic, sociological novel dealing with a middle-aged bank teller's work for his union, and incidentally with politics of the 1930's.

BELLAMY, EDWARD, 1850–1898

*Looking Backward (1888). The most popular Utopian novel. Pictures a perfect socialist state in the year 2000. Some comment on political life of 1887.

*Equality (1894). A sequel to *Looking Backward*. Gives more details and shows how the revolution came about.

BINNS, ARCHIE, 1899–

The Timber Beast (Scribner, 1944). Story of an elderly man, an old "timber beast," and his sons. A quiet, intimate tale of family life, with interesting glimpses of the logging business.

BISNO, BEATRICE

Tomorrow's Bread (1938). Of Russian Jews and their struggles as immigrants, the garment-worker's union, and the making of a labor leader.

BISSELL, RICHARD, 1913?–

A Stretch on the River (Little, 1950). A rollicking report of towboat workers on the upper Mississippi in the early 1940's. Gives glimpses of interesting characters afloat and ashore.

7½ Cents (Little, 1953). Light, comic treatment of labor-management relations and a strike at the Sleep Tite Pajama Company, in an Iowa river town.

High Water (Little, 1954). Another high-spirited towboat story, from St. Louis north, in flood time. Like Clemens, Bissell is entranced by local color and riverbank vernacular.

BOYD, THOMAS, 1898–1935

*In Time of Peace (Minton, 1935). The story of one man's struggles from 1919 to 1929. He meets unemployment, boom times, labor violence. The title is ironic. The hero is becoming a radical at the end of the story.

BRINIG, MYRON, 1900–

The Sun Sets in the West (Farrar, 1935). The setting is Copper City, a large mining town, in which the characters, who spend their lives underground, spend much of their time talking and thinking of their unrealized dreams.

BRODY, CATHARINE

Nobody Starves (Longmans, 1932). A story of workers in an industrial city. Realistic portrayal of a man and his wife, their work, their tragedy growing out of the Depression. A better feeling of actuality than in most such novels.

BURMAN, BEN LUCIEN, 1895–

The Four Lives of Mundy Tolliver (Messner, 1953). Of a veteran who moves among the lower classes in the South and is in turn a towboat deck hand, a moonshiner, a partner in a truck store, and a shrimp fisherman. Picaresque, simple, folklorish, and allegorical.

CANTWELL, ROBERT, 1908–

Land of Plenty (Farrar, 1934). Realistic story of a lumber mill. Good portraits of brutalized workers, owners, and their families.

CHURCHILL, WINSTON, 1871–1947

The Dwelling Place of Light (Macmillan, 1917). Of American industrialism, the harsh lot of women caught in its toils, and the alleged misdoings of the Industrial Workers of the World.

COLMAN, LOUIS, 1904–

Lumber (Little, 1931). Laid in a lumber-mill town in the Northwest. A drifting and uneducated jobber marries and starts a home. Strikes lead to economic difficulties. He is unable to adjust himself to the demands of modern industry.

DAHLBERG, EDWARD, 1900–

Bottom Dogs (Simon, 1930). A realistic indictment of American institutions and the futility of life for the lower classes. The story of one who spent his early life in an orphan's home and his later life as a salesman and hobo.

DARGAN, OLIVE TILFORD (FIELDING BURKE, pseud.)

Call Home the Heart (Longmans, 1932). Leans on old-style romance for hill traditions. A proletarian novel of the hill woman from the Blue Ridge who goes down into the factory town to work.

A Stone Came Rolling (Longmans, 1935). Sequel to *Call Home the Heart*. Tract-like in argument.

DOS PASSOS, JOHN, 1896–

*U.S.A. (Harcourt, 1938). Contains *The 42nd Parallel* (1930), *1919*

(1932), and *The Big Money* (1936). A trilogy which captures much of American life during the first thirty years of the century. Life stories of six men and six women from various social and occupational groups. Contains brief, vivid biographies of national leaders of the time and fragments of the news and songs of the time.

DREISER, THEODORE, 1871–1945

*An American Tragedy (Boni, 1925). An outstanding American novel with a naturalistic philosophy. The ironic title refers to the sordid life and pathetic death of the main character, a weakling—the only sort of life and death a common man could have when controlled absolutely by his environment and his biochemic machine—the sort of "tragedy" modern America produces, according to the Naturalists.

DUNCAN, DAVID, 1913–

The Serpent's Egg (Macmillan, 1950). Focuses on a labor-dispute panel that is arbitrating a controversy about overtime pay for bus drivers. Crosscuts into several lives. A clear, firm story with a residuum of theatricality.

EDMUNDS, MURRELL, 1898–

Between the Devil (Dutton, 1939). Of a young minister in a small Virginia industrial town who finds that besides his religious work he also has to battle on the political and social fronts of labor's war for recognition.

FREEMAN, MARY E. WILKINS, 1862–1930

The Portion of Labor (1901). One of the first labor novels. The struggle between capital and labor in a New England town.

GARSIDE, EDWARD B.

Cranberry Red (Little, 1938). A proletarian novel which shows poor Irish workers, among others, oppressed by a Yankee landlord in the Cape Cod cranberry region.

GELLHORN, MARTHA E., 1908–

The Trouble I've Seen (Morrow, 1936). Of four sets of people from divergent backgrounds who are driven on to the relief rolls.

GILKYSON, THOMAS WALTER, 1880–

Oil (Scribner, 1924). Vivid details of the actual scouting and drilling for oil and of the ruthless business methods of some oil men.

GREENE, JOSIAH E., 1911–

Not in Our Stars (Macmillan, 1945). Relationships between individuals and between families working for a dairy farm in the East.

HALPER, ALBERT, 1904–

The Foundry (Cassell, 1936). Seemingly realistic picture of all classes and individuals working in a foundry.

The Chute (Viking, 1937). Human character study of ordinary people, young Jews, swallowed up in continually feeding the package chute in a Chicago mail-order house. A gifted high-school student sees his dream of an architect's drawing board disappear as he is forced to become an order picker. Good material, but pedestrian writing.

The Little People (Harper, 1942). Depicts the lives of the employees of a huge department store. Shows half-inarticulate people on the job and at home. Sympathetic literary treatment of the repressed and exploited.

HAVIGHURST, WALTER, 1901–

Pier Seventeen (Macmillan, 1935). A shipping strike in the Northwest from a sailor's viewpoint.

HAY, JOHN, 1838–1905

The Bread-Winners (1884). Pictures a provincial town realistically. Conservative in ideas.

HEMINGWAY, ERNEST, 1896–

To Have and Have Not (Scribner, 1937). Both a satire on the idle rich and a brutally realistic depiction of the desperate plight of the unemployed. Contrasts the underdogs of Key West with decadent socialites down for the winter season.

HERBST, JOSEPHINE, 1897–

The Rope of Gold (Harcourt, 1939). Deals with the economic conditions in America from 1933 to 1937. Story centers around a farm organizer, his wife, and an automobile manufacturer.

HULL, MORRIS

Cannery Anne (Houghton, 1936). Cannery workers in central California. Of the hope of the workers some day to own homes of their own, a seemingly hopeless dream.

HUXLEY, ALDOUS, 1894–

***Brave New World** (Harper, 1932). A sharp and pointed satire on human beings in America, in the Machine Age.

IDELL, ALBERT EDWARD, 1901–

Stephen Hayne (Sloane, 1951). Pennsylvania anthracite miners after the Civil War when there was bitter economic conflict, stirred up by overlords, between Pennsylvania Germans and Irish immigrants. Goes into a strike and the charges made in court against "Molly Maguires." Shows how scapegoats were made of the Irish.

KIRKBRIDE, RONALD DE LEVINGTON, 1912–

Spring Is Not Gentle (Doubleday, 1949). See below, p. 158.

LANHAM, EDWIN, 1904–

Thunder in the Earth (Harcourt, 1941). Of Texas oil fields in the 1930's, the oil business, and industrial relations. Graphic accounts of wildcat oil promotion and production.

LEE, EDNA L., 1890–

The Southerners (Appleton-Century-Crofts, 1953). The heart of the book is a series of labor and promotion problems faced by the owner of a cotton mill. Scenes portray the liberalization of labor policies, the facing of financial and marketing issues, and the good fortune of hitting the trend toward "good-looking cottons." Deals with *some* Southerners, in Atlanta and nearby, 1900–1917.

LEVIN, MEYER, 1905–
> **Citizens** (Viking, 1940). Little Steel and the Memorial Day massacre in South Chicago in 1937.

LUMPKIN, GRACE, 1898
> **To Make My Bread** (Macaulay, 1932). Of mountaineers who became part of the factory system when it reached the South. An account of the Gastonia strike.

McCORMICK, JAY, 1919–
> **November Storm** (Doubleday, 1943). Describes life on a Great Lakes freighter, in the bunkrooms, the messrooms, the pilothouse, and the stokehold. Clear portraits of picturesque freshwater sailors and of a boy who is seeking self-confidence.

McINTYRE, JOHN T., 1871–
> **Ferment** (Farrar, 1937). A Philadelphia story of strikebreakers, racketeers, and labor spies. Expresses the hopelessness of the struggle of insignificant little people against Fascism.

McKENNEY, RUTH, 1911–
> *Industrial Valley** (Harcourt, 1939). A vivid pro-labor account of rubber workers in Akron, Ohio. Shows the birth of the sit-down strike and the turbulent growth of the C.I.O.
> **Jake Home** (Harcourt, 1943). The story of "a sort of laboring-class superman." Dramatizes in colorful detail American labor history in the 1920's and early 1930's. Interprets life in a remote Pennsylvania coal patch, trade-unionism, and the radical philosophy.

MALTZ, ALBERT, 1908–
> *The Way Things Are** (International, 1938). Eight short stories of underdogs, underprivileged or abused persons, who the Marxist author implies are victims of the capitalist system. Contains the moving and much-reprinted story of the ravages of silicosis at Gauley Bridge, West Virginia, "Man on a Road."
> **The Underground Stream** (Little, 1940). The struggle for union recognition in Detroit in 1936 before the C.I.O. and before the validation of the Labor Relations Act. A book centering on the lives of real people rather than the propagation of "proletarian" theory.

MARQUAND, JOHN PHILLIPS, 1893–
> **B.F.'s Daughter** (Little, 1946). Of an industrialist and his daughter. She tried to dominate her husband's life as her father had dominated hers.

MELLINGER, MAY
> **Splint Road** (Putnam, 1952). Laid in a shingle mill camp in the Louisiana cypress swamps, before and after 1900, among very simple people. Emphasis on the problems of the children and wives of sawyers and shingle weavers.

MEYERSBURG, DOROTHY, 1902–
> **Seventh Avenue** (Dutton, 1941). Of a New York garment manufacturer who fights the unions and finally becomes a "runaway manufacturer."

MORGAN, MURRAY C., 1916–

Viewless Winds (Dutton, 1949). Of the murder of the wife of a labor leader in an Oregon lumber town and the violent tensions that build up between the workers and the mill owners as the crime comes under investigation.

MORLEY, CHRISTOPHER, 1890–

*Kitty Foyle (Lippincott, 1939). Of the life and loves of an office girl in Philadelphia. Centers upon her mental conflicts.

NATHAN, ROBERT, 1894–

One More Spring (Knopf, 1933). A fantasy of a girl, a musician, a second-hand dealer, and a banker, and how they met the depression. A comedy-satire on the economic beliefs of these people. Artistic but thin.

NICHOLS, EDWARD J., 1900–

Danger! Keep Out (Houghton, 1943). Laid in a Midwest oil refinery; a clear, human story of industrialists and the industrial system. Tellingly dramatizes personnel problems, labor problems, the psychology of industrialists, and especially technological unemployment.

NORRIS, CHARLES G., 1881–1945

Flint (Doubleday, 1943). A melodramatic but illuminating account of strife between capital and labor on the San Francisco waterfront in the 1930's. Sets forth impartially the claims of employers and strike leaders but predicts ultimate, bloody victory for labor.

POOLE, ERNEST, 1880–1950

The Harbour (1915). The story of New York harbor through three stages: individual ownership, monopolistic ownership, and finally worker control (not yet realized).

ROLLINS, WILLIAM, 1897–

The Shadow Before (McBride, 1934). An excellent account of the effects of a strike in a large American textile mill. The major characters are a wealthy neurotic, a winding-room girl, a Puritanical reformer, a "playboy" proletarian sympathizer, and an ambitious young immigrant.

SANDOZ, MARI, 1899–

*Capital City (Little, 1939). Politics, labor, and strife in the capital of a high-plains state, Kanewa, a city with its Hooverville, its upper set, and all classes in between. The "radicals" (laborites) are punished by the forces of "law and order" (a horse doctor is elected governor). Excellent.

SAXTON, ALEXANDER

The Great Midland (Appleton-Century-Crofts, 1948). A thesis story of the labor struggle from 1919 to 1941, told in terms of railroaders in the Chicago yards and of various labor and radical organizations.

SCHULBERG, BUDD, 1914–

Waterfront (Random, 1955). A realistic narrative about New York harbor—about the exploited lives of longshoremen in "a jungle" of quiet murders, the iniquities of the "shape-up" method of hiring for the day, and the tie-in of rackets to the city administrations and the ecclesiastical hierarchy. Shows the problems faced by decent workers, sincere priests, and official investigators. A mixture of artistic creation and reporting on the way things are.

SINCLAIR, UPTON B., 1878–

*The Jungle (1906). Of packing houses in Chicago early in the century. Exposes filthy conditions and the mistreatment of workers. The hero becomes a socialist.

King Coal (Regan, 1917). Of greedy capitalists and their exploitation and maltreatment of workers. The coal fields of Colorado.

Oil (Boni, 1927). Of the son of a wealthy oil man. Southern California.

"Co-op" (Farrar, 1936). Of the establishment of a California co-operative community. Various people who are in dire straits and who would be helped by such a system proceed logically to help themselves.

Little Steel (Farrar, 1938). A dramatic story of attempts to organize unions and of the steel baron's fight to protect "the old ways."

SKIDMORE, HUBERT, 1911–1946

*Hawk's Nest (Doubleday, 1941). An indignant recounting of the famous tunnel-drilling episode at Gauley Bridge, West Virginia, that gave silicosis its first wide publicity.

SLADE, CAROLINE, 1886–

The Triumph of Willie Pond (Vanguard, 1940). An indignant and convincing presentation of the plight of the unemployed with families.

Job's House (Vanguard, 1941). An honest and starkly realistic picture of one man's solution of the problem of poverty in old age.

Lilly Crackell (Vanguard, 1943). Novelized social history. An understanding case study of a generous and beautiful woman born to a life of horrible poverty. Detailed and convincing, this story plumbs a weakness in the American economic system.

SMITTER, WESSEL, 1894–

F.O.B., Detroit (Harper, 1938). Of an automobile factory. Shows what the "machine" does to man.

SPADONI, ANDRIANA

Not All Rivers (Doubleday, 1937). Story of a woman's decision to fight for social justice, after realizing that being an "indignant intellectual" is not enough. Good descriptions of strikes and the methods used by the employer to combat them.

STEGNER, WALLACE, 1909–

The Preacher and the Slave (Houghton, 1950). Fictionalizes and expands the biography of Joe Hill, the Wobbly poet and musician, for the final years, 1910–16. Illuminates a violent phase of the labor movement in the Western states.

STEINBECK, JOHN, 1902–

In Dubious Battle (Viking, 1936). See above, p. 69.

The Grapes of Wrath (Viking, 1939). See above, p. 69.

STONE, IRVING, 1903–

Adversary in the House (Doubleday, 1947). See below, p. 141.

STORM, HANS OTTO

Count Ten (Longmans, 1940). The story of one man's relationships to members of the "exploited" and "exploiter" class, of his love for members of each class, and his plea for human dignity.

TIPPETT, THOMAS, 1894–

Horse Shoe Bottoms (Harper, 1935). An English miner comes to the Illinois coal fields and becomes a leader in the early unionization movement. Presents the problems of a man who sees a relation between his work and human happiness. Competent presentation.

TRAVEN, BRUNO

***The Death Ship** (Knopf, 1934). The adventure of an American who is stranded in Europe without identification, is shunted from place to place, and finally gets on a ship which is being sunk for its insurance. A strong picture of the toughened worker ripe for such doctrines as anarchism.

WALKER, CHARLES RUMFORD, 1893–

Bread and Fire (Houghton, 1927). Excellent sociological material, telling of actualities in steel mills and labor conditions in mill towns. Radical and intellectual groups.

WARD, ELIZABETH S. PHELPS, 1844–1911

The Silent Partner (1871). The wrongs of labor in New England. Our oldest American labor novel of any significance.

WHITCOMB, ROBERT

Talk United States! (Smith, 1935). Story of a skilled American workman, covering the last thirty years. Told in the semiliterate language of the worker.

WHITE, STEWART EDWARD, 1873–1946

The Blazed Trail (1902). Of an unscrupulous lumber corporation in Michigan. A realistic picture of logging and timber-getting.

WILLIAMS, BEN AMES, 1889–1953

Owen Glen (Houghton, 1950). The story takes place in the Ohio mining region in a small town that could be "any one of ten thousand other little towns." The book is careful social history, 1890 to 1898, picturing the problems of coal miners and the rise of the United Mine Workers.

WOLFF, MARITTA, 1918–

Night Shift (Random, 1942). A ruthless, dramatic, fatalistic picture of cruelty and fear in a small factory town in wartime. Naturalistic treatment of boardinghouse, restaurant, hospital, factory, night club. A studied representation of how the other half lives.

ZUGSMITH, LEANE, 1903–

A Time to Remember (Random, 1936). A novel of the strike of white-collar workers in a large New York department store. Many detailed descriptions of the life of the employees and the execution of a strike.

2. BUSINESS AND FINANCE
(ALSO BIG MONEY AND LITTLE ENTREPRENEURS)

An attempt has been made here to list books that deal directly with the handling of business and financial matters. Necessarily the list will to a great extent overlap the lists on labor, city life, and the leisure class. The first books of this type were written by William Dean Howells and H. E. Hamblen in the 'eighties and 'nineties; but a real deluge of such books appeared after the "muckrakers" of the Progressive Era had shown the corrupting influence and undemocratic methods of American business. In the 1920's the attitude toward business was often satirical, as in Sinclair Lewis, and in the 1930's it was generally antagonistic, but numerous books in the 1950's are neutrally realistic or downright compassionate portrayals of businessmen—who are shown as realizing too late that man does not live by commercial values alone. Most novels about businessmen are antidotes for the Horatio Alger tradition and the success-story myth.

ANDERSON, SHERWOOD, 1876–1941

Windy McPherson's Son (Cape, 1916). The tale of an Iowa village boy who goes to Chicago and becomes a millionaire, only to rebel against a life of greed for money. Theme: the utter futility of modern America's ideals.

ASCH, NATHAN, 1902–

The Office (Harcourt, 1925). The story of a broker's office that failed and of the subsequent actions of twenty separate members of the office force.

ASINOF, ELIOT, 1919–

Man on Spikes (McGraw, 1955). About professional baseball as seen by a minor-league player who ends up in the sporting-goods department of a hardware store. Fresh insight into the sports business.

BEZZERIDES, A. I., 1908–

Long Haul (Carrick, 1938). An account of the economic and social plight of the wildcat produce trucker in California. Gives a sense of the exhausting, sleepless life of men who haul oranges and asparagus between Los Angeles and Oakland. Simple and somewhat melodramatic.

Thieves' Market (Scribner, 1949). A melodramatic version of the hard life of an independent fruit and vegetable trucker and his troubles at the San Francisco wholesale market. A novel in the hard-boiled genre.

BRACE, ERNEST, 1893–

Buried Stream (Harcourt, 1946). Interesting analysis of the head of a public relations agency and his attempt to understand his own loneliness.

BRINIG, MYRON, 1900–

The Sisters (Farrar, 1937). A story of the lives and loves of the three daughters of the local druggist of Silver Bow, Montana. Plenty of local color.

BROMFIELD, LOUIS, 1896–1956

Escape (Stokes, 1927). A series of four novels dealing with the founders of a factory town and their descendants. Shows the decay of the Puritan tradition and the rise of Western industrialism. The individual titles are: *The Green Bay Tree, Possession, Early Autumn,* and *A Good Woman.*

BROOKS, JOHN, 1920–

The Big Wheel (Harper, 1949). On the editorial offices of a big and successful news magazine called *Present Day.* Concerned with the ethics and integrity of the journalistic magazine business.

BROOKS, RICHARD, 1912–

The Producer (Simon, 1951). A brisk, topical, nonsatirical novelizing of all major phases of the making and distribution of an independent motion picture.

BURLINGAME, ROGER, 1889–

The Heir (Scribner, 1930). Shows the development of a great chemical business through the war of 1914–1918 and also the thwarting of a son's artistic inclinations by a father's enforcement of a business career.

CAHAN, ABRAHAM, 1860–

*The Rise of David Levinsky (Harper, 1917). An excellent portrait of an immigrant adjusting himself to the American business world. He is quite successful in business but spiritually unsatisfied.

CALDWELL, JANET TAYLOR, 1900–

Dynasty of Death (Scribner, 1938). Follows the lives of two families —the Barbours and the Bouchards—armament makers, from 1837 until 1914. A detailed and forceful account of death merchants.

The Eagles Gather (Scribner, 1940). Sequel to *Dynasty of Death;* continues the story of the Bouchard family from 1918 to President Hoover's election.

The Final Hour (Scribner, 1944). Continues the story of a family of rapacious opportunists who hate democracy and love fascism. A lone humanitarian stands against the forces of evil.

CARSE, ROBERT, 1903–

The Beckoning Waters (Scribner, 1953). Built around "empire builders" in lumbering, shipping, and iron in Great Lakes states in the period 1865–1930. A realistic, sympathetic portrait of an Ulsterman become millionaire.

CARSON, ROBERT, 1909–

The Magic Lantern (Holt, 1952). A novelized history that should have been nonfiction; of all aspects of the movie industry before and after 1920, including the making and financing of pictures, distribution problems, the star system, and scandals. Developed around a producer and his "boy wonder" of a son, who succeeds him.

CHIDESTER, ANN, 1919–

The Long Year (Scribner, 1946). Story of the turmoil caused in a small Minnesota town by a ruthless woman who is part owner of its factory, and who comes to live for one year in the town. The ethics of modern business is a major theme.

Mama Maria's (Scribner, 1947). A tense, brief story about a tourist camp on Route No. 61, between Duluth and New Orleans, the proprietress, her employees, and guests. Real people.

CHURCHILL, WINSTON, 1871–1947

*The Inside of the Cup (Macmillan, 1912). Dramatizes the struggle of a young clergyman against the control of his church by business interests. One of the best and most popular of the muckraking novels.

A Far Country (1915). Of a corporation lawyer, a man who "sells his intellect" to get on in the world.

COHEN, LESTER, 1901–

Sweepings (Boni, 1926). Traces the commercial success of a family, from the time of the Revolution until after the Chicago fire. A picture of ruthless business in the golden age of roughshod competition.

COLWELL, MIRIAM, 1917–

Day of the Trumpet (Random, 1947). Story of the development of a ruthless business man, 1873–1888, who sacrifices friendship and other values for success.

COURNOS, MRS. JOHN (SYBIL NORTON, pseud.), 1893–

The Winthrops (Brentano's, 1927). An ethical study of the evils of living for money. A young man dreams of doing with automobiles what Carnegie and Rockefeller did with steel and oil. Laid in Reading, Pennsylvania.

DAVENPORT, MARCIA, 1903–

*The Valley of Decision (Scribner, 1942). A long chronicle of four generations in an intelligent, honest industrial family who mill steel in Pittsburgh. Dramatizes the struggles between titans, ownership and labor, and shows the growing place of science and enlightened labor policy in American heavy industry since the Civil War. Shows the role played by Slovaks and "Hunkies."

DELAND, MARGARET, 1857–1945

The Iron Woman (1911). Story of an American business woman who holds her own in the driving world of industrial competition, but even more the story of another character who holds everybody in line with Puritan tradition in regard to marriage.

DOS PASSOS, JOHN, 1896–

*The 42nd Parallel (Harper, 1930). Presents the financial-economic setup around 1900. Uses the author's new techniques—the "camera eye," the "news reel," etc.

*The Big Money (Harcourt, 1936). The business world, as well as the laboring classes and the leisure class, is a part of this excellent kaleidoscopic picture of the "roaring 'twenties."

DOWNING, J. HYATT, 1888–

Anthony Trant (Putnam, 1941). A story of business in the corn belt. Set in Sioux City, 1890–1920.

DREISER, THEODORE, 1871–1945

***The Financier** (1912). Shows the methods of big business and the ruthlessness demanded of the man who succeeds. Story of a broker in Philadelphia about 1870. Rich detail.

The Titan (1914). Sequel to *The Financier*. Another detailed account of a grasping capitalist. Laid in Chicago and dealing much with the fight for control of street railways.

The Stoic (Doubleday, 1947). Continues *The Financier* and *The Titan*. In this the central character, Cowperwood, attempts to gain control of London's transportation system. He dies as his fortune begins to dissolve, but much of his money goes into a great hospital that he has dreamed of. The three novels make a complete unit showing Dreiser's conception of modern American business.

FARRELL, JAMES T., 1904–

Gas House McGinty (Vanguard, 1933). Of routine in a large distributing company. The lives of employees and their boss, McGinty.

FERBER, EDNA, 1887–

Emma McChesney & Co. (1915). Experiences of a shrewd traveling saleslady, who meets men on their own ground.

Come and Get It (Doubleday, 1935). In terms of a chore boy who becomes a paper-mill baron, tells of the rise and fall of the lumber industry in Wisconsin and Michigan from 1850 to 1930.

FITZGERALD, F. SCOTT, 1896–1940

The Last Tycoon (Scribner, 1941). An uncompleted novel that gives insight into the Hollywood movie industry. Shrewdly analyzes a picture producer. The volume also contains "May Day" and five other Fitzgerald stories.

FLAVIN, MARTIN, 1883–

***Journey in the Dark** (Harper, 1943). A careful, artistic tale of an Iowa boy in his rise to success in business (wallpaper) and his failure in spiritual adjustment. Neither dishonest nor greedy, the hero is in essence a lonely man in the dark.

FOWLER, GENE, 1891–

***Timber Line** (Covici, 1933). Sensational fictionized biography of the builders of the *Denver Post*, Bonfils and Tammen. Gives an impressive insight into "yellow journalism."

GARRETT, GARET, 1878–

Satan's Bushel (Dutton, 1924). An attack on the speculation in agricultural products in America that despoils the farmer.

GARTH, DAVID

Fire on the Wind (Putnam, 1951). Competent writing on the development of timberland and the lumbering business in the 1860's on the Upper

Peninsula of Michigan. Standard romantic elements, too, including a beautiful, proud Irish-Chippewa girl.

GLASS, MONTAGUE M., 1877–1934

Abe and Mawruss (1911). Two cloak-and-suit men discuss current events in the phraseology and imagery of men "in the trade." Humorous observations on American life in a "Jewish" version of the old cracker-box tradition.

GRAHAM, DOROTHY, 1893–

The China Venture (Stokes, 1929). Tale of three generations of a New England family engaged with China in a trading business unbroken from 1835 to the present.

HALL, OAKLEY, 1920–

Mardios Beach (Viking, 1955). A critical though superficial picture of a self-made man in the used-car business in San Diego, with his lack of understanding and happiness, his impatience, his crass attitude toward women, and his "slavery to the California opium of the automobile."

HARRIMAN, JOHN, 1904–

The Career of Philip Hazen (Howell, Soskin, 1941). A story of high finance and ruthless competition in Wall Street. A picture of the rich struggling for survival.

HARVIN, EMILY (pseud.)

The Stubborn Wood (Ziff-Davis, 1948). An autobiographical novel by a woman whose husband railroaded her to a private insane asylum. An exposé, weak as fiction, strong as nonfiction, of a medical racket.

HAWLEY, CAMERON

Executive Suite (Houghton, 1952). Of the struggle among vice presidents to succeed to the top position in a furniture company. A clever, knowing, closely timed story that is quasi-satirical toward top executives.
Cash McCall (Houghton, 1955). A plot-filled, slickish story of suspense. About businessmen—their private lives, ethical codes, and methods of work—and especially about a man who buys and sells whole enterprises.

HERBST, JOSEPHINE, 1897–

The Executioner Waits (Harcourt, 1934). Deals with a large scattered American family of the middle class, after the Armistice of 1918. Condemns the economic condition after the war—days which saw strikes, unrest, and the I.W.W.

HERGESHEIMER, JOSEPH, 1880–1954

The Three Black Pennys (Knopf, 1917). Of three generations of Pennsylvania iron founders. Over-ornate in style.
Tampico (Knopf, 1926). A melodramatic story of American oil business in Tampico, Mexico. Of a roughneck who double-crossed his boss and gained control of a big business.
The Foolscap Rose (Knopf, 1934). Of the development of a Pennsylvania paper mill from the time when handmade papers were produced by its owners until a hundred years later when the mill had become a slave of Wall Street and the one-time owning family was destroyed.

HERRICK, ROBERT, 1868–1938

*The Memoirs of an American Citizen (1905). On the ethics of modern business. The story of a man's rise in the Chicago meat-packing business, told by the character himself.

Together (1908). Mainly on the failure of marriage as an institution, but contains attacks on railroad mergers and on discriminatory freight rates.

Waste (Harcourt, 1924). Through his hero, Herrick shows the "waste" and shortcomings of the United States since 1880. Shows the psychological effects on mother and son of a low economic standard which never gives him the opportunity for creative work.

HERRMANN, JOHN, 1900–

The Salesman (Simon, 1939). Story of the average traveling salesman —the hard-working one who worries about balancing his family budget on his meager salary.

HOBART, ALICE TISDALE (NOURSE), 1882–

Pidgin Cargo (Century, 1929). About a Yankee trader on the upper Yangtze during the war of 1914–1918.

Oil for the Lamps of China (Bobbs, 1933). American business in China. Centers on the struggle of a young man to better his position in Shanghai.

Their Own Country (Bobbs, 1940). Continues *Oil for the Lamps of China*. The main character manages an industrial alcohol plant in Kansas. A study of man's search for security.

HOBSON, LAURA Z., 1900–

The Celebrity (Simon, 1951). A humorous story of a commercially successful writer and a take-off on the synthetic fame that results when a book is taken by a book club and subsequently made into a movie.

HOWELLS, WILLIAM D., 1837–1920

*The Rise of Silas Lapham (1885). One of our earliest books about American business. A careful portrait of a paint merchant in Boston who aspires to crash Beacon Hill society.

*A Traveller from Altruria (1894). An adroit satire on American business ideals and the rationalizations used by the well-to-do to justify their wealth and power. Howells uses the device of having a man from a utopia visit a fashionable resort town in Maine and converse with representatives of the "upper" and "lower" classes.

JONAS, CARL

Jefferson Selleck (Little, 1952). A sympathetic novel about a "successful" but not happy real estate man, community leader (in Gateway), and manufacturer (the Yaw-Et-Ag Company). Loaded with social history for the period 1915–1950 and discerning about the discrepancies in American civilization. Told by means of a new fictional device: an autobiographical tape recording.

KAUP, ELIZABETH (DEWING), 1885–

Not for the Meek (Macmillan, 1941). A portrait of a rugged indi-

vidualist, a Danish immigrant, rising in capitalistic society. Comparable
to *The Financier* and *The Titan* of Theodore Dreiser.

KELLAND, CLARENCE B., 1881–
Hard Money (Harper, 1930). Tells of the career of a financier in New
York in the days of Jefferson, Jackson, and the first Vanderbilt.

KIRKBRIDE, RONALD DE LEVINGTON, 1912–
Only the Unafraid (Duell, 1953). See below, p. 158.

KOBER, ARTHUR, 1900–
That Man Is Here Again (Random, 1946). Sketches from the *New
Yorker* that create Benny Greenspan, a Hollywood artists' agent, who is
colorful and ungrammatical in his speech.

LAING, ALEXANDER, 1903–
The Sea Witch (Farrar, 1933). Competition in shipping in old New
York. The "Sea Witch," built in 1846, was destroyed at sea in 1856.

LAING, FREDERICK
The Giant's House (Dial, 1955). Of a tough man who builds up a
chain of grocery stores by dominating his employees and independent
grocers.

LAWRENCE, JOSEPHINE
The Sound of Running Feet (Stokes, 1937). Of clerks and bosses in
a small real estate office where no one is actually secure. The worries and
burdens of middle-class America.
If I Have Four Apples (Grosset, 1938). Discusses the economic difficulties of a family who cannot budget their income. A worker in the
financial department of a newspaper and her suggestions in solving the
problems of this family.
No Stone Unturned (Little, 1940). The story of a realtor who was
prosperous in the 1920's but whose business was gone in the 1930's. He
continues, Micawber-like, to believe he is important.

LEE, HARRY, 1914–
No Measure Danced (Macmillan, 1941). A grim story of a woman
business executive who gains success but loses happiness. A detailed
picture of high-pressure business and ruthless opportunism.

LEWIS, SINCLAIR, 1885–1951
*****Babbitt** (Harcourt, 1922). Real estate business. A famous book about
the "average business man." Babbitt is an individual, however; it is the
town that is portrayed as a "type." Babbitt attempts to revolt but rejoins
the herd. A deservedly popular work.
The Man Who Knew Coolidge (Harcourt, 1928). A series of mono-
logues, spoken by Lowell Schmaltz, a deadly dull devotee of "democracy,
manly sports, family life, efficiency, culture, and religious uplift." Written
in the actual language of the little businessman.
*****Dodsworth** (Harcourt, 1929). Of an automobile magnate who escapes
from American business to Europe in order to preserve his individuality
and find freedom for his personality.

Work of Art (Doubleday, 1934). A hotelkeeper's life. Gets in a number of satirical jabs at business in general and conveys practical information about what goes on behind the scenes in hotels.

Gideon Planish (Random, 1943). Of an organizer of charities, uplift societies, etc. Rich satire on organizations of the 1930's.

LONDON, JACK, 1876–1916

*The Iron Heel (1908). A story of the remaking of America into a collective society, called a "plutocracy" by London. A forerunner of books on the coming of fascism, like Sinclair Lewis' *It Can't Happen Here.*

Burning Daylight (1910). Of a young man who makes millions.

LORIMER, GEORGE HORACE, 1868–1937

Letters from a Self-made Merchant to His Son (1902). An old-style philosophy of life and business not unlike that of David Harum.

LYNDE, FRANCIS, 1865–1930

The Helpers (1899). Business and politics in Denver and the Colorado mining regions.

The Grafters (1904). Business and politics in Denver and the mining regions.

The Quickening (1906). The Tennessee coal and iron fields. The conflicts of commercialism.

Empire Builders (1907). Railway building in the West, plotting contractors in Denver, and the New York Stock Exchange.

MACLIESH, FLEMING, 1911–

The Eye of the Kite (Random, 1952). Of a transcontinental flight during very bad weather and of a tycoon with an "ice-cold, diamond-hard center of egotism."

MARKS, PERCY, 1891–

And Points Beyond (Stokes, 1937). A successful businessman finds a pattern for happiness. Pictures city types such as artists, brokers, Harlemites, and office workers.

What's a Heaven For? (Stokes, 1938). Story of the average college man out of school and of his problems in making the proper economic and social adjustments and in compromising some of his ideals in order to get security.

MARQUAND, JOHN PHILLIPS, 1893–

Sincerely, Willis Wayde (Little, 1955). Exhibits a man's rise from mill hand to industrialist—his habits of behavior and the crises he meets. Told with many flashbacks and sure craft.

MAYO, ELEANOR R., 1920–

Swan's Harbor (Crowell, 1953). A pleasant tale, laid in Maine and concerned with twins and their fish and shellfish business.

MERWIN, SAMUEL, 1874–   , and WEBSTER, HENRY K., 1875–

Calumet "K" (1901). Of the building of a two-million-dollar grain elevator by the main character, who is hampered by his opponents and by "walking delegates."

The Short-Line War (1901). A fight for the possession of a line connecting two great railways.

NORRIS, FRANK, 1870–1902

The Octopus (1901). See above, p. 68.

The Pit (1903). Of wheat speculation in the stock market of Chicago.

O'MEARA, WALTER

The Grand Portage (Bobbs, 1951). See above, p. 11.

ORNITZ, SAMUEL BADISCH, 1890–

Haunch, Paunch, and Jowl (Boni, 1923). A record of the process of becoming rich and politically powerful. The main characters are Jewish, and there is discussion of the Jews' place in America.

PARSON, ALICE BEALE, 1886–

John Merrill's Pleasant Life (Dutton, 1930). A penniless, clever, and promising young engineer becomes manager of a factory on the Hudson River; he ends up a successful leading citizen, comfortable and prosperous, but spiritually conventional and frustrated.

PAYNE, WILL, 1865–

The Money Captain (1898). The central story is the struggle between the gas king of Chicago, aided by corrupt aldermen, and a fighting, muckracking editor. A thoughtful, realistic novel that presents the case for and against industrial captains.

PHILLIPS, DAVID G., 1867–1911

The Master Rogue: the Confessions of a Croesus (1903). A clerk in a dry-goods store becomes a millionaire. A sordid and brutal story of success and unhappiness.

Light-Fingered Gentry (1907). Of the inner workings of great insurance companies.

The Second Generation (1907). Of a self-made man who does not provide for his children, wishing them to be hardened by struggle.

RICE, ELMER, 1892–

A Voyage to Purilia (Cosmopolitan Book Corporation, 1930). A satire on the motion-picture industry told in terms of the emotionally standardized types who inhabit the planet of Purilia. Contains some pointed social criticism.

RUBINS, HAROLD (Harold Robbins, pseud.), 1912–

The Dream Merchants (Knopf, 1949). Follows a group of fictional persons set against a real background of the rise of the motion picture business from 1909 to 1938. A social history in disguise, needlessly chaotic in literary form, confined mostly to New York City.

SEIFERT, ELIZABETH, 1897–

A Great Day (Dodd, 1939). A detailed account of what was to have been the greatest day in the life of a self-made millionaire who had made his money on fake advertising and doped patent medicines. An effective indictment of corrupt careers but an artificial plot.

SHIEL, MATTHEW P., 1865–1947

Contraband of War (1899). High finance and politics during the Spanish-American War (1897–1899).

SINCLAIR, UPTON B., 1878–

A Captain of Industry (1906). A Sinclair indictment of the capitalistic system.

The Money Changers (1908). An attack on the methods used by Wall Street to refinance steel companies and railroads.

***Oil!** (Boni, 1927). Picture of the oil industry of southern California, based on the oil scandals during the Harding administration, the bribery of public officials, class antagonism, and the rivalry of big businesses. Glimpses of Senators, oil men, and a Los Angeles evangelist who remind the reader of people actually living.

Boston (Boni, 1928). See below, p. 141.

"Co-op" (Farrar, 1936). Here Sinclair attacks the capitalistic system only by implication. Positively, he shows the case for consumer and producer co-operatives.

SPRAGUE, JESSE R., 1872–

The Making of a Merchant (Morrow, 1928). The rise of a large department-store merchant.

The Middleman (Morrow, 1929). Social history in fiction form of the wholesale-hardware business.

SULLIVAN, OSCAR MATTHIAS, 1881–

The Empire Builder (Century, 1928). A novel based on previous studies of James J. Hill, on newspaper files, and on other firsthand materials. Glorifies the methods and attitudes of the railway builders, and argues for the development of monopoly in the railway field.

TARKINGTON, BOOTH, 1869–1946

Growth (Doubleday, 1927). This is a trilogy of the growth of a Middle Western city, including *The Magnificent Ambersons, the Midlander, The Turmoil*.

TRUMBO, DALTON, 1905–

The Remarkable Andrew (Lippincott, 1941). Of a young clerk who is at outs with the corrupt business world about him, is accused of embezzlement, and is visited by the shade of General Andrew Jackson, who gives him practical advice.

TURNBULL, AGNES SLIGH, 1888–

Remember the End (Macmillan, 1938). A young Scot arrives in Pennsylvania with only a few dollars and stern determination. By ignoring the welfare of his fellowmen and by suppressing his artistic instincts and human emotions he becomes a millionaire in the steel and railway businesses.

WAKEMAN, FREDERIC, 1909–

The Hucksters (Rinehart, 1946). A satire, with some of the thinness of its subject, on radio advertising. Laid in Radio City, New York, it depicts aspects of life and manners among the rich business class.

WESTCOTT, EDWARD N., 1847–1898
  David Harum (1898). See above, p. 33.

WHITE, WILLIAM ALLEN, 1868–1944
  A Certain Rich Man (1926). See above, p. 45.

WILSON, SLOAN, 1920–
  The Man in the Gray Flannel Suit (Simon, 1955). An interpretation
  of business executives, junior and senior, and the problems they face and
  the pressures they endure both on the job and at home. A study of conflicts within men over issues of materialism, love, and self-respect.

WOUK, HERMAN, 1915–
  Aurora Dawn (Simon, 1947). A satire on radio advertising. Deftly,
  smoothly written.

YAFFE, JAMES, 1927–
  What's the Big Hurry? (Little, 1954). About an expedient businessman who was an accountant until the crash of '29 and after that "never
  stayed in one business long enough to lose too much money." Charac-
  terizes him in his family and social environment, in Chicago and elsewhere.

3. CITY LIFE (ALSO DEAD END AND BROADWAY)

City life is a twentieth-century theme, begun in this country by
Henry B. Fuller's The Cliff Dwellers (1893). The second important
work dealing with city life directly was Stephen Crane's Bowery Tales
(1900), which included his two masterly stories, "George's Mother"
and "Maggie, A Girl of the Streets." Although this list overlaps the
ones on labor, immigrants, leisure class, etc., the emphasis here is on
how people live in the city and the peculiar folkways, attitudes, and
problems that have grown up as a consequence of urban life in contrast
to the rural-life pattern of the nineteenth century. While some writers
give pleasant or admiring pictures of American cities, a majority of
novelists are strikingly in agreement in their insistence on seaminess,
vice, crime, brutality, ugliness, frustration, mental illness, or poverty
of spirit and culture! In some books, as in Rice's Imperial City and
Bromfield's Twenty-four Hours, the multiplicity of city life itself is
the sociological theme.

ALBERT, KATHERINE
  Remember Valerie March (Simon, 1939). Realistic, debunking
  glimpses of the private life of a movie star.

ALGREN, NELSON, 1909–
  The Neon Wilderness (Doubleday, 1947). Naturalistic stories of Chicago slums, mostly of prostitutes, thugs, and dope addicts.
  The Man with the Golden Arm (Doubleday, 1949). Of a gambler
  who hangs out in a Chicago tavern in the Polish district. A book rich in

reportage on jail life, contemporary low life, and city life with its palliatives and frustrations.

ALMAN, DAVID, 1919–

World Full of Strangers (Doubleday, 1949). The scene is a grim section of New York City inhabited largely by immigrants and their children. A documentary treatment of fatigue, defeat, and corruption.

APPEL, BENJAMIN, 1907–

Brain Guy (Greenberg, 1936). A study of the murderous stupidity of gangsters and of their hopes and motivating ideas.

Runaround (Dutton, 1937). A story of the vote-getting racket in the melting-pot of Hell's Kitchen, New York City.

The Power House (Dutton, 1939). Vivid, realistic, melodramatic picture of the politically protected underworld rackets of New York City. Close-ups of fixers, mondaines, machine bosses, judges, ward-heelers, mobsters.

ASCH, SHALOM (SHOLEM), 1880–

*East River (Putnam, 1946). A moving story of modern New York, of Jews and Catholics and the twentieth-century factory system. Excellent in portraying the motivations of factory owners as well as workers. The religious life of the main characters is given emphasis.

Passage in the Night (Putnam, 1953). See below, p. 152.

BARNES, MARGARET AYER, 1886–

Years of Grace (Houghton, 1930). Set in the "Years of Grace" (the nineteenth century) and in the jazz age. Chicago.

Within This Present (Houghton, 1933). A family chronicle of Chicago life, from the Civil War to the New Deal.

BASSO, HAMILTON, 1904–

Days Before Lent (Scribner, 1939). Story of a young scientist in New Orleans during the week of Mardi Gras. He has to decide whether to go to India to do research or to stay at home and marry the girl he loves. Realistic details of New Orleans night life.

BEER, THOMAS, 1889–1940

The Road to Heaven (Knopf, 1928). About a man who is waiting for his father's death in order to return to the farm in Ohio. He feels out of place among the complexities of New York City.

BELL, THOMAS

All Brides Are Beautiful (Little, 1936). A realistic story of life in the Bronx. Shows a wholesome young married couple solving their economic problems.

Till I Come Back to You (Little, 1943). Of a typical family of the "plains of Brooklyn" east from Borough Hall. Presents typical attitudes at the beginning of World War II.

BERCOVICI, KONRAD, 1882–

Against the Sky (Covici, 1932). Story of gypsy life on the East Side in New York City today; a gypsy's love for a member of an old New York family.

BODENHEIM, MAXWELL, 1893–1954
Naked on Roller Skates (Liveright, 1931). Story of the dirty and dangerous underworld of Harlem as seen through the eyes of a twenty-four-year-old widow, Ruth Riatt, and her fifty-six-year-old friend, Terry Barberlib, as they go "slumming."

BRADLEY, MARY HASTINGS
Old Chicago (Appleton, 1933). Four novelettes showing the life of Chicago from the War of 1812 to the opening of the Chicago Fair of 1893.

BRINIG, MYRON, 1900–
***May Flavin** (Farrar, 1938). The story of a young woman who comes to New York in the early 1900's with her husband. This couple is forced to live in the slums; and, in the surrounding of saloons, thieves, gambling houses, and prostitutes, one of May's sons becomes a gangster. Shows the various strata of life in a big city.

BROMFIELD, LOUIS, 1896–1956
***Twenty-four Hours** (Stokes, 1930). Traces the lives of six people for twenty-four hours after they attend a dull dinner party given in a beautiful New York apartment. The following twenty-four hours bring a crisis to each of these six society figures. Suggests the dramatic contrasts in New York life.

BURNETT, WILLIAM RILEY, 1899–
Little Caesar (Dial, 1929). The first highly successful novel of Chicago gangsters, told from the point of view and in the language of a gangster. "Little Caesar" bosses his gunmen until he kills a cop during a night-club holdup; the gang then breaks up, several becoming squealers.
Nobody Lives Forever (Knopf, 1943). Careful characterizations of crooks, con-men, gangster leaders, "babes," and cheap racketeers make this a good crime-and-sex novel.
The Asphalt Jungle (Knopf, 1949). A rattling good tale of the underworld of a large Midwestern city and of how the honest police commissioner runs down a notorious criminal *et al.*
Little Men, Big World (Knopf, 1951). A fast-moving yarn of crooked politicos, gamblers, and hoodlums in a Midwestern city that Chicago gangsters are moving in on.

BURT, MAXWELL STRUTHERS, 1882–1954
The Interpreter's House (Scribner, 1924). Comments on the shifting standards and new adjustments of the postwar society of New York City.

CALDWELL, JANET TAYLOR, 1900–
There Was a Time (Scribner, 1947). This recounts the story of an artist struggling to emerge from the midst of the frustrations and illusions of present-day life in a northern New York city.

CARROLL, LOREN, 1904–
Wild Onion (Dodd, 1930). Of the career of a Chicago bootlegger and gangster. He becomes wealthy and powerful and meets death at the hands of a rival mob.

CATHER, WILLA SIBERT, 1876–1947

Lucy Gayheart (Knopf, 1935). Lucy Gayheart desires to live in Chicago away from those she knows, so that she may have time to think. A pathetic story.

CHEEVER, JOHN, 1912–

The Enormous Radio, and Other Stories (Funk, 1953). Fourteen discerning, clever probings into contemporary manners.

CHILD, NELLISE, 1901–

If I Come Home (Doubleday, 1943). A study of a marriage between a rich southern California girl and a poor slum-raised boy. Contrasts the wealthy and the pauperized, fascist and democratic, intolerant and sympathetic that can be found in Los Angeles. Implies the need for social reorganization in postwar America.

COATES, ROBERT M., 1897–

The Farther Shore (Harcourt, 1955). A subtle novel about loneliness, a shy courtship, a marriage that fails, and obsession—about an emotion from birth to death. Sensitive writing about Manhattan materials in the best *New Yorker* tradition.

CRANE, STEPHEN, 1871–1900

*Bowery Tales (1900). Contains "George's Mother" and "Maggie, A Girl of the Streets." Among our earliest naturalistic stories. Uses the language of the people. Realistic and full of pathos.

Twenty Stories (Knopf, 1940). Contains "Maggie" and "An Experiment in Misery."

CROY, HOMER, 1883–

Headed for Hollywood (Greenberg, 1934). An account of the struggles of a young small-town girl who came to Hollywood to find success and met only disillusionment and heartbreaks. Shows Hollywood as the city of pain—those who are already set strive to maintain their status and those who are not yet in strive futilely to be acclaimed.

DAHLBERG, EDWARD, 1900–

From Flushing to Calvary (Harcourt, 1932). Realistic picture of slum life around Calvary Cemetery, New York.

DAVENPORT, MARCIA (GLUCK), 1903–

East Side, West Side (Scribner, 1947). New York shortly after World War II. Mostly on the west side.

DELL, FLOYD, 1887–

The Briary Bush (Doran, 1921). Deals with the early married years of a young couple in postwar Chicago. Suggests some of the Bohemian art life of the time and dramatizes the contemporary concern with sex and marriage.

Souvenir (Doubleday, 1929). The relationship between a divorced man and his son by his former wife. Good on American family life and social phenomena.

DE VOTO, BERNARD AUGUSTINE, 1897–1955

We Accept with Pleasure (Little, 1934). A satire on the so-called "educated gentleman." A history teacher returns from the war shell-shocked but has too much pride to accept charity. All the characters strive for happiness but are so confused by habit and convention that they fail to find it. A detailed picture of people and events in Chicago and Boston after the war of 1914–1918.

Mountain Time (Little, 1947). Two Westerners by birth and New Yorkers by transplantation overcome emotional conflicts by returning to their native city and by gaining insight into each other's problems. A romantic story using modern speech and customs.

DOBIE, CHARLES C., 1881–1943

Portrait of a Courtesan (Appleton, 1934). San Francisco in the late 1890's. A picture of economic unrest, ethnic contrasts, Bohemian art life, fancy houses, practical politics.

San Francisco Tales (Appleton, 1935). Eighteen romantic short stories of the foreign quarter, of Chinatown, and of Nordic Americans in San Francisco. Psychological overtones.

San Francisco Adventures (Appleton, 1937). Nine short stories of foreigners in San Francisco, from the point of view of a Bohemian baker. Impressionistic local color.

DOS PASSOS, JOHN, 1896–

*****Manhattan Transfer** (Harper, 1925). Good on new folkways. Episodic, with diverse characters being brought together by the chaotic, unplanned happenings of the early 1920's. Catches the seething vitality and enormous variety of the city.

The Big Money (Harcourt, 1936). See above, p. 82.

DREISER, THEODORE, 1871–1945

*****Sister Carrie** (1901). Of the adventures or the mishaps of an eighteen-year-old girl in Chicago. Considered a shocker at the time of its publication.

*****Jennie Gerhardt** (1911). A story of a girl who retains admirable qualities, even though she violates some of our "sacred conventions." Regarded as a good example of the naturalistic attitude.

The Genius (1915). Story of an artist who gives up art to be successful in journalism. Much of modern folkways.

FARRELL, JAMES T., 1904–

*****Studs Lonigan: A Trilogy** (Vanguard, 1937). The three stories are *Young Lonigan, The Young Manhood of Studs Lonigan, Judgment Day*. A realistic, forceful presentation of the life of a boy growing up in the culturally impoverished middle-class district of Chicago. A stenographic report on the speech of streets, playgrounds, and pool halls. Excellent for characterization, motivation, and implication.

Father and Son (Vanguard, 1940). Story of an Irish youth in Chicago's South Side. Continues *A World I Never Made* (1936) and *No Star Is Lost* (1938).

Ellen Rogers (Vanguard, 1941). Interprets "an emergent man of ill will." Of an ill-educated, shrewd jackal, Ed Lanson, who preys on others via deceiving, cheating, and debauchery.

Bernard Clare (Vanguard, 1946). Shows a young Chicago Irish-American trying to get started as a writer in New York City. He works as a cigar-store clerk and an advertising salesman, seeks love and self-discovery, sympathizes with Sacco and Vanzetti, and is "wildly rebellious."

The Face of Time (Vanguard, 1953). Presents the central character of *Father and Son,* Danny O'Neill, at the age of five, among a variety of O'Neills, O'Flahertys, and other Irish-Americans in Chicago's South Side.

FAST, HOWARD MELVIN, 1914–

Place in the City (Harcourt, 1937). Vivid, realistic pictures of a few people and their intimate lives. Presents the commoner types of New York's East Side, including Jews and Irish.

FEARING, KENNETH, 1902–

The Hospital (Random, 1939). A concentrated picture of a few hours in the lives of the doctors, nurses, patients, service helpers, etc., who make up a functioning hospital. Shows the effect on all concerned in this institution when a drunken janitor turns off the power for several minutes.

FERBER, NAT. J., 1889–

The Sidewalks of New York (Covici, 1927). Story of the life of a Russian boy who came to America with his foster parents and grew up on the East Side of New York. Shows the life of the ghetto and its effect.

FULLER, HENRY B., 1857–1929

The Cliff Dwellers (1893). Dwellers in a large building in modern Chicago. Satirizes social ambitions. Our first important novel with city life as its central theme.

GORHAM, CHARLES O., 1911–

The Future Mister Dolan (Dial, 1948). A naturalistic, straightforward, and brutal account of a ruthless G.I., product of an Irish slum in New York City, who returns home and sets out with "savagery and sadistic meanness" to work up the scale of money and power.

GRAHAM, CARROLL, and GRAHAM, GARRETT

Queer People (Vanguard, 1930). An example of the muckraking sex shocker about the "grotesquery and bestiality" said to be rampant in Hollywood.

HALPER, ALBERT, 1904–

Union Square (Viking, 1933). An episodic novel of the people who live around Union Square. These episodes are united in a Communist riot and the burning of a firetrap tenement house.

Only an Inch from Glory (Harper, 1943). On the loneliness of life in New York City. Thin story of a young Middle Westerner who preferred life with his frustrated New York friends to his former life.

HARNDEN, RUTH PEABODY

I, a Stranger (Whittlesey, 1950). A subtle presentation of a misunderstood child growing up amid the society of Beacon Hill.

HARRISON, HENRY SYDNOR, 1880–1930
  Queed (Houghton, 1918). A young journalist is disillusioned by his experiences while working for the yellow press.

HECHT, BEN, 1894–
  Erik Dorn (Putnam, 1921). A realistic novel of the successful empty life of a brilliant journalist.
  1001 Afternoons in New York (Viking, 1941). The best of a series of daily columns written for *PM*. Sketches of bums, neurotics, anti-Semites—a piecemeal portrait of New York.

HELTON, ROY ADDISON, 1886–
  Nitchey Tilley (Harper, 1934). Shows New York through the eyes of an unsophisticated mountain couple.

HOLM, JOHN CECIL, 1904–
  Sunday Best (Farrar, 1942). Recreates a whole middle-class Philadelphia neighborhood in the period 1900–1920.

HUNEKER, JAMES, 1860–1921
  Painted Veils (1920). A story of a girl's rise to success as a singer in New York City. A candid and highly sexed picture of hard-drinking, wise-cracking Bohemians of the Greenwich Village variety.

HURST, FANNIE, 1889–
  Lonely Parade (Harper, 1942). An ironical, objective study of the careers of "bachelor women" in New York. A crowded history of "success" and defeat.

HUXLEY, ALDOUS, 1894–
  ***After Many a Summer Dies the Swan** (Harper, 1940). A satire on Los Angeles and on man's search for comfort and immortality as conducted by many Angelenos.

IDELL, ALBERT E., 1901–
  Centennial Summer (Holt, 1943). Amusingly recreates the Philadelphia of 1876, its manners and morals, with capitalism rampant and the Grant scandals in the background. Light reading.

JACKSON, CHARLES REGINALD, 1903–
  The Lost Weekend (Farrar, 1944). A sustained, realistic study of an alcoholic. Takes the reader into bars, Bellevue Hospital, and apartment houses; explains a chronic drinker's behavior in the urban civilization often labeled as "neurotic."

JANEWAY, ELIZABETH, 1913–
  Leaving Home (Doubleday, 1953). Of two sisters and their brother as they all come of age between 1933 and 1940. Objective observation of everyday emotions of middle-class persons in a big city.

KANTOR, MACKINLAY, 1904–
  Diversey (Coward, 1928). Story of the underground world of Chicago and its cabaret life, City Hall politics, bootleg feuds, etc. Shows the effect of this city on a "dreamy" country boy.

Signal Thirty-two (Random, 1950). Good on the training, routines, practical procedures, excitements, and temptations of patrol-car policemen in New York City. Lively reporting, limited to the 23rd Precinct, of life in the city and in the police force.

KARIG, WALTER, 1898–

Lower Than Angels (Farrar, 1945). A realistic and unsparing account of the life story of one Marvin Lang, whose father ran a delicatessen shop on Staten Island. A tale of poverty and drabness.

KEYES, FRANCES PARKINSON, 1885–

Crescent Carnival (Messner, 1942). Covers three generations in the lives of two families, one of them Creole, in and around New Orleans, 1890–1940.

Joy Street (Messner, 1950). A long, expert women's novel about present-day Beacon Hill and liberals' attempts to bring together members of old families and members of new Italian, Irish, and Jewish families. Scenes centered on law, Society, love, and marriage.

KRAMER, DALE, 1910–

The Heart of O. Henry (Rinehart, 1954). A "dramatic narrative" with invented conversations that fictionalizes the life of William Sydney Porter, the Southerner-Westerner who ends up in Manhattan and makes much use of its materials in writing his popular short stories.

LARDNER, RING W., 1885–1933

You Know Me, Al (1916). The letters of a semi-literate ballplayer. Lardner captures the psychology of a lowbrow and reproduces his language in a manner at once accurate and amusing.

LEVIN, MEYER, 1905–

The Old Bunch (Viking, 1937). Set in Chicago, the book traces the activities of a bunch of Jewish high-school graduates from 1921 to 1934, giving an idea of the "justice" of this city and the education, racketeering, business, and politics of the time.

LEWIS, OSCAR, 1893–

I Remember Christine (Knopf, 1942). A satiric novel of a woman, a tycoon, and the city of San Francisco, 1850 to the present.

LEWIS, SINCLAIR, 1885–1951

*Ann Vickers (Doubleday, 1933). The story of one woman's adjustment to modern life. She represents the most advanced notions as to prison reform, charity work, and personal morality.

Cass Timberlane (Random, 1945). A story of modern marriage, centering on the psychological problem of a middle-aged judge and his wife, who is seventeen years his junior. Satirizes the country-club set. Partly commentary instead of story, in the usual Lewis style.

LIPTON, LAWRENCE, 1898–

Brother, the Laugh Is Bitter (Harper, 1942). Of a would-be businessman. Gangsterism, anti-Semitism, and also orthodox Jewish home life

LONG, MARGARET, 1911–
   Louisville Saturday (Random, 1950). Parallels the lives of eleven girls
and women of various ages during one afternoon and evening in 1942.
Shows the impact of the war on various types of city women who illustrate Genesis 3:16.

McINTYRE, JOHN T., 1871–
   "Slag" (Scribner, 1927). Of "the refuse of the melting-pot," the immigrant poor, their hard lives, their amusements, and their difficulties with
the police. Realistic and dramatic.
   Steps Going Down (Farrar, 1936). A realistic novel of the underground world in an American city of today. The very amiable hero manages to keep ahead of the police for the several months which cover the
time of the story.

MOFFETT, LANGSTON, 1903–
   Devil by the Tail (Lippincott, 1947). A well-written, detailed novel
of alcoholism. Excellent detail in regard to effects, attempted cures, and
final rehabilitation.

MORLEY, CHRISTOPHER, 1890–
   Swiss Family Manhattan (Doubleday, 1932). A Swiss family called
Robinson takes a ten-day airship cruise while vacationing from their business with the League of Nations. They have an accident and finally land
on top of the Empire State Building. Tells of their adventures with the
uncivilized New Yorkers.

MOTLEY, WILLARD, 1912–
   Knock on Any Door (Appleton, 1947). A naturalistic novel about an
Italian-American boy in Chicago, tracing his gradual descent into a
world of crime. Cause and effect relationships of an environmental study
are all present, but human motivations are unconvincing.
   We Fished All Night (Appleton-Century-Crofts, 1951). A disillusioned picture of disillusioned Chicagoans—laborers, strikers, members
of minority groups, veterans of World War II—persons who fancy themselves to be in a cheap, betrayed world. "Lord, we fished all night and
caught nothing." Heavily reportorial and naturalistic.

NORRIS, FRANK, 1870–1902
   ***McTeague: A Story of San Francisco** (1899). A masterpiece of
early American naturalism, interesting for its use of symbols to develop
the thesis that greed ruins personality and character. Studies the degeneration of a stupid ex-dentist through unemployment, loveless wedlock,
and insensate lust for gold.

O'HARA, JOHN, 1905–
   Butterfield 8 (Harcourt, 1935). A very realistic tale of New York during the early 1930's, when speakeasies were in their last years. A bitter
account of a young girl who led a rather fast life.
   Hope of Heaven (Harcourt, 1938). Partly satiric, partly melodramatic treatment of Hollywood.

PARKER, DOROTHY, 1893–

Here Lies (Viking, 1939). A collection of two dozen skillful short stories, epigrammatic, with suggestive dialogue. Full of wicked insight into modern urban types and social levels, and also into the human heart.

PAUL, LOUIS, 1891–

Breakdown (Crown, 1947). Story of a female alcoholic, finally cured by psychoanalysis and exposure to the group therapy of "Alcoholics Anonymous."

PORTER, WILLIAM SYDNEY (O. HENRY, pseud.), 1862–1910

The Four Million (1906). Stories about New York's common people (a contrast to "the 400"). Twenty-five short stories, including many of O. Henry's best.

RICE, ELMER L., 1892–

*Imperial City (Coward, 1937). A kaleidoscopic story of a New York financial family and the various people of all classes related to it through business, social circles, professional relations, and casual contacts. One of our finest books on the city.

RIESENBERG, FELIX, 1879–

*East Side, West Side (Harcourt, 1927). A fine picture of New York City, of both its East and West sides since 1900. Story of a man who rises from the slums of the East Side, goes to Columbia, becomes a civil engineer, and cracks the West Side.

ROSAIRE, FORREST, 1902–

Uneasy Years (Knopf, 1950). Of family life—of the parents and the emergence of their children to facing adult realities—in Chicago.

ROSENBERG, ETHEL, 1915–

Go Fight City Hall (Simon, 1949). A humorous novel of Brooklyn, showing the provincial customs of a subregion with characters restricted by place and by their cultural and ethnic backgrounds. Centers on a Jewish family. Excellent for speech and dialect.

RUBINS, HAROLD (HAROLD ROBBINS, pseud.), 1912–

79 Park Avenue (Knopf, 1955). A literary case history of a prostitute and madam that dramatizes the call-girl racket in New York City and shows its tie-in with the police and the gangsters.

RUSSELL, RUTH

Lake Front (Rockwell, 1931). Traces an Irish family from its arrival in Chicago in 1835 through the presidential campaign of 1840, the Civil War, the Haymarket riots, the railway strike of 1894.

ST. JOHNS, ADELA R.

Skyrocket (Cosmopolitan Book, 1925). A young girl rises from poverty to dizzy stardom. An example of early writing about Hollywood.

SANDOZ, MARI, 1899–

Capital City (Little, 1939). See above, p. 77.

SCHULBERG, BUDD, 1915–

What Makes Sammy Run? (Random, 1941). A sharp, realistic picture of many-sided Hollywood, focused on a Jew who rises from childhood in a New York slum to power and prominence as a movie producer.

SCOTT, NATALIE ANDERSON, 1900–

Story of Mrs. Murphy (Dutton, 1947). Story of a man "married to booze." A study of the folkways of modern city life.

SLADE, CAROLINE, 1886–

Sterile Sun (Vanguard, 1936). Story of the economic conditions that forced four young New York girls into becoming prostitutes.

Margaret (Vanguard, 1946). The story of a sixteen-year-old delinquent girl, whose mainsprings of action were fear, hatred, and greed. Society, which has failed to reach her through church or school, fails also in its repair services, leaving nothing for Margaret but an institution.

SLESINGER, TESS, 1905–

The Unpossessed (Simon, 1934). A group of short stories, loosely connected, about the life of a group living in Greenwich Village: a novelist, a weary radical, a society matron who is a little too romantic, etc.

SMITH, BETTY, 1904–

A Tree Grows in Brooklyn (Harper, 1943). Portrays the varied life among the Irish and others in Williamsburg, Brooklyn, in the years leading up to World War I. The pain and poetry of tenement life as seen by an adolescent girl.

STREETER, EDWARD, 1891–

Daily Except Sundays (Simon, 1938). A light satire on the modern suburban commuter. Full of sharp observations.

VAN DOREN, DOROTHY G., 1896–

Strangers (Doran, 1926). Story of the marriage entanglements of two wealthy, cultured couples. Theme: no matter how close people are, there is still a barrier between them; so they remain "strangers."

Dacey Hamilton (Harper, 1942). The story of a woman worker on a newspaper in New York and of her gradual awakening to a fuller emotional life.

VAN VECHTEN, CARL, 1880–

Spider Boy (Knopf, 1928). Satirical story of the mad rush of Hollywood. A man writes a Broadway hit, becoming famous overnight, and the movie world stampedes toward him.

WARD, MARY JANE, 1905–

The Snake Pit (Random, 1946). Describes the experiences in a sanitarium for the mentally ill of an ambitious Evanston girl who has gone to New York City. Implies that her breakdown came from the strains and worries of marriage and ambition in the big city. Superficial but serious and suggestive.

WARNER, CHARLES D., 1829–1900

A Little Journey in the World (1889). Of the spiritual disintegration of a girl who marries a financier.

The Golden House (1894). Of the complexity and heartlessness of city life, the financial ruin of some characters and the villainy of others. Continues *A Little Journey in the World*.

That Fortune (1899). The main characters of *The Golden House* are in conflict with the next generation.

WAUGH, EVELYN, 1903–

The Loved One (Little, 1948). Satirizes the American standard of dying, specifically, the prolific—and profitable—funeral business in metropolitan Los Angeles.

WEIDMAN, JEROME, 1913–

I'll Never Go There Any More (Simon, 1941). A young man from Albany goes to New York City, where he lives among some very undesirable people from whom he finally escapes to return to Albany. Good character delineation.

WEST, EVELYN

Animal Fair (Lippincott, 1945). A simply told story of an adolescent girl's adjustment to independent adult life in the city of Baltimore, Maryland.

WEST, NATHANAEL

The Day of the Locust (Random, 1939). A sensational picture of the lunatic fringe in Hollywood. A psychological study of suppressed violence and spiritual emptiness.

WIENER, WILLARD, 1900–

Four Boys and a Gun (Dial Press, 1944). A tough story of the lives of the boys in a neighborhood gang which kills a policeman. Convincingly reconstructs a demoralized era we think of as past.

WILSON, EDMUND, 1895–

Memoirs of Hecate County (Doubleday, 1946). Six stories, mostly about sophisticated business and artistic people, in New York City and the rich rural suburbs. Notable for "The Princess with the Golden Hair," which contrasts rich and poor, and "The Milhollands and Their Damned Soul," which satirizes the literary racket. Time: the 1920's and '30's. Excellent realism on sexual folkways.

WILSON, WILLIAM EDWARD, 1906–

Crescent City (Simon, 1947). Struggles of a small-town editor of the Middle West against the Klan and other corrupt forces.

WOLFERT, IRA

Tucker's People (Fischer, 1943). Of New York's underworld and the numbers racket. A story of the frustrations of little people.

ZUGSMITH, LEANE, 1903–

The Reckoning (Smith, 1934). A novel dealing with New York social conditions and the making of social outcasts.

4. THE LEISURE CLASS
(ALSO UPPER CRUST AND CLIMBERS)

The novel of the social climber and the novel of the idle rich have both been prominent and persistent for the past three generations. Among the earliest books of this type are W. D. Howells' *The Rise of Silas Lapham* and Henry James's *The American.* The most popular writers about society folk at the turn of the century were Gertrude Atherton and David G. Phillips. Since that time Edith Wharton, Booth Tarkington, F. Scott Fitzgerald and J. P. Marquand have been among the most popular, with a host of younger writers making their contributions since the late 1920's. The prevailing tone of most of this writing is satiric.

ATHERTON, GERTRUDE, 1857–1948
 Aristocrats (Lane, 1901). Satirizes the affectations of the overrefined, emasculated, "most exclusive" American society.

BARNARD, J. LAWRENCE, 1912–
 Revelry by Night (Doubleday, 1941). A satirical picture of the upper crust on Long Island in 1940—of imported English mannerisms, decadent jokes, expensive sports, promiscuity, and so on.

BASSO, HAMILTON, 1904–
 In Their Own Image (Scribner, 1935). Story of the effect of a textile strike and the death of a worker on a group of social and superficial individuals vacationing in the neighboring winter resort. Gives a good insight into the lives of the bored and idle rich.

BEER, THOMAS, 1889–1940
 Sandoval: A Romance of Bad Manners (Knopf, 1924). Covers a few days in the life of a seventeen-year-old son of a Civil War profiteer. New York in the 1870's.

BRACE, GERALD WARNER, 1901–
 The Garretson Chronicle (Norton, 1947). Often reading like an autobiography, this traces the conflict in ideas through three generations of a Massachusetts family, from the Victorian period to the present. Shows in clear portraits the admirable—and the stuffy—in the Brahmin.

BRIGHT, ROBERT, 1902–
 The Olivers (Doubleday, 1947). Details the tangled lives of Americans —artists, writers, pleasure lovers, and celebrity seekers—in a French seaside village.

BURT, MAXWELL STRUTHERS, 1882–1954
 The Diary of a Dude Wrangler (Scribner, 1938). About the wealthy and fashionable who disport themselves on a Wyoming "guest" ranch.
 Along These Streets (Scribner, 1942). A slow-paced but amply filled novel of the life of the well-bred (and well-heeled) society folk in Phila-

delphia. Excellent reporting on kindly and brainless aristocrats—noble traditions, wasted opportunities, clubs, cuisines.

CATHER, WILLA SIBERT, 1876–1947

*A Lost Lady (Knopf, 1923). A lady lost between the nineteenth century and its values and the hurly-burly and changing modes of the twentieth century. In an age when woman's life consisted of dependence on man, she would have been a lady; in the twentieth century, she was scarcely that.

CHURCHILL, WINSTON, 1871–1947

A Modern Chronicle (1910). Dealing with marriage and divorce. Reflects our changing social pattern.

COOPER, LOUISE (FIELD), 1905–

Summer Stranger (Harper, 1947). Of a Long Island Sound summer resort, as seen by an unsophisticated young girl who is visiting wealthy relatives.

FINLETTER, GRETCHEN

The Dinner Party (From the Journal of a Lady of Today) (Harper, 1955). A light, clever treatment of parties, home decoration, socialite visits to army bases, official decorum, child rearing, and so on.

FITZGERALD, F. SCOTT, 1896–1940

Flappers and Philosophers (Scribner, 1920). Eight stories of socialites, who range from small-town elite to yacht-owning millionaires. Clever tales of the early Jazz Age.

This Side of Paradise (Scribner, 1920). A picture of well-to-do youth before and after World War I. Shows sensitive and intelligent young people reacting to new sex customs, new literary ideas, and prosperity. A sensation in its day, the book now seems both "dated" in content and inexpert in construction.

The Beautiful and Damned (Scribner, 1922). Of an aristocratic, subsidized, Harvard graduate and his beautiful wife, before, during, and after World War I. A readable picture of high life in the early Jazz Age.

Tales of the Jazz Age (Scribner, 1922). A group of eleven stories ranging from broad burlesque to somber tragedy.

*The Great Gatsby (Scribner, 1925). A polished Fitzgerald story about love and bootlegging in fashionable Long Island society.

Tender Is the Night (Scribner, 1934). Of wealthy, sophisticated Americans on the French Riviera. A story of underlying despair and psychological degeneration.

FOSTER, HANNAH WEBSTER, 1759–1840.

The Coquette, or, the History of Eliza Wharton (1797; Columbia University, 1939). A dramatic narrative, "founded on Fact," of the seduction of a gay, "volatile," well-bred young woman of good family. Intended as a warning to virtuous young ladies, the book is also a mirror of eighteenth-century notions of the conflict between sensibility and passion.

FREEMAN, MARY E. WILKINS, 1862–1930
Jerome: A Poor Man (1897). A realistic romance of a poor young man in love with a member of the well-to-do class.

GLASGOW, ELLEN, 1874–1945
The Romantic Comedians (Doubleday, 1926). A satire on aging and romantic Southern gentlemen.

GRANT, ROBERT, 1852–1914
Unleavened Bread (Scribner, 1900). The story of a social climber and her three marriages in attempts to reach "high society."

GRONDAHL, KATHRYN
The Mango Season (Morrow, 1954). Of American diplomatic representatives and their wives in Bangkok, Thailand, showing them more interested in their personal relationships, intrigue, and leisure-time activities than in serving the U.S.A.

HEMINGWAY, ERNEST, 1896–
To Have and Have Not (Scribner, 1937). See above, p. 75.

HERGESHEIMER, JOSEPH, 1880–1954
The Three Black Pennys (Knopf, 1917). See above, p. 84.
Tropical Winter (Knopf, 1933). A collection of ten short stories about the inhabitants of an exclusive winter colony near Palm Beach. Tells what these people—whose only reason for living is their immense wealth —do, say, drink, wear, and think.

HORGAN, PAUL, 1903–
The Fault of Angels (Harper, 1933). Social comedy of a wealthy American and the community he endowed with an opera, a symphony orchestra, and a school of music.
No Quarter Given (Harper, 1935). Social satire on the sophisticates of Santa Fé, New Mexico.

HOWE, HELEN, 1905–
We Happy Few (Simon, 1946). A satire on the cultivated upper ranks of society in Cambridge, Massachusetts. Cruelly dissects the nature of a sophisticated woman and also the conversation of Harvard literary coteries.

HOWELLS, WILLIAM D., 1837–1920
The Rise of Silas Lapham (1885). See above, p. 85.
*A Hazard of New Fortunes (1890). A social-climber novel in which a couple come to New York and rise steadily in society.

ISHERWOOD, CHRISTOPHER, 1904–
The World in the Evening (Random, 1954). The story ends in a Hollywood divorce for the main character, a homosexual, whose life is traced through a first marriage to a woman writer twelve years his elder and a second marriage to a "Hollywood play girl." A major thesis seems to be an argument for understanding of the homosexual and less rigorous legal attitudes.

JAMES, HENRY, 1843–1916

The American (1877). A self-made American goes to Europe to enjoy his wealth and to essay entrance into the upper stratum of French society.

Daisy Miller: A Comedy (1878). The story of an American girl who scandalizes Rome society by her defiance of conventions.

***The Portrait of a Lady** (1881). A subtle psychological novel of an American girl being wooed among the elite of international society. Scene laid mostly in Europe. An artistic masterpiece but for most persons quite slow reading.

Washington Square (1881). Of a fortune hunter in wealthy New York society. Artistic and ironical. By a very genteel realist.

LA FARGE, CHRISTOPHER, 1897–1956

The Wilsons (Coward, 1941). A deft account of the rise of a pretty, semipoisonous, relentless social climber.

LINCOLN, VICTORIA, 1904–

Celia Amberley (Rinehart, 1949). Laid in a Rhode Island town and a women's college in Cambridge, this is a picture of a girl's growing up in the 1910's and 1920's—the development of her personality and her capacity for love.

MARKS, PERCY, 1891–

The Plastic Age (Century, 1924). An account, considered realistic in its day, of college students in the postwar period. Shows new attitudes toward religion, sex, booze, college snobbery.

MARQUAND, JOHN PHILLIPS, 1893–

***The Late George Apley** (Little, 1937). The story of a simon-pure Bostonian, from 1866 to 1933. Brings out in detail the code of family integrity, public responsibility, and so on, of the Beacon Hill aristocrat. Subtly ironical.

Wickford Point (Little, 1939). A family chronicle depicting a self-satisfied but inefficient family at Wickford Point, north of Boston.

H. M. Pulham, Esquire (Little, 1941). A humorous, satiricial picture of present-day Boston, contrasting its prevailing folkways with those of New York.

NIN, ANAIS, 1903–

Ladders to Fire (Dutton, 1946). A strange psychological study of the "confused and twisted nature" of women in the artistic leisure class, in Hollywood, New York, and Paris. Poetizes the psychiatric data on sexual sophisticates.

O'HARA, JOHN, 1905–

Appointment in Samarra (Harcourt, 1934). Of a fast-moving, country-club set in a Pennsylvania town. A ruthless and sardonic presentation of social leaders.

PHILLIPS, DAVID G., 1867–1911

The Great God Success (1901). A realistic picture of the luxuries, follies, and sins of the upper class.

The Fashionable Adventures of Joshua Craig (1909). A blatant, self-made politician marries a refined lady of the highest Washington society. Realism in character drawing.

PINCKNEY, JOSEPHINE, 1895–
Three O'Clock Dinner (Viking, 1945). Built around the making and breaking of a marriage between the scion of an old Charleston family and the daughter of relative newcomers to South Carolina. Interesting for contrasts of the old and new, for drama and wit, and for the careful literary texture of the style.

RICE, ELMER L., 1892–
Imperial City (Coward, 1937). See above, p. 99.

RINEHART, MARY ROBERTS, 1876–
A Light in the Window (Rinehart, 1948). A chronicle of the events in several generations of a wealthy and prominent family during the years 1919–1945. Illuminates the publishing world, modern marriage, the conflicts between conservatives and liberals, and the problems of leading the good life.

SANTAYANA, GEORGE, 1863–1952
The Last Puritan (Scribner, 1936). Ironical and philosophical analysis of a talented blue-blood who has been suppressed by tradition to the point of futility in all of his personal relationships.

SINCLAIR, UPTON B., 1878–
World's End (Viking, 1940). A study of fascism in the world. The son of a munitions maker finds his world of culture crashing about him, owing to the way of life represented by his father and modern big business.

SMITH, ROBERT, 1905–
Hotel on the Lake (Farrar, 1943). A crowded behavioristic novel of life in a summer hotel in Maine. A naturalistic satire.

STAFFORD, JEAN, 1915–
Boston Adventure (Harcourt, 1944). A psychological novel of Boston bluebloods, their virtues and errors, as seen by the daughter of an immigrant. In the tradition of Marcel Proust, the book reads slowly like an elaborate reminiscence.
The Catherine Wheel (Harcourt, 1952). Analytical study of a woman in love with her friend's husband. She seems to think herself a martyr, but to regret her martyrdom at the last. Called "an engrossing unsuccessful novel" by *The Nation*.

TARKINGTON, BOOTH, 1869–1946
*Alice Adams (Doubleday, 1921). The unsuccessful "social climbing" of a small-town American girl.
The Plutocrat (Doubleday, 1927). An American artist, very prissy, goes to Europe and North Africa on a tour. He feels very superior to a Midwest *nouveau riche* family on the same tour but ends by marrying the daughter: Americans are alike after all, and different from those "bad old Europeans."

The Heritage of Hatcher Ide (Doubleday, 1941). A comedy of manners that shows a young man, his family, and their neighbors, all once well-to-do, bungling through the maladjustments and disillusions of the Great Depression and its aftermath.

Van Vechten, Carl, 1880–

Peter Whiffle (Knopf, 1922). Biography in fiction of a versatile, restless, and curious boy born in Ohio in the 1880's. He travels to Paris and amuses himself with his group of New York friends on the money he inherits from his uncle. Mentions numerous literary personalities.

Wharton, Edith Newbold (Jones), 1862–1937

The House of Mirth (1905). Of a woman who belongs to the leisure class in New York. Shows the emptiness of society life and the need for money to keep up appearances.

The Custom of the Country (1913). An account of a beautiful but unscrupulous social climber and her sequence of marriages.

*The Age of Innocence (Appleton, 1920). New York society in the 1870's. A pale and restrained picture of an emotion-denying, code-bound elite.

Twilight Sleep (Appleton, 1927). New York's "fast set" of today. The main character is a woman who follows an incessant routine of important trifles.

The Buccaneers (Appleton, 1938). A story of American families trying to "crash" society in New York and London.

Williams, William Carlos, 1883–

The Build-Up (Random, 1952). The story centers around a Norwegian woman married to a German, and their rise in American society in a small New Jersey town in the years leading up to World War I.

Winslow, Anne Goodwin

The Springs (Knopf, 1949). The place is a resort hotel in the country near Memphis that draws planters from the Delta. The time is around 1900. The subject is the psychic growing-up of a lovely, literate girl. A quiet, subtle study of emotional coming-of-age.

Wister, Owen, 1860–1938

Lady Baltimore (1906). A sympathetic picture of the life of Charleston and its urbane society with roots deep in the past.

5. MODERN WAR

(ALSO ORGANIZED DESTRUCTION AND MASS MURDER)

The Spanish-American War, World War I and World War II are so much a part of the modern industrial world that books about them are included here. A few books about Americans taking part in other wars have also been included. Novels about the Spanish-American War are scarce, but there was a steady stream of fiction about World War I from 1917 until 1940. Few among the writers were apologists for our entry into that war, or for the war itself, for that matter. Many accepted Scott Nearing's definition, "war: organized destruction and mass murder by civilized nations." The war which we formally entered in 1941 stimulated at once the writing of nonfiction, but a scattering of fictional accounts began to appear, and after V-E and V-J days participants wrote a great many interpretations of their wartime and postwar experiences.

ALLEN, HERVEY, 1889–1949
   It Was Like This (Farrar, 1940). Two stark and realistic stories of World War I: "Report to Major Roberts" and "Blood Lust."

APPEL, BENJAMIN, 1907–
   Fortress in the Rice (Bobbs, 1951). Story of an American who is married to a Filipina wife and who joins the guerrilla forces in the Islands during the war.

BEACH, EDWARD LATIMER, 1918–
   Run Silent, Run Deep (Holt, 1955). Built around the anxiety and danger of four patrols of a submarine in the Pacific during World War II. Lacks psychological depth but is sturdy in plot and in reporting the details of work, life, and terror in a submarine.

BELLAH, JAMES WARNER, 1899–
   Ward Twenty (Doubleday, 1946). A frank and unexpurgated picture of "clipped" veterans (maimed ones and amputees) in a military hospital. Stresses their problem of social and sexual acceptance. Reproduces their language and records their acts. An indictment of our thinking on rehabilitation.

BINNS, ARCHIE, 1899–
   The Laurels Are Cut Down (Reynal, 1937). Of two brothers sent to Russian Siberia after 1918. One is killed; one returns embittered to an America which seems to have lost its ideals.

BOWEN, ROBERT O., 1920–
   The Weight of the Cross (Knopf, 1951). A highly personal story of a man committed to the hospital as a psycho. He is captured by the Japanese and regains sanity and a satisfactory religion of his own as he helps take care of the helpless. Psychologically excellent. Well written.

BOYD, JAMES, 1888–1944
   Roll River (Scribner, 1935). Compares the 1914–1918 generation with the one immediately preceding it.

BOYD, THOMAS, 1898–1935
   *****Through the Wheat** (Scribner, 1923). A realistic picture of war. Called the "least partisan and most brilliant of doughboy reminiscences." Very accurate day-by-day description of actuality. How an average man, a very real character, takes part in a war.
   Points of Honor (Scribner, 1925). Eleven stories of American soldiers in France, showing how insufferable World War I appeared to the average man.

BOYDEN, FREDERICK, 1924–

The Hospital (Farrar, 1951). Vivid story of three disfigured airmen and their hospital life after the war. The various psychological effects of their situation are well handled.

BRISTOW, GWEN, 1903–

Tomorrow Is Forever (Crowell, 1944). Concerns a widow of World War I who lives in dread that her eldest son will be drafted. Discussion of our aims in World War II.

BROWN, HARRY, 1917–

A Walk in the Sun (Knopf, 1944). A brief, poetic, evocative tale of the landing of one platoon on a dangerous Italian beachhead. Pictures ordinary privates in the presence of death.

Artie Greengroin, Pfc. (Knopf, 1945). Sketches of an ex-Brooklyn hearse driver in numerous situations—in the guardhouse, at the movies, waiting to meet an English duchess—and expressing in Brooklynese the gripes of soldiers on a hundred matters. Reprinted from *Yank*.

BURNS, JOHN HORNE, 1916–1953

*The Gallery (Harper, 1947). Reports on Italians and Americans in Naples and North Africa. A powerful and ruthlessly realistic version of hospitals, dives, hotels, city streets. A bitter novel of the conquerors and the conquered.

BUTTERFIELD, ROGER, 1907–

Al Schmid Marine (Norton, 1944). The biography of a marine who fights at the battle of Tenaru. Almost completely blinded, he struggles for reintegration into the society he left.

BYWATER, HECTOR C., 1884–1940

The Great Pacific War (Houghton, 1925, 1942). On a war between the United States and Japan, written when such a struggle was hypothetical. Interesting ideas on the economic and strategic aspects of the conflict. Plausible tactics and effective fiction.

CALMER, NED

The Strange Land (Scribner, 1950). Story of six days in an attack on the Siegfried Line in 1944. Story told from the various points of view of twelve participants ranging from privates to a general. Some women characters.

CAMPBELL, WILLIAM E. MARCH, 1894–1954

*Company K (Random, 1933). A unique story of one company. Short sketches of many individuals of the company, telling what happened to each and his reactions. Structure similar to that of Evelyn Scott's *The Wave*.

Some Like Them Short (Little, 1939). A collection of twenty short stories concerned chiefly with the experiences of the unhappy and unfortunate; expresses the author's hatred of war.

CARSE, ROBERT, 1903–

Deep Six (Morrow, 1946). An American vessel is sunk off the African coast, and the survivors are marched into the desert by a German-commanded band of Vichy French. The novel describes their experiences and those of a group that escape.

CATHER, WILLA SIBERT, 1876–1947
One of Ours (Knopf, 1922). See above, p. 42.

CHARLES, JOAN, 1914–
And the Hunter Home (Harper, 1946). A returned veteran faces the problem that life at home has remained the same while he, as a result of what he has undergone, has matured.

COZZENS, JAMES GOULD, 1903–
*****Guard of Honor** (Harcourt, 1948). Of World War II as it related to officers and their friends in an air training camp in Florida. A careful and intense picture of interrelationships, including a Negro officer. The best analysis among recent war novels of forces at work in American society.

CRANE, STEPHEN, 1871–1900
Wounds in the Rain (1900). A collection of stories of the Spanish-American War.

CUMMINGS, E. E., 1894–
*****The Enormous Room** (Boni, 1922). An excellently written narrative of a man held in a huge camp for those suspected of being spies, etc. The prison was an "enormous room," the nave of an old church. Realistic and thoughtful.

DAVIDSON, DAVID, 1908–
The Steeper Cliff (Random, 1947). About a public relations officer in defeated Germany, a man of generous and liberal mind, who finds the courage and integrity necessary for his task of helping redirect German civilization.

DEEPING, WARWICK, 1877–
No Hero—This (Knopf, 1936). The diary of a sensitive man's reactions to Army existence. Tale of a doctor who leaves his practice to serve with a medical unit.

DELL, FLOYD, 1887–
An Old Man's Folly (Doran, 1826). Presents some of the early radical movements in postwar America. About a disbeliever in war, whose lover fought in it.

DOS PASSOS, JOHN, 1896–
*****Three Soldiers** (Doubleday, 1921). Gives the military history of three men of dissimilar backgrounds, from their days at training camp through demobilization and disillusionment. Told from the point of view of common soldiers. Considered brutal and sordid in its day.
The 42nd Parallel (Harper, 1930). See above, p. 82.
1919 (Harcourt, 1932). An episodic treatment of the 1914–1918 years and those immediately after. Similar in style to *The 42nd Parallel.*

EMPEY, ARTHUR GUY, 1883–
Over the Top (Putnam, 1917). Gives some of the details of war. Glorifies America's part.

Helluva War (Appleton, 1927). Light-headed novel of the war. Presents the slapstick-comedy antics of a brawny Irish-American private.

FAULKNER, WILLIAM, 1897–

Soldier's Pay (Boni, 1926). Of the homecoming of a mutilated soldier. How he was received by his father, his fiancée, and others.

A Fable (Random, 1954). See below, p. 157.

FISHER, DOROTHY CANFIELD, 1879–

The Deepening Stream (Harcourt, 1930). About a woman and her husband doing war work in France.

FOX, PAUL

Four Men (Scribner, 1946). Follows the destinies of four members of a submarine crew in World War I through the next quarter of a century. An illuminating commentary on American civilization.

FRANK, PAT, 1908–

Hold Back the Night (Lippincott, 1952). Well-written story of one company of Marines as they fight on until cut down to a mere handful of men.

GELLHORN, MARTHA, 1908–

The Wine of Astonishment (Scribner, 1948). A strong novel about American infantrymen in the final winter of war, 1944–45, in the campaigns from the Luxembourg border to Munich and eastward. Studies the effect of war on men's inner lives.

GOODRICH, MARCUS, 1897–

Delilah (Farrar, 1941). A wordy but interesting novel of an old coal-burning destroyer and its crew on duty on various assignments around the Philippine archipelago. Stringent analysis of the officers and men.

HAGEDORN, HERMANN, 1882–

The Rough Riders (Harper, 1927). Contains candid details of the mismanagement, disorder, and waste which characterized America's entrance into the struggle with Spain in 1898.

HAINES, WILLIAM WISTER, 1908–

Command Decision (Little, 1947). A fast-moving adventure story of World War II, of the struggle between the believers in red tape and the believers in "command decision." Points up the problems a brigadier general faces, including how to conduct operations so as to get good newspaper coverage.

HAYES, ALFRED, 1911–

The Girl on the Via Flaminia (Harper, 1949). A symbolic picture of the relations between conquered and conqueror in a story about an affair between an American GI and a Roman girl.

HEATTER, BASIL, 1918–

The Dim View (Farrar, 1946). About the commander of a PT boat, an Australian girl, and other war-born types. A love story, in the Hemingway tradition, that catches the frank talk of fighting men.

HEGGEN, THOMAS, 1919–1949

Mister Roberts (Houghton, 1946). Moving and hilarious sketches of life in the Pacific on a drab Navy cargo vessel that never sees action. Tales of young men who are victims of frustration, and particularly boredom—one of the chief conditions and horrors of war.

HEMINGWAY, ERNEST, 1896–

The Sun Also Rises (Scribner, 1926). Story of frustrated men and women of the wealthy class drifting about after the war. The main characters get drunk in a different place each day. Incisive realism.

*A Farewell to Arms (Scribner, 1929). A notable love story laid against a realistic background of fighting and war tension in Italy and Switzerland. About an American volunteer. Told in a staccato style.

HERSEY, JOHN, 1914–

Into the Valley: A Skirmish of the Marines (Knopf, 1943). Vividly and tersely reports one small battle on Guadalcanal. Shows the reality of war at close quarters.

A Bell for Adano (Knopf, 1944). A journalistic sketch of the important work of Allied Military Government in occupied territory. Set in an Italian town, the story shows the problems faced by both American officials and native Italians as the idea is applied that government is the servant—not the master—of the people.

HETH, EDWARD HARRIS, 1909–

Told with a Drum (Harper, 1945). A story of the effect of World War I on the mayor of a German-American city. Pathetic and appealing.

ILYIN, BORIS

Green Boundary (Houghton, 1949). Love story of a Russian-American and a Russian girl during the cold war. Explores mental attitudes of displaced persons and escapees from Russia.

JONES, JAMES, 1921–

From Here to Eternity (Scribner, 1951). A novel with a bit more plot than *The Naked and the Dead* but emphasizing the same general type of phony "realism." Setting, the army in Hawaii before Pearl Harbor.

LAWRENCE, JOSEPHINE

There Is Today (Little, 1942). A realistic account of a young couple who, with the draft staring them in the face, decide to get married. A timely discussion of the issues involved in a war marriage, set against a lively American background.

A Tower of Steel (Little, 1943). Told in terms of four women on the staff of an old lawyer, this is a study of the private life of young women during the war.

LEE, MARY, 1891–

It's a Great War (Houghton, 1929). Praised by Löhrke in *Armageddon* as one of the two best war novels written in America in the 1920's, the other being Dos Passos' *Three Soldiers*. From the standpoint of an American Y.M.C.A. hostess. Realistic and interesting.

LONG, MARGARET

Louisville Saturday (Random, 1950). See above, p. 98.

LOWRY, ROBERT JAMES, 1919–

Casualty (New Directions, 1946). A story of savage boredom and the mean injustices suffered by men in a photo reconnaissance wing stationed in an Italian town. A bitter indictment of officers.

MCLAUGHLIN, ROBERT, 1908–

The Side of the Angels (Knopf, 1947). A realistic interpretation of fast living and frantic furloughs in New York and Washington, and of barrack and battle life. Contrasts two brothers, one an idealistic enlisted man, the other an amoral advertising man in the OSS.

MAIER, HOWARD

Undertow (Doubleday, 1945). A psychological novel about an American soldier who ends his Army career in the psychiatric ward.

MAILER, NORMAN, 1924?–

The Naked and the Dead (Rinehart, 1948). Of the capture of a Japanese island in the Pacific by amphibious assault and jungle fighting. Studies the relationship of the individual soldier within the Army organization, shows what the act of fighting does to character, and explores the forces and philosophies that create men's fates.

MARQUAND, JOHN PHILLIPS, 1893–

So Little Time (Little, 1943). Clever writing of high society in America as the country drifted into the war against the Axis. Of a writer whose life was disrupted by World War I and whose son faces the same situation of "so little time." Biting, timely.

MATTHEWS, ALLEN R.

The Assault (Simon, 1947). By one of three survivors of a thirteen-man squad during the first twelve days of assault on Iwo Jima, this is an account of the Marines in a war of attrition. A picture not of highly mechanized war but of close personal fighting with rifle, machine gun, and hand grenade. Painfully authentic details of the "desperate little confusions" of war. The author says he finds combat to be "completely unglamorous, a foul business full of fear and loneliness, and misery."

MAXWELL, JAMES, 1912–

I Never Saw an Arab Like Him (Houghton, 1948). Thirteen stories related to the activities of a CIC agent in Tripoli, during 1944–45. Concise tales of the pattern of relationships involving Americans, British, French, Italians, Jews, and Arabs.

MERGENDAHL, CHARLES H., 1919–

His Days Are As Grass (Little, 1946). The life and world of a man who lived for twenty-three years and died on Tarawa in November 1943. An honest book.

MERRICK, GORDON

The Strumpet Wind (Morrow, 1947). A story of World War II during the invasion of southern France. About an Intelligence officer who is spying on Vichyite activities. A competent treatment of sensitive, idealistic men drafted into the business of killing.

MICHENER, JAMES A., 1907–

Tales of the South Pacific (Macmillan, 1947). Nineteen stories of a trouble shooter in aviation maintenance on atolls and islands. Shows nurses, Seabees, Marines acutely and adroitly.

The Bridges at Toko-ri (Random, 1952). Well-told action story about the bombing of the bridges. Good psychological handling of character.

Sayonara (Random, 1954). A rather contrived story dealing with love affairs between American soldiers and Japanese girls before intermarriage was officially permitted.

MILLER, MERLE, 1918–

Island 49 (Crowell, 1945). A short novel describing the personal experiences of a group of American soldiers during a three-day fight for possession of a small coral island.

That Winter (William Sloane Associates, 1948). A skillful, honest account of combat soldiers, their social and personal adjustments. In the background is a magazine organization similar to that of *Time*. In the foreground are credible people. A novel with both artistic skill and important contents.

Reunion (Viking, 1954). Eight members of an army company hold a reunion eight years after World War II. A picture of after-the-war effects of war on each, as well as analysis of present-day society.

NABLO, JAMES BENSON, 1910–

The Long November (Dutton, 1946). A grim, realistic portrayal of what a private thought as he lay wounded in an Italian house. Traces his life of hard work and disillusion in Illinois and Canada, and the realizations and convictions he gained during the war.

NASON, LEONARD H., 1895–

Chevrons (Doran, 1926). A clear picture of World War I—battles, states of mind of the soldiers, etc. Written in an amusing, familiar style.

A Corporal Once (Doubleday, 1930). A colorful and lively study of a representative American doughboy in the trenches. Little of the glamor of war; only the experiences of boys behind the line.

The Fighting Livingstons (Doubleday, 1931). About two brothers' activities at the front. The one wishing action was sent to a French instruction camp; the other, who joined the militia to dodge the draft, was called on for active service at once.

NEWHOUSE, EDWARD, 1912–

The Iron Chain (Harcourt, 1946). Contains twenty-one short stories, most of them about the iron chain of circumstances in modern war. Sad, ironic, artistic accounting of what war does to civilians and also to the professionals in disaster.

ODUM, HOWARD W., 1884–

Wings on My Feet (Bobbs, 1929). Deals with the experiences of

"Black Ulysses" in the war. To Ulysses the hardships he suffered were by no means new, for he had been cold and hungry before and he knew what violence meant. An effective account of an American Negro told in poetic prose.

OPPENHEIM, E. PHILLIPS, 1866–1946

The Pawns' Count (1918). Story of international intrigue and of German-American activities and propaganda during 1914–1918. The interest is centered on the conveying of three important war documents.

PARSON, ALICE BEAL, 1886–

I Know What I'd Do (Dutton, 1946). Shows the incidents and the psychological momentum that drive a returned soldier to murder the man who he believes has brutally assaulted his wife.

SCANLON, W. T.

God Have Mercy on Us (Houghton, 1929). Story of the part the submarine played in adding to the horror of World War I. Presents the psychology of a good soldier getting pleasure in serving.

SHAPIRO, LIONEL, 1908–

The Sealed Verdict (Doubleday, 1947). Of a young major who must prosecute and convict Nazi war criminals, and his mental conflict between his civilian sense of justice and his military duty to win by any means. A story involving justice and also a love affair.

SHAW, IRWIN, 1913–

The Young Lions (Random, 1948). A novel of World War II, in which the major characters are symbolic and somewhat overdrawn. The complete and valorous Nazi is pitted against the simple, persecuted, honest American Jew.

SHIEL, MATTHEW, 1865–1947

Contraband of War (1899). See above, p. 89.

SINCLAIR, UPTON B., 1878–

100%: The Story of a Patriot (Regan, Chicago, 1920). Of a man who becomes a spy upon Communist and Socialist groups during World War I. The Mooney case is part of the background.

Between Two Worlds (Viking, 1941). Continues *World's End*. Starts with the Treaty of Versailles and ends with the crash of 1929. A long, comprehensive study of the period. Vigorous and dramatic and fair, despite socialistic zeal.

Dragon's Teeth (Viking, 1942). Third novel in the series, this covers the years 1930–1934. Combines journalism and history to cover in story form the background of Hitlerism. In terms of Lanny Budd and the other characters, presents national attitudes, class attitudes, and personal attitudes toward world-shaking events.

Wide Is the Gate (Viking, 1943). Continues the *World's End* series, with Lanny Budd engaging in anti-Nazi activities during the beginning of the Popular Front and through part of the Spanish Civil War. A stirring, adventurous novel enriched (or slowed up) by editorializing and social philosophy. An unquestionably honest book.

Presidential Agent (Viking, 1944). See below, p. 141.

Dragon Harvest (Viking, 1945). Lanny Budd marches on through European history from Munich to the fall of Paris, while an apprehensive world watches Europe yield to the German war machine.

STALLINGS, LAWRENCE, 1894–

Plumes (Harcourt, 1924). The story of a family who have fought in all the American wars. The hero departs from family tradition in his revolt aganist the pseudo-patriotism rampant in postwar America.

STEVENS, JAMES, 1892–

Mattock (Knopf, 1927). A clever satire about a soldier who wanted to remain a "Christian American gentleman" but fell from grace in France. Upon his return to Kansas, he embraced the Klan, married the deacon's daughter, and again became pure.

STURGIS, ROBERT

Half-Past Yesterday (M.S. Mill, 1945). Tells of a young journalist's first year in uniform and of the decisions he reaches about life, including marriage.

THOMASON, JOHN WILLIAM, 1893–1944

Fix Bayonets (Scribner, 1926). An account of the actual fighting man in World War I. Shows how wars can make brutes of the best of men.

A Few Marines (Scribner, 1943). A Kiplingesque collection of Thomason's stories from World War I to 1939.

TOWNER, WESLEY, 1907–

The Liberators (Wyn, 1946). Shows what happens when American occupational forces move in on a small German city. Shows human frailty triumphing over the effort "to punish constructively." Important for contents rather than artistry.

TRAIN, ARTHUR, 1875–1945

The Earthquake (Scribner, 1918). Portrays the effect of the war on a wealthy family of America and on their friends. The news of war reaches the family while they are traveling in the Orient. The book describes the changes they see in New York City when they return.

TRUMBO, DALTON, 1905–

Johnny Got His Gun (Lippincott, 1939). Vivid story of a boy who lost his sight and hearing and his limbs in the war, and who lies in bed and thinks over the events of his life.

VIDAL, GORE, 1925–

In a Yellow Wood (Dutton, 1947). One day in the life of an ex-soldier who works in a New York brokerage house. With careful, precise artistry the author dramatizes the veteran's psychological conflicts and his split personality.

WARRICK, LA MAR

Yesterday's Children (Crowell, 1943). Concerns one American boy who reaches adulthood and is sent off to war by his parents. An American parallel to *Mrs. Miniver*.

WHARTON, EDITH NEWBOLD (JONES), 1862–1937

A Son at the Front (Scribner, 1923). Told from the point of view of those at home and written for the parents of American boys who died at the front. The picture of wartime Paris is interesting.

WHARTON, JAMES B.

Squad (Coward, 1928). A very realistic account of eight members of the A.E.F. in France—each a very distinct type, from the San Francisco high-school boy to the corporal from Ohio.

WOLFE, DON M. (editor), 1902–

The Purple Testament: Life Stories by Disabled War Veterans (Stackpole, 1947). Of life at home, at work, and at war. Full of plain talk on love, friendship, hate, vulgarity, and so on.

WOLFERT, IRA, 1908–

An Act of Love (Simon, 1948). A psychological novel of the war, laid on a jungle island. On the surface, a story of an aviator in love and war. Beneath it, a study of a man finding himself.

WOUK, HERMAN, 1915–

***The Caine Mutiny** (Doubleday, 1951). A novel dealing with the question of a junior officer's right or duty to relieve his senior who becomes incompetent. Effective characterization and plot. One of our better war novels.

WYLIE, PHILIP, 1902–

Tomorrow (Rinehart, 1953). A novel tracing the course of our prospective war with Russia, and showing both countries left prostrate after atomic attacks. Characters well presented. Interesting criticism of our recent foreign policies.

POLITICS AND INSTITUTIONS

Fiction dealing with politics in the United States has appeared off and on throughout the life of the Republic. The writers have been idealists, believers in republican and democratic forms, in "the American dream" as James T. Adams explains it in *The Epic of America*. They have supported the cause of the common man in his rightful search for security, happiness, and self-respect. Their writing, aside from that on the Revolution and the Civil War, has tended to expose or satirize conditions that abuse the average citizen and corrupt his political life. The ideals of the writers, then, have often been indirectly expressed in protest against unintelligent democracy, "practical politics," or minority control of government.

Subjects widely treated in the nineteenth century were Jacksonian democracy, the abolition movement, the Civil War, and reconstruction. The Progressive Era, 1901–1917, produced a large school of writers about politics, who wrote of the proposed or attempted reforms of the period and of the colorful political leaders and their followers, and who raked the mud of corruption. The 1920's, 1930's, and 1940's produced a miscellaneous crop of satires, realistic studies, and historical re-examinations of the "founding fathers" and their era.

In this section we also include books about hospitals, schools and other institutions dealing with segments of the general public.

I. COLONIAL AND REVOLUTIONARY AFFAIRS

Our major political war, the Revolution, has been abundantly used by fiction for over a century. Almost always until lately the treatment was heroic and romantic. A recent tendency is toward straight realism, as in James Boyd, Howard Fast, and Kenneth Roberts, the books being the result of critical historical research. Increasingly, too, novelists are showing that there is a case for the Tories and the English.

In addition to the Revolution, frontier democracy and the Hamilton-Jefferson controversies have been popular subjects.

ATHERTON, GERTRUDE, 1857–1948

The Conqueror (1902). A fictionized biography glorifying Alexander Hamilton.

BARKER, SHIRLEY

Fire and the Hammer (Crown, 1953). A story centering on a group of Quakers who became outlaws after being mistreated by the rebels. Rather believable characters in a romantic plot.

118

BELLAMY, EDWARD, 1850–1898
The Duke of Stockbridge (1879, 1900). A fictionized account of Dan Shays's Rebellion, an uprising of oppressed farmers in Massachusetts, in 1786, against unbearable taxes and inadequate justice.

BOYCE, BURKE, 1901–
The Perilous Night (Viking, 1942). Of the lives of farm folk in the Hudson Valley in Revolutionary days.

BOYD, JAMES, 1888–1944
*Drums (Scribner, 1926). An epoch-making book, breaking the steady tradition of romantic treatment of the Revolution. Makes people and events real. Shows that the Revolution was an economic civil war.

BRACKENRIDGE, HUGH H., 1748–1816
Modern Chivalry (1792, 1815). A rollicking but wordy satire on the overexuberant democracy of the frontier in western Pennsylvania.

BRICK, JOHN
The Raid (Farrar, 1951). Vivid well-told story of one pioneer and his wife, and his adventures in helping to fight Butler's Rangers.
The King's Rangers (Doubleday, 1954). The usual old-fashioned treatment of the Revolution, but in this one the heroes are Loyalists, including Walter Butler.

CHURCHILL, WINSTON, 1871–1947
Richard Carvel (1899). A stereotyped romance, very popular in the early 1900's, against the background of society in eighteenth-century Maryland and London. Introduces Charles Fox and John Paul Jones.
The Crossing (1904). See above, p. 3.

COOPER, JAMES FENIMORE, 1789–1851
The Spy (1821). A romantic tale of a patriotic peddler who masquerades as a British agent in order to get information for the Revolutionary cause. A fairly good portrait of Washington himself, and realistic hints as to the political struggle between rebels and Tories. This book established the formula for treatment of the Revolution.
The Pilot (1823). Contains stilted Cooper love scenes, also a narrative of adventure on a frigate. The mysterious pilot is John Paul Jones.

DEGENHARD, WILLIAM
The Regulators (Dial, 1943). Of Shays's Rebellion in Massachusetts in 1786 and its political significance.

EATON, EVELYN SYBIL MARY, 1902–
The Sea Is So Wide (Harper, 1943). A story of one Acadian family which was allowed to settle in Virginia and of their readjustments to life there.

EDMONDS, WALTER DUMAUX, 1903–
Drums Along the Mohawk (Little, 1936). See above, p. 22.

ERSKINE, JOHN, 1879–1951
Give Me Liberty (Stokes, 1940). Deals with the fortunes of a young Virginian who is not much interested in politics but who is drawn into

pre-Revolution politics and becomes an ardent admirer of Patrick Henry. Sprightly conversation.

FAST, HOWARD MELVIN, 1914–

*Conceived in Liberty (Simon, 1939). Realistic story of the Revolution, told from the viewpoint of a private from Mohawk Valley, of the incredible hardships of the American army during the winter spent in Valley Forge.

*The Unvanquished (Duell, 1942). A story of George Washington, covering the time from August 1776 to the defeat of the Hessians at Trenton on Christmas night. Good characterization.

Citizen Tom Paine (Duell, 1943). Vivid montage of scenes from the life of Tom Paine. A debatable interpretation of Paine's character.

The Proud and the Free (Blue Heron, 1950). Story of a Pennsylvania regiment in revolt against their officers. Good detail about men of various cultures working together in what was called a Foreign Regiment.

FEUCHTWANGER, LION, 1884–

Proud Destiny (translated by Moray Firth; Viking, 1947). Unfolds a panorama of pre-Revolutionary France and the rebellious American colonies. A broad, flowing narrative dominated by such characters as Franklin, Beaumarchais, and Marie Antoinette.

FLETCHER, INGLIS, 1888–

Raleigh's Eden (Bobbs, 1940). A crowded, romantic novel of Revolutionary days in North Carolina. Gives a picture of Colonial society, plantation life, and—with some historical inaccuracies—the doings of such notables as Nathaniel Greene and Lord Cornwallis.

Toil of the Brave (Bobbs, 1946). Set in the Albemarle district of North Carolina. Begins with the spring of 1779 and comes to a climax with the Battle of King's Mountain. The hero is a staff officer of the Continental Line.

FORBES, ESTHER, 1894?–

Johnny Tremain (Houghton, 1943). Boston at the outbreak of the Revolution. Of a teen-age boy who rode for the "Committee of Safety." Alive and realistic.

FORD, PAUL LEICESTER, 1865–1902

Janice Meredith (1899). A standard romance set against a realistic background of the times, making clear the selfish motivation of many American "patriots."

FREDERIC, HAROLD, 1856–1898

In the Valley (1890). A historical romance of the Mohawk Valley during and after the Revolution.

GESSNER, ROBERT, 1907–

Treason (Scribner, 1944). A vigorous cynical novel about the American Revolution. Arnold's treason made understandable. Pointed and effective parallel to contemporary America.

GRAVES, ROBERT, 1895–

Sergeant Lamb's America (Random, 1940). Historical novel from the point of view of a British soldier who came here in 1776. A good picture of the British army and a commentary on the causes of the Revolution.

Proceed, Sergeant Lamb (Random, 1941). Sergeant Lamb, British soldier, escapes from prison camp, goes from New England to Virginia, and serves under Cornwallis.

HARRIS, CYRIL, 1891–

Trumpets at Dawn (Scribner, 1938). Shows the conflicting loyalties of a New York family. Set during the American Revolution, demonstrates how it destroyed the old society, disrupted families, and changed conventions of the soldiers and the civilians. There is the conflict between the newer and poorer people and the older and more wealthy families.

HERGESHEIMER, JOSEPH, 1880–1954

*Balisand (Knopf, 1924). A vivid story of Federalists fighting Jefferson's new Democratic-Republican party.

HOUGH, FRANK OLNEY, 1899–

Renown (Carrick, 1938). A sympathetic picture of Benedict Arnold is given in this fictionized story of his career.

If Not Victory (Carrick, 1939). Psychological study of a farm boy in the Hudson Valley campaigns of the Revolution.

The Neutral Ground (Lippincott, 1941). A nonpartisan narrative of the events of the war in Westchester County, New York. An exciting plot.

JOHNSTON, MARY, 1870–1936

Lewis Rand (Houghton, 1908). A vivid and entertaining narrative of Jefferson's time, involving Aaron Burr as a character.

KARIG, WALTER, 1898–   , and BIRD, HORACE

Don't Tread on Me (Rinehart, 1954). An old-type, swashbuckling-hero-type story about the Revolution, capably written.

KENNEDY, JOHN P., 1795–1870

*Horseshoe Robinson (1835). A romantic tale of bravery and patriotism in the Southern forests. One of the most popular of the early treatments.

LANCASTER, BRUCE, 1896–

Guns of Burgoyne (Stokes, 1939). Deals with the expedition and defeat of Burgoyne's expedition at Saratoga from the viewpoint of a Hessian officer of the English army. The story is an old formula, but the history is fresh and vigorous.

MASON, F. VAN WYCK, 1897–

Three Harbours (Lippincott, 1938). A study of confusion and conflicting interests before the American Revolution in 1774–75. Set in Norfolk, Virginia, Boston, Bermuda, and a few other places. Concerned with seacoast merchants.

Stars on the Sea (Lippincott, 1940). A romantic tale of privateering during the American Revolution. Set in Rhode Island, South Carolina, and the Bahamas.

Rivers of Glory (Lippincott, 1942). Of events of the fourth and fifth years of the Revolution, occurring on the Hudson, Montego, and Savannah rivers. A competent brew of romance and historic realism.

MELVILLE, HERMAN, 1819–1891

Israel Potter (1855). Fictionized biography of a Revolutionary soldier. Much adventure. Enlivened scenes with Franklin, Ethan Allen, and John Paul Jones. Good realistic scenes.

MITCHELL, SILAS WEIR, 1829–1914

Hugh Wynne, Free Quaker (1897). A fairly realistic story of the events of the Revolution in and about Philadelphia. Several strong characters, and considerable drama.

The Red City: A Novel of the Second Administration of President Washington (1907). A skillful dramatization of the English and French factions in political conflict during Washington's administration. A good portrait of Washington and some of the life in the Philadelphia of that time.

MORROW, HONORÉ WILLSIE, 1880?–1940

Let the King Beware (Morrow, 1936). The hero of the story is a Massachusetts Tory who returns to England because he cannot agree with the Revolution. He gains entrance to court, where he becomes the King's trusted friend. Presents a fresh interpretation of the character of George III. Gives the views of Franklin, Burke, Penn, and Lord North.

PAGE, ELIZABETH, 1889–

The Tree of Liberty (Farrar, 1939). A story of the planting and the growing of the American tree of liberty from 1750 to 1800. Contrasts Hamilton, who had no faith in the people, and Jefferson, who knew and understood the role of the masses and fought for the establishment of American democracy. Better history than fiction.

ROBERTS, KENNETH L., 1885–

*Arundel (Doubleday, 1933). A realistic and convincing reconstruction of Benedict Arnold's march on Quebec.

Rabble in Arms (Doubleday, 1933). Sequel to *Arundel*. Here Roberts continues his story of the American Revolution and of Benedict Arnold, who the author feels was misjudged. A fine account of the country and the atmosphere of the time with some fine descriptions of the Indian and navigation.

Oliver Wiswell (Doubleday, 1940). A historical novel of the Revolution as seen through the eyes of a colonel who is loyal to the Crown. Presenting "the other side" of the story of the Revolution, showing that the Revolutionaries were not always angels. Informative and challenging.

Lydia Bailey (Doubleday, 1947). A romantic, historical novel of troubled Haiti under Toussaint L'Ouverture and of the "war" between the United States and the pirates of Tripoli. An example of popular story telling based on original, scholarly research.

SAFFORD, HENRY B., 1883–

That Bennington Mob (Messner, 1935). Of the settlers of the New

Hampshire grants, which later became Vermont. Shows their attitudes toward Indians. A swashbuckler.

SANDBURG, CARL, 1879–

Remembrance Rock (Harcourt, 1948). A bulky novel, really three novels in one, that sweeps from early Puritan days to the Civil War. A multitudinous historical pageant, strong in reiterating humane ideals.

SCRUGGS, PHILIP LIGHTFOOT, 1898–

Man Cannot Tell (Bobbs, 1942). A clear picture of Bacon's Rebellion and the causes leading thereto. The first of a projected trilogy on early Virginia.

SHAFER, DONALD C., 1881–

*Smokefires in Schoharie (Longmans, 1938). Fictionized, exciting history of the border wars in New York during the Revolution. Friendly Indians as well as hostile ones.

SIMMS, WILLIAM GILMORE, 1806–1870

The Partisan (1835). A vigorous, old-fashioned tale narrating Gates's defeat at Camden and giving a picture of camp life in the Carolina swamps.

The Scout (1854). A tale of the rivalry of a Whig and a Tory, half-brothers, for the same girl, against the background of fighting in the South Carolina woods.

Woodcraft (1856). A realistic account of economic and political conditions near Charleston at the end of the war. Indicates that many common men gained nothing after undergoing the dangers of fighting.

STERNE, EMMA G., 1894–

Drums of the Monmouth (Dodd, 1935). A story of the American Revolution set in New Jersey and New York and dealing with the role of the Huguenots, the Quakers, etc. Also includes some interesting comments on the role of the students at Princeton. The central character is Philip Freneau, the poet.

SWANSON, NEIL H., 1896–

The First Rebel (Farrar, 1937). Of unruly Scotch-Irish who came to Pennsylvania in the beginning of the eighteenth century and began to assert themselves before the time of the Revolution. Deals mostly with the years from 1763 to 1767.

The Forbidden Ground (Farrar, 1938). See above, p. 8.

The Silent Drum (Farrar, 1940). Deals with the first armed rebellion against the Crown at the time of the Stamp Act, ten years before the Revolution. Set in the backwoods of Pennsylvania and Maryland. Gives (a bit too lengthily) the conversation of the time.

THOMPSON, D. P., 1795–1868

The Green Mountain Boys (1839). One of the popular early treatments of the Revolution.

THOMPSON, JAMES MAURICE, 1844–1901

Alice of Old Vincennes (1901). A dilated but long-popular romance of the George Rogers Clark expedition of 1779.

TURNBULL, AGNES SLIGH, 1888–

The Day Must Dawn (Macmillan, 1942). A light, cheerful portrayal of brave, solid people of Revolutionary days in a western Pennsylvania town. Full of movement and adventure.

VINING, ELIZABETH (GRAY), 1902–

The Virginia Exiles (Lippincott, 1955). Historical novel of a little-known Revolutionary War episode: the arrest, detention, and, upon their refusal to sign a loyalty oath, the banishment without trial of twenty Philadelphia Friends.

2. THE CIVIL WAR AND RECONSTRUCTION

The range of writers and attitudes in regard to the Civil War and the Reconstruction is from the sentimental to the realistic, as it is for the plantation. The sentimental and romantic portrayal has been continuous since the war. J. W. De Forest's *Miss Ravenel's Conversion* excepted—for it was unpopular when written—increasingly realistic treatment of the war begins with Crane's *Red Badge of Courage.*

ALLEN, HERVEY, 1889–1949

Action at Aquila (Farrar, 1938). A story of the Civil War told from the standpoint of a contemporary character, centering on the frustrations and chaos of the war.

BACHELLER, IRVING A., 1859–1950

A Man for the Ages (Bobbs, 1919). A sentimental character study of Lincoln.

Father Abraham (Bobbs, 1925). Sequel to *A Man for the Ages.*

BENNETT, JOHN

So Shall They Reap (Doubleday, 1944). An action-filled story of an Alabama poor white in the Confederate Army who never really comprehends the issues of the war. Sometimes rich with description.

BILL, A. H., 1879–

The Beleaguered City (Knopf, 1946). Of Richmond during the years 1861–1865. Presents stereotyped Negroes and Virginia masters, and is concerned mostly with the well born, but does present the maladministration of affairs by the Confederacy.

BOYD, JAMES, 1888–1944

*Marching On (Scribner, 1927). Sturdy re-creation of history, despite a standard-type love plot. Recounts the war from the point of view of a yeoman-farmer's son who is held back socially and economically by the plantation system. One of our best Southern novels.

BRICK, JOHN

Troubled Spring (Farrar, 1950). A down-to-earth treatment of a triangle which develops when a woman marries the brother of her fiancé, who has been thought killed in the Civil War. The stay-at-home brother has developed a money-making craze contrary to his brother's ideals. More realistic in tone than the other books by Brick.

BRIER, ROYCE, 1896–

Boy in Blue (Appleton, 1937). Set in the Cumberland Valley. Climaxed in the Battle of Chickamauga. Story of an ordinary Union private, giving a picture of the actual men who fought the battles—their thoughts, emotions, and desires.

BRISTOW, GWEN, 1903–

The Handsome Road (Crowell, 1938). Continues the story of *Deep Summer*. In this book the family history is carried through Civil War times. Strong in traditional themes—the "lost state" of the gentleman class, the emergence of the poor white, the villainy of Yankees.
This Side of Glory (Crowell, 1940). Continues the story of *The Handsome Road*.

CHENEY, BRAINARD

Lightwood (Houghton, 1939). A novel of farmers in the pine barrens of southern Georgia and of the Yankee lumber company which evicts them from their lands during "Reconstruction days." Realistic and dramatic.

CHURCHILL, WINSTON, 1871–1947

The Crisis (1901). The Old South of Missouri and its defeat during the Civil War. Makes clear the part German immigrants played in saving the Union.

COOKE, JOHN E., 1830–1886

Surry of Eagle's Nest (1866). A pro-Southern account of the early campaigns in Virginia. Re-creations of Stonewall Jackson, Jeb Stuart and other Confederate leaders. A liberal interpretation of McClellan. Interesting to read along with the nonfiction *I Rode with Stonewall* by H. K. Douglas (University of North Carolina, 1940).
Mohun: or the Last Days of Lee and His Paladins (1869). A rather realistic account of Richmond during the last days of the war, including sketches of unpatriotic blockade runners.

CRABB, ALFRED LELAND, 1884–

Supper at the Maxwell House (Bobbs, 1943). The characters of *Dinner at Belmont* struggle with the problems of Reconstruction and carpetbag rule. Effective romance.
Breakfast at the Hermitage (Bobbs, 1945). Of Tennessee after the war and a poor boy who realizes his life's ambition—to build beautiful houses.
Lodging at the Saint Cloud (Bobbs, 1946). Of Nashville harassed by the Yankees. A lively adventure story concerned with three daring young musketeers detached from the army of General Nathan Bedford Forrest and annoying the Union authorities.

CRANE, STEPHEN, 1871–1900

*The Red Badge of Courage (1895). A sensitive account of the psychological effect of battle on a Northern boy. Often called the first realistic American war novel.

Twenty Stories (Knopf, 1940). Contains four of Crane's Civil War sketches—the same emphasis on the pictorial and on psychology as in *The Red Badge of Courage.*

DE FOREST, JOHN WILLIAM, 1826–1906

*Miss Ravenel's Conversion from Secession to Loyalty (Harper, 1867, 1939). A vigorously realistic account of the war, honestly portraying the carnage of battle, political chicanery, and sexual immorality. The principal scenes are laid in Connecticut and Louisiana, which are effectively contrasted. Notable for the characterizations of Colonel Carter, a Virginian Loyalist, and Mrs. Larue, his Creole mistress.

DIXON, THOMAS, 1864–1946

The Leopard's Spots (1902). Violent pro-Southern and anti-Negro propaganda. A melodramatic tale of Reconstruction in South Carolina during the rule of "Black Republicans."

The Clansman (1905). An apology for the K.K.K. and an attack on Negroes. Important as the basis for David W. Griffith's famous motion picture, *The Birth of a Nation.*

The Traitor (1907). A sequel to *The Clansman.* Shows the dissolution of the Klan.

The Southerner (1913). Presents a wordy description of Abe Lincoln and the antagonism toward him during the Civil War. The romantic interest is furnished by Betty Winter, who is loved by two brothers, one fighting for the North, the other loyal to the South.

DOWDEY, CLIFFORD, 1904–

Bugles Blow No More (Little, 1937). Richmond defends itself for years against the campaigns of McClellan and Grant, and finally falls, taking with it a way of life. Vividly impressionistic.

FAST, HOWARD MELVIN, 1914–

*Freedom Road (Duell, 1944). An answer to Reverend Thomas Dixon's books, this is partisan historical fiction of Reconstruction. It gives an anti–Southern-white version of the South Carolina Constitutional Convention, post-bellum plantation life, and the Klan. A much less balanced view of Reconstruction than *Gone With the Wind.*

FOX, JOHN W., 1862–1919

The Little Shepherd of Kingdom Come (1903). Perhaps the most widely read love story of a mountain boy during the Civil War who proves himself to be just as good as "those down below"—a traditional theme.

GLASGOW, ELLEN, 1874–1945

The Voice of the People (1900). Life in Virginia during Reconstruction.

*The Battle-Ground (1902). Shows how the Virginia plantation realized the "American dream" for the aristocratic owners, fostering love, gallantry, comfort. Pictures noncombatants during the war until the fall of Richmond.

GORDON, CAROLINE, 1895–

None Shall Look Back (Richter, 1937). Set in the western part of the South. The central points are the battles of Chickamauga and Donelson.

HARRIS, JOEL CHANDLER, 1848–1908

Free Joe and Other Sketches (1887). Tales of Northerners and Georgians during and after the war.

Gabriel Tolliver: A Story of Reconstruction (1902). A reasonably dispassionate version, by a Southern writer, of the post-bellum South under military rule, and of the struggle for power between the Union League of the Freedman's Bureau on one side and the Klanlike Knights of the White Camellia on the other. Old-fashioned story telling, more like an essay than like the present-day historical novel.

HARRIS, L. F., 1922–   , and BEALS, F. L., 1881–

Look Away, Dixieland (Robert Speller, 1936). Study in Mississippi local color and problems during Reconstruction. The hero returns from the war to find his wife dead and his plantation wasting. It takes his daughter to make the necessary adjustments to the new industrial age.

HERGESHEIMER, JOSEPH, 1880–1954

The Limestone Tree (Knopf, 1931). A pioneer family chronicle and an epic of early Kentucky, which also includes interpretative history of Civil War and Reconstruction days.

HEYWARD, DuBOSE, 1885–

Peter Ashley (Farrar, 1932). Pictures a brief period in the history of Charleston in the 'sixties. Peter Ashley, returning from Oxford to a city whose political and social life was almost disrupted by the impending war, found that his cosmopolitan education had resulted in a sympathy for the Union, making it impossible to give himself wholeheartedly for the South.

JOHNSTON, MARY, 1870–1936

***The Long Roll** (1911). A vivid picture of the Civil War from a Virginian's point of view. Very careful sketches are given of Stonewall Jackson. Deals mostly with a Confederate captain who not only must fight for the "cause" but also for the hand of the woman he loves. A fine picture of the Southerners during Reconstruction.

Cease Firing (1912). Picture of the hideous and inglorious side of the Civil War and of sacrificing individuals.

KANTOR, MACKINLAY, 1904–

Long Remember (Coward, 1934). The battle of Gettysburg as seen by a resident pacifist.

Arouse and Beware (Coward, 1936). A tale of the hunger, destruction, and brutality of the Civil War. Effective realism.

KIRKLAND, JOSEPH, 1830–1894

The Captain of Company K (1891). A strongly realistic account of camp life and of haphazard military strategy in the attack on Fort Donelson and the battle of Corinth.

KREY, LAURA, 1890–
*And Tell of Time (Houghton, 1938). A detailed and convincing picture of the problems of Texas whites during the decades of Yankee military control.

LANCASTER, BRUCE, 1896–
The Scarlet Patch (Little, 1947). About the service of the foreign-born volunteers who fought on the Union side. Good in action but not in characterization.

LOCKE, DAVID ROSS, 1833–1888
The Nasby Papers (1864). An ironic, savage, often coarse attack on the Southern cause and on Southern sympathizers in the North during the Civil War. The experience and opinions of "Petroleum V. Nasby," a perennial office seeker.

MITCHELL, MARGARET, 1900?–1949
Gone with the Wind (Macmillan, 1936). See above, p. 49.

NOBLE, HOLLISTER, 1900–
Woman with a Sword (Doubleday, 1948). A solid fictionalizing of the life of Anna Ella Carroll, who was a spy, an adviser to Lincoln, a political and military mastermind, and a charming Victorian woman. Presents the men and events of the Civil War from a fresh point of view.

PAGE, THOMAS NELSON, 1853–1922
Red Rock (1898). Constituting one of the solider old treatments of Reconstruction.

PERENYI, ELEANOR SPENCER (STONE), 1918–
The Bright Sword (Rinehart, 1955). A careful historical novel built around Confederate General Hood from his victory at Chickamauga to his defeats at Nashville. Much on politics and social life in Richmond.

ROBERTSON, CONSTANCE (NOYES)
Fire Bell in the Night (Holt, 1944). A historically accurate account of the Underground Railroad in Syracuse, New York, just before the Civil War. Better as history than as creative literature.

The Unterrified (Holt, 1946). Concerned with the bitter struggle between Northerners who supported the war and the Copperhead Democrats, who favored a negotiated peace. Tells a story of the political conflicts that led to the bloody draft riots in New York City in 1863. Makes clear the political roles of farmers, laborers, and merchants.

SCOTT, EVELYN, 1893–
The Wave (Smith, 1929). A unique story of the Civil War, showing how "the wave" passed over all sorts and conditions of people and how it affected their lives.

A Calendar of Sin (Harrison, 1931). Stories of the Reconstruction period, especially of the work of the Klan.

SINCLAIR, UPTON B., 1878–
Manassas (1904). An inaccurate debunking of men and events, yet a presentation of the war as a clash of all-important principles.

SINGMASTER, ELSIE, 1879–

Gettysburg (1913). A collection of short stories about the Civil War: three about the first three days of the Battle of Gettysburg, one about the day on which Lincoln gave his famous address, and the others about the days after the war and the older people who couldn't forget it.

SMITH, CHARD P., 1894–

Artillery of Time (Scribner, 1939). The Civil War era from the point of view of upstate New Yorkers. A Northern counterpart of the long-winded Southern romance.

STERN, PHILIP VAN DOREN (PETER STORME, pseud.), 1900–

The Drums of Morning (Doubleday, 1942). Of a young man who joined the abolitionists and fought through the Civil War. "The conflicting and tragic elements" leading to the war are well presented.

STONE, IRVING, 1903–

Love Is Eternal (Doubleday, 1954). The love story of Mary Todd and Abraham Lincoln, emphasizing the strong character traits of each and the enduring nature of their love. A sympathetic portrait.

STREET, JAMES HOWELL, 1903–

Tap Roots (Dial, 1942). Centers on a group of Southern abolitionists in Jones County, Mississippi. Skillful romance.

STRIBLING, THOMAS SIGISMUND, 1881–

*The Forge (Doubleday, 1931). The Civil War affects a representative Southern family, the Vaidens.

THOMASON, JOHN WILLIAM, JR., 1893–1944

Gone to Texas (Scribner, 1937). Presents the struggle for readjustment in Texas after the Civil War. Shows the problems of reuniting the North and South. Mentions the dream of Sam Houston, the work of Juarez, the Mexican raiders, and the conditions of army life.

Lone Star Preacher (Scribner, 1941). A chronicle of the acts of Praxiteles Swan, a Methodist preacher from Texas in the Northern Army of Virginia, a he-man parson who engaged in many battles.

TODD, HELEN, 1912–

A Man Named Grant (Houghton, 1940). Fictionized biography of an enigma who was a failure before Shiloh and after Appomattox.

TOURGEE, ALBION W., 1838–1905

A Fool's Errand (1879). A story of a Northerner who settles in the South after the war and tries to solve some of the problems of Reconstruction. An interesting political discussion that criticizes both North and South.

*Bricks Without Straw (1880). A propaganda novel, containing much social history, which makes clear that the Negroes needed aid from the North and tolerance from the South. Scenes of Negroes adjusting during the period of the Freedman's Bureau and the Ku Klux Klan. Compactly sums up the aspirations of Negroes and the fears of Southern whites.

The Invisible Empire (1883). Of the carpetbagger period and the Ku Klux Klan.

TUCKER, NATHANIEL BEVERLEY, 1784–1851

The Partisan Leader (1836; Knopf, 1933). A love-and-war story full of patriotic propaganda for Virginia. For Calhoun, and against Jackson and "King Martin the First" Van Buren. Expresses the states' rights doctrine in extreme form and shows disdain for democracy, industrialism, and Yankees. Prophesies secession and civil war.

WARD, SAMUEL, 1814–1884, supposed author

The Diary of a Public Man (1879). Part fiction, part facts about high life in Washington during the winter of 1860–61. Famous for his Lincoln stories. See F. M. Anderson: *The Mystery of "A Public Man"* (University of Minnesota Press, 1948).

WILLIAMS, BEN AMES, 1889-1953

House Divided (Houghton, 1947). A solid and complicated novel about the war as seen from a Virginian point of view. Concerned with major political and military events between 1859 and 1865. Combines much historical research with some standard romantic trappings, and glosses over the evils of slavery.

The Unconquered (Houghton, 1952). A Reconstruction novel set in New Orleans. The major characters are a Southern officer who co-operates with the occupation forces and a Northern major who marries the Southerner's daughter. Various points of view adequately presented.

3. THE NINETEENTH CENTURY

Nineteenth-century political matters, other than those concerning the Civil War, which have received wide treatment in fiction are: the Jacksonian era; political corruption of the 'seventies, 'eighties, and 'nineties; the rise of the "Robber Barons"; the agrarian crusade; the feminist movement; and the political maneuvers surrounding the Spanish-American War.

ADAMS, HENRY, 1838–1918

Democracy (1880). Cold, subtle satire on legislators in Washington during a very corrupt period.

ADAMS, SAMUEL HOPKINS, 1871–

The Gorgeous Hussy (Houghton, 1934). On Andrew Jackson and Peggy O'Neill.

ATHERTON, GERTRUDE, 1857–1948

Senator North (1900). Shows American politics in Washington while affairs in Cuba were making possible the build-up for the Spanish-American War.

BENSON, RAMSEY, 1866–

Hill Country (Stokes, 1928). The background is a Swedish pioneer settlement in northwestern Minnesota, and the story is concerned with a young Swede, who ran a country newspaper and went to the legislature; and the Farmers Alliance, its political influence and effect.

BURNETT, FRANCIS H., 1849–1924

Through One Administration (1883). A solid account of political corruption in Washington.

CHURCHILL, WINSTON, 1871–1947

Coniston (1906). Combines romance and muckraking. A study of a village boss in New Hampshire who sells political control to the highest bidder. Laid in the time between Jackson and Grant.

CLEMENS, SAMUEL LANGHORNE, 1835–1910, and WARNER, CHARLES D., 1829–1900

*The Gilded Age (1873). A sharp, entertaining satire on corruption in Washington during the Grant administration. The book, which is a gallery of American types, including the Western land boomer and the boondoggling Senator, gave the name "Gilded Age" to the '70's and '80's.

COOPER, JAMES FENIMORE, 1789–1851

The Redskins (1846). Attacks Puritanism and the agrarianism of the Anti-Rent Party.

DE FOREST, JOHN WILLIAM, 1826–1906

Honest John Vane (1875). A strong satire on fraud in Washington in 1871–1872, this shows a well-intentioned man becoming a prosperous vulgar rogue.

DUNNE, FINLEY PETER, 1867–1936

Mr. Dooley in Peace and in War (1898). Humorous sketches giving the ideas expressed by Mr. Dooley to his friend, Mr. Hennessey, on a variety of political and social subjects at the time of the war with Spain.

Mr. Dooley in the Hearts of His Countrymen (1899). A satirical account of the political and social events around 1900. Shows some of the failings of our democracy and gives a picture of home life of the times.

Mr. Dooley at His Best (Scribner, 1938). A posthumous selection from the numerous Dooley papers, immensely popular in their day and very readable and pertinent even now.

FAST, HOWARD MELVIN, 1914–

The American: A Middle Western Legend (Duell, 1946). A fictionalized biography of John Peter Altgeld, the governor of Illinois, who pardoned the Haymarket anarchists. Dramatizes his political career, especially his conflicts with big business and President Cleveland. Skips eleven crucial and formative years of Altgeld's life.

FORD, PAUL LEICESTER, 1865–1902

The Honorable Peter Stirling (1894). Deals with a Harvard graduate who started on his political career in the East Side of New York and in sixteen years was elected governor by popular acclaim. He won the people's faith by bettering the poor's milk supply. A sympathetic study of a good "boss."

GARLAND, HAMLIN, 1861–1940

A Spoil of Office (1892). A picture of the rise of the Grange and the Farmers Alliance against the Republican party.

JAMES, HENRY, 1843–1916

The Bostonians (1886). A condescending and mild satire on feminists, in which they are allowed to expose their illogicality through their conversation.

KANE, HARNETT T., 1910–

New Orleans Woman: A Biographical Novel of Myra Clark Gaines (Doubleday, 1946). Of a woman's long legal fight (1832–1896) against the city of New Orleans to reclaim her lost inheritance. Parallels the nonfiction in Nolan B. Harmon, Jr., *The Famous Case of Myra Clark Gaines* (1946).

LEWIS, ALFRED HENRY, 1842–1914

The Boss (1903). A clear account of the Tammany machine and its tie-in with corporations. Shows how a man gets to be a boss.

LIPSKY, ELEAZAR

Lincoln McKeever (Appleton, 1953). Story of a highly ethical lawyer fighting the cause of the Spanish-Americans in New Mexico when one of them is accused of murder. Well-written and appealing.

MCSPADDEN, JOSEPH WALKER, 1874–

Storm Center: A Novel About Andy Johnson (Dodd, 1947). Shows a homespun politician, one interested in the welfare of farmers and workingmen, rising in a vigorous and fruitful career, in Tennessee and national politics. Especially rich in its treatment of life, politics, and the Civil War in East Tennessee.

MARSHALL, JAMES, 1896–

Ordeal by Glory (McBride, 1927). A novel about John P. Altgeld, the governor of Illinois, who "defied Cleveland" and pardoned "the anarchists."

MASTERS, EDGAR LEE, 1869–

The Tide of Time (Farrar, 1937). See above, p. 38.

NICHOLSON, MEREDITH, 1866–1947

The Cavalier of Tennessee (Bobbs, 1928). A story of Andrew Jackson in the early days of Tennessee. In the romantic tradition.

SHIEL, MATTHEW P., 1865–1947

Contraband of War (1899). Of high finance and politics during the Spanish-American War (1897–1899).

STONE, IRVING, 1903–

*Immortal Wife: The Biographical Novel of Jessie Benton Frémont (Doubleday, 1944). This fictionalized life gives substantially reliable pictures of Senator Benton of Missouri and his daughter and an effective interpretation of John C. Frémont as explorer, businessman, general, and presidential candidate.

The President's Lady (Doubleday, 1951). A biographical novel based on the lives of Andrew and Rachel Jackson, making them both very heroic. Interesting plot which makes their marital affairs central in the lives of both.

TARKINGTON, BOOTH, 1869–1946

The Gentleman from Indiana (1899). The gentleman is a likable country editor who crusades against political terrorists.

TROLLOPE, ANTHONY, 1815–1882

The American Senator (1877). A long Victorian novel of the Senator who spent a winter on a landed estate in England and had some sharp things to say to the English on their economic and political usages. Pedestrian in style but somewhat interesting. Senator Gotobed of Mikewa is incredible.

WILLIAMS, BEN AMES, JR., 1915–

"Mr. Secretary" (Macmillan, 1940). A fictionized biography of Edwin M. Stanton, showing his desire, all through the war, to utterly crush the South. Not a convincing portrait.

4. THE TWENTIETH CENTURY

Major topics for treatment in the field of politics and public institutions in the twentieth century have been: Utopias, socialism, liberalism, communism, progressivism, fascism, graft, the evils of capitalism, and modern war and its causes. The gangsterism of the 'twenties and the revival of the Ku Klux Klan were subjects for several novels, as were the rabble-rousers of the Bilbo–Huey Long type. The New Deal, McCarthyism, schools, atomic war, Congressional investigations—have all been popular topics in the late 'forties and early 'fifties.

ADAMS, SAMUEL HOPKINS, 1871–

Revelry (Boni, 1926). A novel about the grafting that went on in Washington during Harding's administration. Details of the oil scandals and the graft of the Veterans' Bureau, giving an inside picture of dishonesty in government.

BASSO, HAMILTON, 1904–

Sun in Capricorn (Scribner, 1942). Revolves around a Louisiana demagogue who resembles Huey Long. Expert local color and a clear delineation of a politician with personal magnetism, lust for power, and genius for self-dramatization.

BELLAMY, EDWARD, 1850–1898

Looking Backward (1888). See above, p. 72.
Equality (1894). See above, p. 72.

BLANKFORT, MICHAEL, 1907–

A Time to Live (Harcourt, 1943). The analysis of a liberal as he is on December 7, 1941, with a recapitulation of his life up to that point.

BOK, CURTIS, 1879–

I Too, Nicodemus (Knopf, 1946). About a judge, by a judge. A fantasy in which a judge rebels against the decree that makes him an administrator of the law, when humanity needs a dispenser of justice.

BOURJAILY, VANCE NYE

*The Hound of Earth (Scribner, 1954). An Oak Ridge scientist, who deserted the army on Hiroshima day because of his feeling of guilt, is finally apprehended. A strikingly critical picture of present-day U.S.A. "wanting to punish the impulse of decency . . . to [praise] the crime." Man's own humanity is "the hound of earth."

BRACE, GERALD WARNER, 1901–

The Spire (Norton, 1952). A year in a New England college. Centers on the internal politics of the school and on the personal lives of two main characters. Attention is paid to New England moralistic notions. Quite satisfactory.

BROWNE, LEWIS, 1897–1951

Oh, Say, Can You See (Macmillan, 1937). A clever satire on American "democracy." Browne tells of the reactions of a Russian communist who visits America.

See What I Mean? (Random, 1943). Portrays an American fascist, revealing in story form the whole technique of American fascism: anti-Semitism, violence, pseudo-patriotism, etc.—its misuse of religion, politics, and the free press. Factual material recognizable on every hand. Written in a dime-novel style. The boys are bad-bad boys and the F.B.I. gets them.

BURNETT, WILLIAM RILEY, 1899–

King Cole (Harper, 1936). The story of six closing days of Governor Read Cole's "honest" campaign for re-election, including a riot planned for publicity.

CALDWELL, JANET TAYLOR, 1900–

The Devil's Advocate (Crown, 1952). A rather fantastic story of a dictatorship in the U.S.A. and how it is overthrown by army officers who are deliberately harsh in order to move people to revolt.

CAMERON, ELEANOR

The Unheard Music (Little, 1950). Careful characterization of a handful of people revolving about a reference librarian in a small town. Mature understanding of people and their motivations.

CHAMPAYNE, MARION MIRA (GROSBERG), 1915–

The Cauliflower Heart (Dial, 1944). Of Smith College in the middle 1930's. Fair presentation of various attitudes toward current events of college students of the time.

CHURCHILL, WINSTON, 1871–1947

Mr. Crewe's Career (Macmillan, 1908). A study of a boss's absentee control of a state legislature and the idealistic revolt of a younger generation.

COHEN, LESTER, 1901–

Coming Home (Viking, 1945). Of a young marine, wounded in the battles of Guadalcanal, who returns to his native city, Pittsburgh, and fights hard against political corruption.

COLBY, MERLE ESTES, 1902–

*The Big Secret (Viking, 1949). A very satisfactory satire of bureaucratic Washington of 1950. Many recognizable pictures of Congressional investigators, bumbling cabinet officers, etc.

CORRIGAN, BARBARA

Voyage of Discovery (Scribner, 1945). Of a girl's four years at Pacific State University, where she discovers almost too much. An outspoken novel of college life in the 1930's.

COZZENS, JAMES GOULD, 1903–

The Just and the Unjust (Harcourt, 1942). The story of a three-day trial of two gangsters, exposing the ways of legal justice and the life of a Connecticut village.

DAVIS, CLYDE BRION, 1894–

The Great American Novel (Farrar, 1938). An unpartisan, human review of the United States over the past forty years, written by a fictionary person who records the events of presidential elections, political machines, and views of the development of five cities—Denver, Kansas City, San Francisco, Cleveland, and Buffalo. Also records the events in his personal life. Interesting episodes about Teddy Roosevelt, Taft's administration, and the suffragettes.

Follow the Leader (Farrar, 1942). An analytical study of a Babbitt from "Pabuloma" who makes good in World War I and later in politics, and goes to Washington in 1942 as a dollar-a-year man with his eye on the presidency.

DAVIS, KENNETH, 1912–

The Years of the Pilgrimage (Doubleday, 1948). Probes the sociological and psychological troubles of small-town Kansas today, especially the conflict between native fascists and native democrats.

DENNIS, NIGEL FORBES, 1912–

A Sea Change (Houghton, 1949). Novel about a journalist who went to Europe in 1939 to report on the Polish crisis for a "liberal" magazine, and found himself in sympathy with a more conservative point of view.

DINNEEN, JOSEPH F., 1899–

Ward Eight (Harper, 1936). Story of the old Irish colony of Boston. Gives much of its local color and shows why this little part of American society is run undemocratically by a boss.

DOS PASSOS, JOHN, 1896–

Adventures of a Young Man (Harcourt, 1939). A young American becomes a communist and finally dies in Spain in the Loyalist army. A story of an idealist's betrayal by the groups he served.

Number One: A Novel (Houghton, 1943). A fictional biography based on the life of Huey Long, this novel is a documentary study of how a sleek hypocrite builds a powerful political machine. The main character powerfully dramatizes the central problem of democracy: how to select good leaders in an age when public opinion is swayed by radios and chain newspapers.

The Grand Design (Houghton, 1949). Third in the series including *Adventures of a Young Man* and *Number One*. A picture of liberals and radicals in Washington during the New Deal as its ideals decline into "expediency, cynicism, and war."

DUNNE, FINLEY PETER, 1867–1936

Mr. Dooley Says (1910). Humorous dialogue between Mr. Dooley and his friend, Mr. Hennessey, about public affairs.

ENGSTRAND, SOPHIA, 1908–

Miss Munday (Dial, 1940). See above, p. 36.

ERSKINE, JOHN, 1879–1951

Uncle Sam in the Eyes of His Family (Bobbs, 1930). Novelization of our national temperament. Sam, Antoinette, John, and the rest stand for America, France, England, and the other members of the family of nations, their reactions and relationships paralleling the reactions among nations.

FAIRBANK, JANET A.,   ?–1951

The Lion's Den (Bobbs, 1930). Of a "radical" Wisconsin farmer, a La Follette Progressive, who goes to Congress and gets tangled up in practical politics.

Rich Man, Poor Man (Houghton, 1936). A plump, realistic novel which tells the story of an ambitious young man and gives pictures of Theodore Roosevelt's Bull Moose campaign, political and economic troubles during World War I, national party machinery, and the fight for woman suffrage.

FERGUSSON, HARVEY, 1890–

*Capitol Hill (Knopf, 1923). A shrewd version of Washington, D. C. A story of an opportunist that gives one a notion of patronage, wire-pulling, pressure groups, Washington society, and the conflict between liberals and vested interests.

FIELD, FRANCIS T.

McDonough (Duell, 1951). A long novel about politics in New Jersey in the early '50's. The story of a political boss who knows all the tricks, but loses his beautiful wife, who has more humanitarian standards than he.

FISHER, DOROTHY CANFIELD, 1879–

Seasoned Timber (Harcourt, 1939). Presents the struggle between democracy and fascism in the symbolic story of a poor academy in rural Vermont. A wealthy graduate leaves the school a million dollars provided some very undemocratic policies are adopted. The whole town takes sides on this important question, and finally a broad-minded policy is accepted.

FRANK, WALDO D., 1889–

The Bridegroom Cometh (Doubleday, 1939). Of a girl who escapes from her New England home, works her way through college, makes an unsuccessful marriage, is divorced, and finally becomes a communist. Theme: economic and political factors that hinder individuality in the United States today.

GESSNER, ROBERT, 1907–

Youth Is the Time (Scribner, 1945). The scene is Metropolitan College, situated in lower Manhattan. A realistic close-up of a campus, and also a mirror for war-bred problems.

GOERTZ, ARTHEMISE

New Heaven, New Earth (McGraw, 1952). The theme of a doctor fighting against superstitions and against private enterprise in order to get good public health in a community near New Orleans. Good in its picture of the Creole of recent times. The time of the story is 1909.

GREENE, WARD (FRANK DUDLEY, pseud.), 1892–

King Cobra (Carrick, 1940). Of a secret organization called the Red Riders (seemingly Ku Klux Klan). A warning against "superpatriotic" organizations.

HACKETT, FRANCIS, 1883–

The Senator's Last Night (Doubleday, 1943). Through the fictional device of a day in a Senator's life, the author introduces rich talk on government, the conduct of the war, and the grave problems of postwar planning. Scathing judgment of society in general and the power-loving Senator in particular.

HALPER, ALBERT, 1904–

Union Square (Viking, 1933). See above, p. 95.

HIMES, CHESTER B., 1909–

Cast the First Stone (Coward-McCann, 1952). A psychological portrayal of men in prison. The major character is a college-trained man who fights to keep a friend away from homosexual activity and is himself misunderstood by others.

HOBART, ALICE TISDALE (NOURSE), 1882–

Venture into Darkness (Longmans, 1955). Idealistic story of an American bank official who knows China well, and his attempts to rescue another American. He gives his life to save two Chinese members of the underground.

HOUSTON, NOEL, 1909–

The Great Promise (Reynal, 1946). Shows the growth of an Oklahoma boom town and what happens on this "last frontier" when have-nots and con men rush in to build overnight. Fast-paced narratives and sulphurous scenes of passion.

HUMMEL, GEORGE FREDERICK, 1882–

Joshua Moore, American (Doubleday, 1943). The stories of five Joshua Moores, stretching from the setting of the first story in 1640 to the last in 1940. Indian wars, the Civil War, and other dramatic events are involved, including recent political events.

HUNTER, EVAN, 1926–

The Blackboard Jungle (Simon, 1954). Supposedly realistic picture of a tough secondary school in New York City. Overdrawn.

HUSTON, McCREADY, 1891–

Dear Senator (Bobbs, 1928). A Midwesterner starts humbly as a lawyer with high ideals and legitimate ambition, rises to senatorial position, and thereafter declines in integrity as he grows more ambitious.

JACKSON, SHIRLEY, 1920–

The Bird's Nest (Farrar, 1954). Unique story of a girl divided between her four personalities, which take over one at a time. With the help of a psychiatrist she achieves integration. Skillful and fascinating.

KANTOR, MACKINLAY, 1904–

God and My Country (World, 1954). Sweet, sentimental little story of a man who was scoutmaster for forty years in an Iowa town and how he accomplished great things for the boys.

KIMBROUGH, EDWARD, 1918–

From Hell to Breakfast (Lippincott, 1941). Less a skillful novel than an excellent job of reporting on the methods and campaign promises of a Southern demagogue. Laid in Mississippi, it is an exposé of hypocrisy, dishonesty, and ruthless egotism. Shows a new element in Southern politics, the C.I.O. union.

Night Fire (Rinehart, 1946). See above, p. 57.

LANGLEY, ADRIA LOCKE

*A Lion Is in the Streets (Whittlesey, 1945). Based on the life of Huey Long, a story of a Southern politician who rises from peddler to state governor by using the tricks and slogans of a demagogue, including "Divide the Riches." The novel shows appreciation of the man's accomplishments without condoning his ruthless methods.

LEWIS, SINCLAIR, 1885–1951

It Can't Happen Here! (Doubleday, 1935). Predicts in startling detail what America would be like under a fascist dictatorship. Suggests the dangerous decay of old-style political idealism in the United States.

LONDON, JACK, 1876–1916

*The Iron Heel (1908). A story of the remaking of America into a type of collective society which London calls a "plutocracy." A forerunner of books on the coming of fascism to America, such as It Can't Happen Here! Perhaps more accurate in picturing how fascism actually could come.

LOSTUTTER, MELVIN SIMMONS, 1895–

High Fever: A Novel of the Sales Promotion Decade (Harper, 1935). Of a mountain preacher and those who used him to promote an organization like the Ku Klux Klan.

LUMPKIN, GRACE, 1898–

A Sign for Cain (Furman, 1935). Story of certain happenings in a small town in the South which involves the deterioration of the former ruling family—and the organization of the Negroes by Denis, a Negro Communist returned from the North.

MACAULEY, ROBIE

The Disguises of Love (Random, 1952). The various attitudes of three people, a college professor, his wife, and his son, in regard to his affair with a co-ed. Interesting psychological study. Realistic presentation.

MANCHESTER, WILLIAM RAYMOND, 1922–

The City of Anger (Ballantine, 1953). A story of political corruption in a northeastern seaport. Central characters are a "numbers" king and an incorruptible police commissioner.

MANKIEWICZ, DON M., 1922–

Trial (Harper, 1955). Communist exploitation of the trial of a young Mexican in a West Coast city. Good glimpses of the prejudices and "way of life" in Southern California. Place names are fictitious.

MASTERS, DEXTER

*The Accident (Knopf, 1955). The accident is the death by radiation of a scientist at Los Alamos. The book is a live discussion of the problems arising out of our production and use of the atom bomb. The various attitudes of scientists, military men, and politicians are well stated.

McDUFFIE, LAURETTE

The Stone in the Rain (Doubleday, 1946). Shows how fascism fostered by a few corrupt men can take hold in an easy-going Southern community; also shows how psychological maladjustments warp character.

MILLER, MERLE

The Sure Thing (Sloane, 1949). The story of thirty-six hours in the life of a young member of the State Department in Washington. During that period he is subjected to an unjust investigation which eventually costs him his job.

MOON, BUCKLIN, 1911–

Without Magnolias (Doubleday, 1949). See below, p. 167.

MORRISON, THEODORE, 1901–

The Stones of the House (Viking, 1953). Story of the trials of the acting president of an eastern college. He succeeds in solving some of his perplexing problems and is made president at the end of the year. Shows real understanding of college life.

NEWHOUSE, EDWARD, 1912–

This Is Your Day (Furman, 1937). A story of a young Communist party worker in America, his personal life, and especially his work organizing striking farmers in upstate New York.

ORNITZ, SAMUEL BADISCH, 1890–

Haunch, Paunch, and Jowl (Boni, 1923). See above, p. 88.

PAUL, ELLIOT HAROLD, 1891–

The Governor of Massachusetts (Liveright, 1930). A pleasant satire showing an honest, simple-minded organ manufacturer as governor of the state and as a victim of graft and political scheming. Nineteenth-century style.

PERKINS, VIRGINIA (CHASE), 1902–
The End of the Week (Macmillan, 1953). A presentation of thirteen grade-school teachers as they spend their time from 3:00 P.M. to midnight on a Friday evening. None of them is happy or satisfied or intelligent enough to be human. They are in a perfect treadmill of semi-intellectual activity.

PHILLIPS, DAVID G., 1867–1911
The Plum Tree (1905). Public-utility bosses in a small town make a political career for a young lawyer.

PHILTINE, ELLEN (CATT), 1910–
They Walk in Darkness (Liveright, 1945). Of a young doctor and his wife and the impact on their lives of conditions in a state hospital for the insane.

PRESTON, JOHN H., 1906–
The Liberals (Reynal, 1938). Deals with the questions of labor unions, anti-Semitism, and the evils of capitalism as seen through the eyes of the liberals on the one hand and the revolutionaries on the other. Definitely takes the part of the revolutionary and is not sympathetic to the "theorist" only. Set in a factory in Connecticut, the story deals with strikes and C.I.O. activities.

RAND, AYN
*****The Fountainhead** (Bobbs, 1943). In a strong, adroit story, crammed with irony and ideas, the author defends the philosophy and morality of individualism and attacks mass-oriented, "humanitarian" institutions.

RYLEE, ROBERT, 1908–
The Ring and the Cross (Knopf, 1947). Of a senator who is the dictator in a seaboard Texas metropolis. Sheds light on the political significance of acts by members of A.F.L. unions, the Klan, conservative churches, and industrialists' associations. A counterattack on books that defend economic fascism.

SANDOZ, MARI, 1899–
Capital City (Little, 1939). See above, p. 77.

SARTON, MAY, 1912–
*****Faithful Are the Wounds** (Rinehart, 1955). Laid at Harvard, symbol of American education at its best, the story explores academic freedom in terms of present-day conflicts between liberals on the one hand and investigators and instigators of subversion on the other. A thesis novel that lays out the several points of view.

SAXTON, ALEXANDER PLAISTED
Grand Crossing (Harper, 1943). The story of a radical youth in Harvard and of his shift to the slums of Chicago. Good discussions of "pacifism, unionism, government, and democracy."

SCOTT, VIRGIL JOSEPH

The Hickory Stick (Morrow, 1948). The story of a teacher who is a fighting liberal in a small town. An angry book, full of insight, on the American system of public education.

SHAW, IRWIN, 1913–

The Troubled Air (Random, 1951). An indictment of McCarthyism and of Communism. The conductor of a radio program is asked to dismiss five members of his cast. He sticks by one member of the cast, who later proves to be a Communist.

SHIRER, WILLIAM LAWRENCE, 1904–

*Stranger, Come Home (Little, 1954). One of the best books about McCarthyism. In a 1949–50 setting, the story of a commentator called before a Senate committee and accused of Communist activity. Follows the pattern of actual hearings quite closely.

SINCLAIR, UPTON B., 1878–

100%: The Story of a Patriot (Regan, 1920). See above, p. 115.

Boston (Boni, 1928). A fictionalized report on the Sacco-Vanzetti case in Massachusetts, one of the famous civil liberties cases of the 1920's. Presents the psychology of the needy worker as contrasted to the desire of the rich to retain power. Shows the different application of justice for the two classes.

World's End (Viking, 1940). See above, p. 106.

Between Two Worlds (Viking, 1941). See above, p. 115.

Dragon's Teeth (Viking, 1942). See above, p. 115.

Wide Is the Gate (Viking, 1943). See above, p. 115.

Presidential Agent (Viking, 1944). The fifth volume in the series, this novel deals largely with events immediately preceding the opening of World War II.

SMITH, CHARD POWERS, 1894–

Turn of the Dial (Scribner, 1943). Money versus ideals in radio.

STEINBECK, JOHN, 1902–

In Dubious Battle (Viking, 1936). See above, p. 69.

STONE, IRVING, 1903–

Adversary in the House (Doubleday, 1947). A fictionalized life of Eugene V. Debs. The historical parts are quite accurate. The relationship with his wife, to which the title refers, seems overdrawn.

STRIBLING, THOMAS SIGISMUND, 1881–

The Sound Wagon (Doubleday, 1935). An exciting and provocative satire on practical politics, including gangster rackets.

These Bars of Flesh (Doubleday, 1938). The story of a Southern politician who goes north to Megapolis to school. Satirizes politics, political groups, and educational institutions.

SYLVESTER, HARRY, 1908–

Moon Gaffney (Holt, 1947). A slice-of-life novel of Irish Catholics in New York City in the 1930's. Shows a young politician torn between the spiritual and materialistic forces in his cultural complex. Exhibits the struggle of an idealist to adjust himself during strife between fascists and anti-fascists. Attacks religion only in so far as it attacks those religious leaders who betray the human spirit.

TARKINGTON, BOOTH, 1869–1946

The Conquest of Canaan (1905). See above, p. 41.

TRAIN, ARTHUR, 1875–1945

Yankee Lawyer; The Autobiography of Ephraim Tutt (Scribner, 1943). The story of an American lawyer's seventy-five years up to 1943. Mr. Train's pictorial character in a full-length portrait. Humorous.

TWERSKY, JACOB, 1920–

Face of the Deep (World, 1952). The author, who is blind, traces the lives of six blind people from early adolescence until each is in his twenties. A real glimpse into the lives of the blind, and of the institutions that work with them and for them.

WALKER, MILDRED

Medical Meeting (Harcourt, 1949). Excellent account of a young doctor doing research on a mold used in the cure of tuberculosis. He has to choose between security in a good institutional job and going on with his research. Well written, compelling.

WARREN, ROBERT PENN, 1905–

*All the King's Men (Harcourt, 1946). Concerns the governor and boss of a Southern state, his urge to power, and his relations with two men and a woman who become attached to him. Follows in part the story of Huey Long's life. Shows the boss rising to supply a local need and then falling victim to his own power over voters and women. The book ignores Negroes but gives crisp views of cynical politicos.

WELLMAN, PAUL ISELIN, 1898–

The Walls of Jericho (Lippincott, 1947). Story of a young lawyer's struggle against political corruption—Old Guard politicians and "piratical utilities and the money power"—in a Kansas town in the early twentieth century. A dramatic picture of the close-knit relationships of the small town and of folkways on the High Plains. Sympathetic to farmers and common people.

WHITE, W. L., 1900–

What People Said (Viking, 1938). See above, p. 45.

WHITLOCK, BRAND, 1869–1934

Big Matt (Appleton, 1928). A generally realistic novel which shows the sense of honor of a state boss and also a governor's inner conflict between serving the state and wanting re-election.

WILDER, ROBERT, 1901–

Flamingo Road (Putnam, 1942). Of Florida in the bootleg era, exposing state and local politics.

The Wine of Youth (Putnam, 1955). An oil town in Texas, especially before and after the crash in 1929. Much on Mexico and Mexican-Americans. Built around political corruption and a Mexican-American boss. Good style.

WILLIAMS, BEN AMES, 1889-1953

Time of Peace (Houghton, 1942). A swift-moving historical novel of American life from 1930 to 1941. Mainly of anti-Roosevelt Bostonians and their changes of opinion as to foreign policy and the war. A propaganda novel, but written with "Galsworthian impartiality."

WILSON, CHARLES M., 1905–

Rabble Rouser (Longmans, 1936). Tells of local politics in Arkansas before 1914. Shows the rise of a sincere man of the people who sides with underdogs and becomes governor. Plot somewhat improbable.

RELIGION

Fiction concerned with religion is miscellaneous. Since Hawthorne began writing, there has been considerable psychoanalysis of American Puritans, in Massachusetts and to the west, which makes clear the powerful force Puritanism is in American life. Evangelical religion has been treated in moods varying from the sentimentality of Lloyd Douglas to the satire of Sinclair Lewis. The various minority religions have been novelized to some extent. Of them, the Church of Jesus Christ of the Latter-day Saints has received the most extensive literary attention, at its best in Fisher's realistic *Children of God* and Scowcroft's *Children of the Covenant*. There have also been many books about the Quakers.

1. PURITANS AND PURITANISM (INCLUDING CONGREGATIONALISTS AND PRESBYTERIANS)

Stories of the Puritans and Puritanism show that Puritan thought has had an influence upon these United States in every stage of our history. There are stories of the settlers of Massachusetts and their attitudes toward Quakers and other dissenters, stories of the great witchcraft delusion, stories of Puritan fundamentalist beliefs and superstitions carried on through the eighteenth and nineteenth centuries. There are such artistic outcroppings as the works of Poe, Melville, and Hawthorne, with their probing of consciences and their obsessions' with the problems of evil and retribution. There are moralistic crusaders like Harriet Beecher Stowe and mystical speculators of many sorts. Finally we come to the twentieth-century revolters against Puritanism, who center on the frustrations and unhappiness of those who are bound by too rigid a code, several of them attempting to picture "the last Puritan."

ANDERSON, SHERWOOD, 1876–1941
Winesburg, Ohio (1919). See above, p. 34.

BARKER, SHIRLEY
Peace, My Daughters (Crown, 1949). Dramatizes Salem during the witchcraft excitement — including the satanic powers that (villagers thought) invaded the town. A picture of terrorism as a means of control.
Tomorrow the New Moon (Bobbs, 1955). An interesting picture of a preacher of the early seventeenth century in New England and his rejection of the Calvinists' doctrine of the elect. His opponents in the clerical world use accusations of sex irregularity to discredit him with the people.

BROMFIELD, LOUIS, 1896–1956

Early Autumn (Stokes, 1926). Shows a rigid aristocratic caste in present-day Massachusetts that stifles freedom of personality and action.

A Good Woman (Stokes, 1927). The "good woman" is a domineering type who spoils her son's life.

CANNON, LEGRAND, 1899–

Come Home at Even (Holt, 1951). A story of a couple who came to Salem to live, because the husband felt God had called him to settle there. The story involves his struggle between visionary "calls" and the common sense which wins out in the end.

CARLISLE, HELEN GRACE, 1898–

We Begin (Smith, 1932). A story of one Separatist family during the years in Holland and the first years in America. Centers on the sex frustration and neurotic condition of the elder brother of the family.

DELAND, MARGARET, 1857–1945

John Ward, Preacher (1888). A mildly interesting story of a gentle but sternly Calvinistic preacher. One of the first novels to treat of the conflict between conservative and liberal ideas in religion during the great debate over evolution.

Dr. Lavendar's People (1903). A portrait of a kindly parson who tries to live by a law higher than human law and to aid distressed people in his community. Decisions made in line with Puritan tradition.

DODGE, CONSTANCE W., 1896–

In Adam's Fall (Macrae, 1946). About the Salem witch hunt. A dramatic and depressing combination of background and plot.

EGGLESTON, EDWARD, 1837–1902

*Roxy (1878). A picture of southern Indiana in the 1840's, when settlers were in the path of a crusading Methodism. Shows strict attitudes of the early Middle Westerners in regard to sex. Realistic for its day, with well-developed characters.

EHRLICH, LEONARD, 1905–

*God's Angry Man (Simon, 1932). A strong, intense, fictionized biography of John Brown, nineteenth-century Kansan, carrying on early Puritan traditions in his burning conscience. Objectifies the austere, illiberal, crusading spirit that the seventeenth-century Puritans planted in America.

FORBES, ESTHER, 1894?–

A Mirror for Witches (Houghton, 1928). Excellent ironic account of the life of one girl who became a witch. Behind the actual words of the tale the reader may see the pathetic, real story of the main character.

*Paradise (Harcourt, 1937). An exciting, well-rounded presentation of seventeenth-century Massachusetts Puritans. *Paradise* gives them flesh and blood. It shows the frontier affecting them.

FREEMAN, MARY E. WILKINS, 1862–1930

Jane Field (1893). A study of conscience, of a woman's awareness of her upright life.

FULLER, EDMUND, 1914–
  Brothers Divided (Bobbs, 1951). A well-told story of the 1930's. The main character becomes a liberal Presbyterian minister and helps to straighten out the chaos created by his Communist brother.

GLASGOW, ELLEN, 1874–1945
  Vein of Iron (Harcourt, 1935). Of a Virginia Presbyterian community, in particular of a father and daughter who were strong enough to break away from the Puritanic code surrounding them.

GREY, ZANE, 1872–1940
  Wanderer of the Wasteland (Harper, 1923). A melodramatic story of a sensitive boy who feels he has committed mortal sin and wanders for a number of years in the deserts of southern California, suffering miserably.

HAWTHORNE, NATHANIEL, 1804–1864
  *****The Scarlet Letter** (1850). The established literary classic of the tortures of a Puritan conscience.

HUGHES, RUPERT, 1872–
  Stately Timber (Scribner, 1939). A historical setting telling in great detail the life of Puritan New England in the 1650's. Presents the fight for freedom in that society that denied it.

JOHNSTON, MARY, 1870–1936
  The Great Valley (Little, 1926). Shows strong faith helping a Scotch Presbyterian woman through hardships during the French and Indian War.

LEWIS, SINCLAIR, 1885–1951
  The God Seeker (Random, 1949). In the 1840's, a devout Congregationalist goes to Minnesota as a missionary working under a Presbyterian. Interesting treatment of the work of missionaries and various reactions thereto. Inconsistent characterization.

MARQUAND, JOHN P., 1893–
  The Late George Apley (Little, 1937). See above, p. 105.

MARQUIS, DON, 1878–1937
  Sons of the Puritans (Doubleday, 1939). See above, p. 38.

MELVILLE, HERMAN, 1819–1891
  *****Moby Dick** (1851). A chaotic masterpiece and a great sea romance which dramatizes the problem of evil in the conflict between Captain Ahab and the white whale. May be taken as a pessimist's reply to Emerson and the optimistic transcendentalists.

PHILLIPS, DAVID G., 1867–1911
  *****Susan Lenox: Her Fall and Rise** (Appleton, 1917). A naturalistic story, shocking to Puritans, since it pictures an "immoral" woman making a success of her life.

POE, EDGAR ALLAN, 1809–1849
  Best Tales (Modern Library, 1924). Poe's stories of death, murder,

and conscience, with their emphasis on the "guilt complex," should be noticed in connection with the "Puritan mind."

REES, GILBERT, 1923–

I Seek a City (Dutton, 1950). A simple, compelling story of Roger Williams as he grows up in England, and of his life in the new world.

SANTAYANA, GEORGE, 1863–1952

The Last Puritan (Scribner, 1936). See above, p. 106.

STONE, GRACE Z., 1896–

The Cold Journey (Morrow, 1934). Story of the attack by French and Indians on a Massachusetts Colonial village (based on the Deerfield Raid of 1704), followed by the journey of captives and victors through the snow to Quebec. Contrasts the rigid piety of the Puritans and the acceptance of life by the French.

STOWE, HARRIET B., 1812–1896

*The Minister's Wooing (1859). A detailed picture of scrupulous Calvinists with well-nurtured consciences. An important presentation of New England, some time after the Revolution, when religion was still a powerful force in the daily lives of people. Introduces several real people, including Aaron Burr and Samuel Hopkins.

Old-Town Folks (1869). A revealing picture of the firm place of many Puritan ideals in the weekday life of New Englanders about 1790. A strong interpretation of a people whose lives centered in the meeting-house.

TURNBULL, AGNES SLIGH, 1888–

Gown of Glory (Houghton, 1952). Story of a Presbyterian pastor and his wife in a small Pennsylvania town in the early 1900's. Emphasizes his place in community affairs.

WALLIS, JAMES HAROLD, 1885–

The Niece of Abraham Pein (Dutton, 1943). A picture of religious bigotry in New England—the inhumanity of the Gentile toward the Jew.

WARD, ELIZABETH STUART PHELPS, 1844–1911

The Gates Ajar (1868). Once tremendously popular in America and Europe, this consists of conversations in which two bereaved women discuss life after death. They make heaven a definite place where earthly affection can be continued. "Human dearness will wax, not wane, in heaven" (chapter xiii). A good specimen of wish-fulfillment via fiction. Appealed to women who had lost husbands, sons, brothers in the Civil War.

WHITTIER, JOHN GREENLEAF, 1807–1892

Leaves from Margaret Smith's Journal in the Province of Massachusetts Bay, 1678–79 (1849). Published anonymously. A vivid account of the second generation in New England. An imaginative piecing together of old records. It gives a day-by-day picture of Puritan life, including maltreatment of Quakers.

WINWAR, FRANCES, 1900–

Gallows Hill (Holt, 1937). Salem in the days of the witchcraft delusion.

2. THE CATHOLICS AND THE LARGE PROTESTANT GROUPS (INCLUDING BAPTISTS, METHODISTS, LUTHERANS, EPISCOPALIANS, AND DISCIPLES OF CHRIST)

The place of the larger church groups in American life has been a subject for fiction for the past two generations, particularly since the appearance of Edward Eggleston's popular *The Circuit Rider* in 1874. The commonest matters written about have been the place of the churches in pioneer times, particularly the development of revivalism and the continuance of "old-fashioned" evangelical religion in certain groups in the South today. Often the discussion of Catholicism is used to accentuate the story of the struggles of Catholics to adjust themselves in what used to be a "Protestant America." Recent books have emphasized the contributions of priests and Protestant ministers to the daily life of the communities they serve.

BATES, ARLO, 1850–1918
   The Puritans (1898). Of two high-minded young Bostonians, both novitiates in an Episcopalian monastic order, and their contrasting solutions to their conflicts between the spiritual and the physical in life. Shows the attitudes of socialites toward religion and religious cults. Old-fashioned in technique but substantial in content.

BERLIN, ELLIN MACKAY
   Lace Curtain (Doubleday, 1948). Presents the deep problems raised by a mixed marriage of Protestant and Catholic. Told against the background of a rich Irish-Catholic family living on a Long Island estate.

BONN, JOHN LOUIS, 1906–
   And Down the Days (Macmillan, 1942). A novel of the life of the daughter of Maria Monk (who wrote *Awful Disclosures,* which led to anti-Catholic riots in America). The daughter becomes a Catholic but never arrives at spiritual peace.

BRADFORD, ROARK, 1896–1948
   Ol' Man Adam an' His Chillun (Harper, 1928). Bible stories as told by illiterate Mississippi Negroes. Humorous yet reverent.

BUCK, PEARL, 1892–
   The Exile (Day, 1936). Story of the author's mother, wife of a stern missionary, whose unquestioning faith she was unable to follow.

CANNON, LEGRAND, 1899–
   A Mighty Fortress (Farrar, 1937). See above, p. 28.

CATHER, WILLA SIBERT, 1876–1947
   *Death Comes for the Archbishop (Knopf, 1927). Makes clear the hardships and accomplishments of Catholic missionaries, particularly Father Latour, in New Mexico and Arizona. The book is more panoramic than dramatic. Excellent writing, and appreciation of the work of the Church.

CHURCHILL, WINSTON, 1871–1947

*The Inside of the Cup (1912). A product of the Progressive Era, this treats the theme of corruption within the Church. Idealism versus snobbery in the Episcopal Church.

A Modern Chronicle (1910). Presents the problem of divorce.

COZZENS, JAMES GOULD, 1903–

Men and Brethren (Harcourt, 1936). An objective but slightly cynical presentation of one type of modern clergyman, the rector of a prominent Fifth Avenue church who is urbane, intelligent, and "liberal" in outlook.

CURRAN, DOYLE, 1917–

The Parish and the Hill (Houghton, 1948). A set of highly personal memories of an Irish-American girlhood in a New England mill town. Shows the inner conflicts of a young person adjusting to parochial narrowness on one hand and the open-opportunity system of America on the other hand.

DOUGLAS, LLOYD C., 1877–1951

Magnificent Obsession (Willett, 1929). An "inspirational novel" of a young waster who is redeemed by following a doctrine of anonymous aid to his fellow men. A fictionized sermon that preaches a sugary doctrine.

Green Light (Houghton, 1935). The story of the Dean of a Midwestern cathedral in present-day America. The Dean has become more understanding because of his suffering due to infantile paralysis in his youth. He gives his understanding and comfort to a young surgeon much in need of it.

White Banners (Houghton, 1936). Douglas presents his sentimental philosophy—that there is material and spiritual peace only in being patient, having courage, and serving humanity—through the character of Hannah Parmalee, who by using the philosophy saved the Ward household from financial failure and brought peace to all the members of it in the twenty years of her employment.

EDMUNDS, MURRELL, 1898–

Between the Devil (Dutton, 1939). See above, p. 74.

EGGLESTON, EDWARD, 1837–1902

*The Circuit Rider (1874). See above, p. 3.

FANTE, JOHN, 1911–

Dago Red (Viking, 1940). Stories of Catholic Italians in a Colorado town. Shows the place of religion in their lives, in parochial schools, at communion, and so on.

FREDERIC, HAROLD, 1856–1898

The Damnation of Theron Ware (1896). A narrow young Methodist minister goes to pieces spiritually and becomes an agnostic.

HEDDEN, WORTH TUTTLE

Love Is a Wound (Crown, 1952). A well-told but too-long story of a Southern triangle, a Methodist preacher loved by two sisters, one of whom he marries. Puritan attitudes toward sex plus Southern romanticism lead to quite a bit of unhappiness for each of the three.

HURLEY, DORAN, 1906–

Monsignor (Longmans, 1936). Scene laid in a small New England factory town inhabited largely by Irish, French-Canadian, and Portuguese Catholics. Shows the day-by-day life of an Irish priest who is fighting a hopeless struggle against the sin of self-pride and desire for power.

The Old Parish (Longmans, 1938). Gives a clear picture of religion in the lives of Irish Catholics in a Massachusetts village.

JOHNSTON, RICHARD M., 1822–1898

Old Times in Middle Georgia (1897). Georgia in the first half of the nineteenth century. Religious squabbles.

KENNEDY, JOHN P., 1795–1870

Rob of the Bowl (1838). A story of early days in Maryland, centering on the conflict between Catholic and Protestant in 1681. Emphasizes the struggle for religious freedom.

LEWIS, SINCLAIR, 1885–1951

Elmer Gantry (Harcourt, 1927). Biting satire on the Protestant churches in America, especially on revivalists.

MACLEOD, LEROY, 1893–

Three Steeples (Covici, 1931). See above, p. 38.

MICHELFELDER, WILLIAM A.

A Seed upon the Wind (Bobbs, 1954). The story of a doctor and a nurse in a Catholic hospital and their rejection of the church. Psychological exploration of the subject of human love and its relation to the life of the spirit.

MURFREE, MARY N. (CHARLES EGBERT CRADDOCK, pseud.), 1850–1922

The Prophet of the Great Smoky Mountains (1885). A tale of Tennessee superstitions and revivalism after the Civil War.

PAAP, OPAL LEIGH (BERRYMAN), 1897–

Pioneer Preacher (Crowell, 1948). A fictionalized account of the author's father, a Baptist minister in a Texas town early in the twentieth century. A tender account of a family facing hardship while the father faced saloon keepers, cattle rustlers, and other sinners.

PETERKIN, JULIA M., 1880–

Green Thursday (Knopf, 1924). Collection of short stories about Negro farm life in the South. In each story there is reference to the Negroes' struggle against poverty and hunger. The book brings out their religion and superstition.

Black April (Bobbs, 1927). Stories of an isolated South Carolina plantation and of the tragic lives of the few hundred Negro people who live on it. An outstanding fine portrayal of the atmosphere and local color of Negro life. Presents the strength and variety of Negro superstition. The main character is Black April, foreman of the plantation.

ROBINSON, HENRY MORTON, 1898–

The Perfect Round (Harcourt, 1945). A fantasy of the conflict between good and evil in modern life. A returned soldier struggles against moral evil in the postwar world and finally regains his faith in the Catholic church.

*The Cardinal (Simon, 1950). A novel based on episodes from the lives of several priests. Good in exposition of Catholic ideas and attitudes.

ROLVAAG, OLE E., 1876–1931

Their Father's God (Harper, 1931). A realistic account of the disintegration of a family due in the main to the religious differences between the Catholic wife and the agnostic husband.

SHELDON, CHARLES, 1857–1946

In His Steps (1897). A statement of the social gospel, advocating that churches concern themselves with social problems rather than with individual salvation. Over 23,000,000 copies sold, in 21 languages.

SPELLMAN, FRANCIS JOSEPH, Cardinal, 1889–

The Foundling (Scribner, 1951). A simply-told, appealing story of a foundling brought up by the welfare agencies of the church, emphasizing what the church does for the unfortunate. Accepts as good, decisions the non-Catholic reader may question.

STREET, JAMES HOWELL, 1903–

The Gauntlet (Doubleday, 1945). The story of a Baptist minister and his search to find his functional place amid church politics in a small Missouri town.

High Calling (Doubleday, 1951). Story of a Baptist pastor in a small Missouri town. Sentimental and appealing, upholding some simple religious doctrines. Sequel to *The Gauntlet*.

SUCKOW, RUTH, 1892–

New Hope (Farrar, 1942). Of a young Methodist minister's two-year pastorate in a small Iowa town about 1900.

SYLVESTER, HARRY, 1908–

Moon Gaffney (Holt, 1947). See above, p. 141.

THOMASON, JOHN WILLIAM, 1893–1944

Lone Star Preacher (Scribner, 1941). A collection of eight stories of a Methodist Episcopal preacher from Texas who accompanied the Texas men in the Army of Northern Virginia in the Civil War. See above, p. 129.

TURNBULL, AGNES SLIGH, 1888–

The Bishop's Mantle (Macmillan, 1947). Of a young rector of the Episcopal Church. A well-integrated study of the life and faith of a modern churchman and of the problems he must face, such as tenements in the city and the tenets of his sermons. Mature and satisfying.

WALWORTH, DOROTHY, 1900–

Nicodemus (Houghton, 1946). Begins with the Easter morning service of a fashionable Fifth Avenue church and ends there on the following Christmas Eve. A composite portrait of people in search of faith.

WELLMAN, PAUL ISELIN, 1898–
The Chain (Doubleday, 1949). A clever, light novel about a serious subject: a spiritually minded Episcopal minister in conflict with his comfortable, materialistic congregation. Set in a Kansas town.

WILDER, THORNTON, 1897–
Heaven's My Destination (Harper, 1934). Shows what happens to a textbook salesman who tries to live up to his religious principles in a world dominated by business ideals.

3. THE JEWS

Although Jews have been present in America since the seventeenth century (the earlier groups were Spanish or Portuguese; the later ones have been German or Russian mainly), it is only within the past generation that a body of fiction has developed dealing directly with them as a group. Many books center about the struggle for adjustment of various immigrant groups as they find their religious traditions in conflict with the customs and habits of America. As in the stories of other religious groups, the revolt of the young against the restrictions of their elders is a common theme.

ASCH, SHALOM (SHOLEM), 1880–
Uncle Moses (Dutton, 1918). Deals with Polish Jews adjusting themselves to an American environment.

The Mother (Liveright, 1930). The tragic story of a young girl who spends her days acting as a mother to the younger members of her family of Polish Jews that migrate to New York. She later is forced to be a "mother" to her husband and is never allowed a normal life.

East River (Putnam, 1946). See above, p. 91.

*Passage in the Night (Putnam, 1953). Centers on one man's search for spiritual peace as he attempts to right a wrong committed when he was young. His struggle is with his son, who puts family prestige above his father's sense of ethics. Quiet and forceful writing. See above, p. 91.

BRINIG, MYRON, 1900–
Singermann (Farrar, 1929). Of a Jewish family that leaves Rumania to settle in Silver Bow, Montana, a mining town resembling Butte. The children all become a part of American life in various ways. The parents are pathetic in their lifelong struggle.

This Man Is My Brother (Farrar, 1932). Sequel to *Singermann*, with much stress on the sexual and other psychological problems of the second generation.

CAHAN, ABRAHAM, 1860–
*The Rise of David Levinsky (Harper, 1917). An excellent biographical portrait of one man adjusting himself to life in America. Vivid pictures of his early life in Russia. Good presentation of Jewish social customs and folk attitudes. Strife of orthodox versus unorthodox, and of German-Jew versus Russian-Jew.

CASPARY, VERA, 1899–

Thicker Than Water (Liveright, 1932). A chronicle of three generations in a Jewish family in Chicago. Shows orthodox religion losing its hold.

COHEN, HYMAN, and COHEN, LESTER, 1901–

Aaron Traum (Liveright, 1930). Of Slavic Jews in America. An excellent realistic picture of life among the garment workers of New York City. The hero and his friends become Unionists.

COURNOS, JOHN, 1881–

The Mask (Boni, 1920). A sensitive account of Russian Jews who transplant themselves to America and find themselves trapped economically in the textile mills of the City of Brotherly Love. *A klug zu Kolumbussen,* "Woe to Columbus !"

The Wall (Boni, 1921). The history of a struggling journalist, from the age of twenty to thirty.

Babel (Boni, 1922). Continues the story of the journalist begun in *The Wall.* Laid mostly in England, *Babel* shows a Jew struggling against poverty, exile, and the inheritance of his Jewish blood. A picture, too, of England and America before the war of 1914–1918.

DAHLBERG, EDWARD, 1900–

Those Who Perish (Day, 1934). A psychological novel of American Jews and their reactions to the coming of German Nazism.

FAST, HOWARD MELVIN, 1914–

Place in the City (Harcourt, 1937). See above, p. 95.

FERBER, NAT J., 1889–

The Sidewalks of New York (Covici, 1927). A story of a Russian boy who grows up with his foster parents on the East Side of New York. Shows the life in the ghetto and the effect on residents.

One Happy Jew (Farrar, 1934). A story of five brothers. The one who remained true to his family traditions was the "happy Jew."

FIELD, BEN, 1901–

The Outside Leaf (Reynal, 1943). About a Jewish tobacco farmer who loves his Connecticut land. This vigorous novel is a non-stereotyped account of the Jew in America.

FUCHS, DANIEL, 1909–

Summer in Williamsburg (Vanguard, 1934). A novel about the people of Williamsburg, the Jewish section of Brooklyn—a dreamer who commits suicide, a racketeer, the leader of a boys' gang, a salesman's wife.

GOLD, MICHAEL, 1894–

Jews without Money (Liveright, 1930). The East Side of New York as Gold saw it in his youth. Pictures of crowded tenements, prostitution, dirt, and crime. Good descriptions of Jewish characters.

GOLLOMB, JOSEPH, 1881–

Unquiet (Dodd, 1935). Presents a man's life from childhood in Russia through adolescence in East Side New York tenements. Indicates the busy life of the streets. Presents the conflict of family loyalty and personal aspiration.

GRAHAM, GWETHALYN
  *Earth and High Heaven (Lippincott, 1944). A lecture in disguise dealing with the psychological problems of a Gentile-Jewish marriage. Covers the standard arguments and basic situations. Laid in Quebec during the war years, 1939–1945. A wise book on love, marriage, and "race" prejudice.

HOBSON, LAURA Z.
  Gentleman's Agreement (Simon, 1947). An outspoken novel about social anti-Semitism in America.

HURST, FANNIE, 1889–
  Humoresque, a Laugh on Life with a Tear Behind It (1919). Eight stories of Jewish life in New York City. The ordinary ups-and-downs of common people in the slightly sentimental tone of the "Progressive Era."

JESSEY, CORNELIA
  Growing Roots (Crown, 1947). Of Russian Jews in Colorado from the 1890's on. The first half of the book is a definitive re-creation of the life of a Jewish immigrant family. The second half talks of anti-Semitism and Zionism. An able, thoughtful novel of the growth of a girl.

LAWRENCE, JOSEPHINE
  Let Us Consider One Another (Appleton, 1945). The love story of a young American girl, of mixed Protestant and Catholic descent, who married a Jewish army officer. Her reactions to unexpected discrimination that follows on their marriage and her struggles with her own family point up this study of American intolerance. Realistic, vivid, and effective.

LEVIN, MEYER, 1905–
  The Old Bunch (Viking, 1937). See above, p. 97.

LEWISOHN, LUDWIG, 1882–
  The Island Within (Harper, 1928). A tragicomedy of the ingrained character of the Jew, with its ethnic pride, ambition, frustration, and compensations.
  Trumpet of Jubilee (Harper, 1937). Story of the conditions of the Jew under Hitler. A young nonreligious lawyer is murdered, and his wife and son flee first to France and then to America. Here in a Midwestern city they live with their relatives whose narrow-mindedness appalls them.
  Breathe Upon These (Bobbs, 1944). A propaganda novel against Nazi brutality and the British treatment of Zionists in Palestine.

LIPTON, LAWRENCE, 1898–
  Brother, the Laugh Is Bitter (Harper, 1942). See above, p. 97.

MILLER, ARTHUR, 1915–
  Focus (Reynal, 1945). Dramatizes anti-Semitism on one block of a city street. A study of nightmarish fear and poisonous prejudice. Makes

anti-Semitism real and comprehensible. Particularly effective because the hero, although taken for a Jew, is not Jewish.

ORNITZ, SAMUEL BADISCH, 1890–

Haunch, Paunch, and Jowl (Boni, 1923). See above, p. 88.

Bride of the Sabbath (Rinehart, 1951). The story of a Jewish boy growing up in New York City from about 1900 to 1930. Critical of Jewish custom and religion, also of Catholic. The main character throws orthodox religion overboard.

ROSENBERG, JOSEPH D.

Kosher Americans (Associated Publishers, 1929). A detailed study of the life of a Jewish-American family, once poor and now rich. Depicts customs, records speech, dramatizes troubles.

ROTH, JOSEPH, 1894–1939

Job (Viking, 1930). Of a devout orthodox Jew who emigrates to America and loses faith in God because of his misfortunes.

SCHNEIDER, ISIDOR, 1896–

From the Kingdom of Necessity (Putnam, 1935). An autobiographical novel which traces a man's life from the time he comes to America at the age of six until he reaches maturity and finds his place in the world.

SEID, RUTH (JO SINCLAIR, pseud.)

*Wasteland (Harper, 1946). Shows the emotional problems of the children of Russian Jews. They dwell in a wasteland between being immigrants and being Americans. The central character "finds himself" with the aid of a psychiatrist. A strong realistic novel.

TODRIN, BORIS

Out of These Roots (Caxton, 1944). Puts into words the polyglot world of Brooklyn and shows a boy growing up. He is the son of an intellectual Jewish family from southern Russia.

YEZIERSKA, ANZIA, 1885–

Hungry Hearts (Houghton, 1920). Stories of the immigrant's struggles in New York's ghetto. Intense, vivid, and appealing.

Salome of the Tenements (Boni, 1923). Of a Jewess unhappily married to a Gentile. Sensational.

Bread Givers (Doubleday, 1925). Of a Jewish girl fighting her way from poverty through college and into the teaching profession. Convincing realism.

Arrogant Beggar (Doubleday, 1927). Of a girl from the tenements and her experience with organized charity. A lively style.

4. RELIGIOUS EXPERIMENTS AND THE SMALL SECTS (INCLUDING MORMONS, QUAKERS, NAVAJOS, CHRISTIAN SCIENTISTS, AND SHAKERS)

There have been an increasing number of novels about religious innovations such as Christian Science, small but permanent groups such as the Quakers and Navajos, bizarre sects, and communal experiments. Of the minor sects in America, the Latter-day Saints have received the most attention, no doubt because of the controversies they once raised and their brave and successful settlement of Utah. In fiction as in folklore the Mormons have appeared as both noble and villainous.

Dancing Saints (Doubleday, 1943). Story of a boy's life from eight to twenty as a member of a "Shaker" group. A convincing narrative about a little-known religious group.

CAMERON, OWEN

The Antagonists (Doubleday, 1946). Of the conflicts between a farmer and a "faith healer" who has a great influence over the farmer's wife and one of his children. Gives a good analysis of the "savior" complex.

CHILD, NELLISE, 1901–

Wolf on the Fold (Doubleday, 1941). Of a woman evangelist, who is supplanted by her immoral brother. Striking characterizations.

COOLIDGE, DANE, 1873–1940

The Fighting Danites (Dutton, 1934). Highly melodramatic story of plot and counterplot in the southern Mormon country along the Arizona line. Unfavorable to the Mormons.

CORLE, EDWIN, 1906–

*People on the Earth (Random, 1937). Deals in large part with a Navajo boy's struggle between his own religion and that of the white man.

DELAND, MARGARET, 1857–1945

The Kays (Harper, 1926). The tale is dominated by an austerely religious "iron woman" (a member of the True Followers), who has the courage to be a conscientious objector in Civil War days, when pacifism was quite unpopular.

The Quakers have been almost as extensively treated, but have always appeared as kindly and gentle, their mistreatment being the most constant theme.

ARMER, LAURA ADAMS, 1874–

Waterless Mountain (Longmans, 1931). Story laid among the Navajo Indians of northern Arizona today. The principal character is a sensitive young man who is training to be a Medicine Priest.

BALDWIN, JAMES, 1924–

Go Tell It on the Mountain (Knopf, 1953). Of the religious experience of a fourteen-year-old Negro boy in Harlem. Flashbacks tell of the early life of his father and others in the South. Seems psychologically sound.

BROWN, CHARLES B., 1771–1810

Wieland (1798). Portrays a religious maniac acting under the command of God. A novel of terror.

CAMERON, LESLIE GEORGIANA (ANN GEORGE LESLIE, pseud.), 1886–

DREISER, THEODORE, 1871–1946

The Bulwark (Doubleday, 1946). This is a patient story of a fine Pennsylvania Quaker, a man with principles "too high for these days," who becomes a wealthy banker but never forgets the example of John Woolman or the precepts of the Book of Discipline. His children react to him in varying ways in the age of automobiles and flaming youth. Gives insight into the Society of Friends.

EGGLESTON, EDWARD, 1837–1902

The Faith Doctor (1891). Satirical treatment of early Christian Science and of the times which gave it its start.

EMERSON, ELIZABETH H.

The Good Crop (Longmans, 1946). A story of a Quaker couple who move their family of eleven children from Tennessee to Illinois in the nineteenth century. A descriptive and enlightening account of Quaker life.

ENGSTRAND, STUART D., 1905–

They Sought for Paradise (Harper, 1939). A fictionized account of the Swedish immigrants who came to Bishop Hill, Illinois, under the guidance of Erik Jansson, a religious fanatic, who claimed to be a Messiah and established a communal settlement. Over-sensationalized on the subject of sex and underdeveloped psychologically.

ERTZ, SUSAN

The Proselyte (Appleton, 1933). Of Mormon missionary work in England, and the emigration of a group of converts to Salt Lake City via chartered boat, railroad, and foot. A good account of the Handcart Expedition across the plains. Details of life in Deseret. Deals with the problems raised in the minds of monogamous Mormons by the plural marriage revelations.

FAULKNER, WILLIAM, 1897–

A Fable (Random, 1954). Story of a group of soldiers who, influenced by a Christ-like fellow-soldier, lay down their arms and refuse to advance. Events paralleling the events of Passion Week in certain respects. Complex.

FISHER, VARDIS, 1895–

***Children of God** (Harper, 1939). A dramatic account of troubles of the Mormons during their early history, especially in Missouri. Notable characterizations of Joseph Smith and Brigham Young. A tribute to the fanatical zeal that founded a substantial civilization in the desert.

GIBSON, JEWEL, 1904–

Joshua Beene and God (Random, 1946). A satire about an elderly Texan—Joshua—who thought he was the center of the universe and that God was made in his image. He was a member of the Church of Christ.

GREY, ZANE, 1872–1940

Riders of the Purple Sage (1912). Melodramatic and romantic story of Utah in 1871, in the days of Mormon authority. In part, picturing the invisible methods of pressure employed by the Church in an attempt to break the will of a faithful but independent woman member.

HAWTHORNE, NATHANIEL, 1804–1864

The Blithedale Romance (1852). A narrative of the persons taking part in the Brook Farm experiment, making clear why it failed.

HOWELLS, W. D., 1837–1920

An Undiscovered Country (1880). An unsympathetic treatment of spiritualism and Shakerism.

The Day of Their Wedding (1895). Two Shakers fall in love, marry, try to live in the "outside world," find adjustment impossible, and return to the colony to live as brother and sister. A mild satire.

The Leatherwood God (Century, 1916). A story of a man who claimed to be God, causing excitement in a small community.

KIRKBRIDE, RONALD DE LEVINGTON, 1912–

Winds Blow Gently (Fell, 1945). A convincing picture of Quaker life and a dramatic exposition of the Quaker creed. About the experiences of a family of Pennsylvania Quakers who move to South Carolina.

Spring Is Not Gentle (Doubleday, 1949). Second in the trilogy about David Jordan. In this one the Quaker family start a co-operative to help their neighbors through the depression. David and his wife are separated when he decides to be a conscientious objector in World War II.

Only the Unafraid (Duell, 1953). Third in the trilogy about David Jordan and his family. In this story David comes home from prison and helps to re-establish a rural co-operative. Differences of religious belief keep him from two women he loves.

LA FARGE, OLIVER, 1901–

***Laughing Boy** (Houghton, 1929). An excellent story of Navajos and their troubled relationships to whites. An appealing presentation of religious ideas and ideals.

***The Enemy Gods** (Houghton, 1937). A story centering directly on a Navajo boy's struggles with the white man's religion, and telling of his return to his own people and their ways.

MARTIN, HELEN REIMENSNYDER, 1868–1939

Tillie, a Mennonite Maid: A Story of the Pennsylvania Dutch (1904). One of the popular dialect stories of the early 1900's. Thesis: the restricted life of Mennonite women.

MORLEY, CHRISTOPHER, 1890–

Thorofare: A Novel (Harcourt, 1942). An episodic, nostalgic account of an English immigrant boy who grows up to be an American citizen among Quakers in Pennsylvania and Maryland. The "thorofare" is a path across the sea connecting two nations and cultures.

MORRIS, HILDA, ?–1947

The Long View (Putnam, 1937). Of a Quaker family from the Civil War to 1929, in a New Jersey village and the Middle West.

PARKER, NORTON S.

Hell and Hallelujah (Dial, 1931). A story of the emigration of the Mormons to Utah. Wooden characters, but appealing story.

PUTNAM, NINA WILCOX, 1904–

The Inner Voice (Sheridan House, 1940). About the role Southern Quakers played in the abolition movement.

ROBERTSON, CONSTANCE

Seek-No-Further (Farrar, 1938). Story of an imaginary community in upstate New York in the 1860's. Presents the relationships between the community and the outside world. Awakens a sense of horror of "the machine." Story deals with the son of the founder of the community and of his struggle to rescue the girl he loves from a scheming intruder.

SCOWCROFT, RICHARD, 1916–

Children of the Covenant (Houghton, 1945). A tender and mature novel about a Mormon family in Ogden. Shows tensions in the church, the family, and individual characters. Realistic reportage on present-day Mormons, but emphasis on the universal rather than the peculiar.

SESSLER, J. J., 1899–

Saints and Tomahawks (Pyramid, 1940). A historical novel of the Moravian settlements in Pennsylvania, 1736–1760.

SINCLAIR, UPTON B., 1878–

They Call Me Carpenter (Regan, 1922). A clever satire in which Jesus comes to Los Angeles in modern times, does and says the things he did and said in his own time, only to be pronounced a freak and denied the right to become a martyr. Nice irony.

SNEDEKER, CAROLINE DALE, 1871–

The Town of the Fearless (Doubleday, 1931). On the socialist experiment at New Harmony, Indiana.

Uncharted Ways (Doubleday, 1935). A thoughtful story of early Colonial days. Gives a picture of the persecutions of the Quakers by tyrannical and bigoted Puritans. Interprets the religious beliefs and faith that motivated the lives of the principal characters.

SNELL, GEORGE D.

Root, Hog, and Die (Caxton, 1937). A novel of an upstate New York farm boy who is inspired by Mormonism to go to the Utah paradise, where in time he becomes prosperous and influential in business enterprises. Laid against the background of the history of the Latter-day Saints, from New York to Salt Lake City.

SORENSON, VIRGINIA (EGGERTSEN), 1912–

A Little Lower than the Angels (Knopf, 1942). Of Mormons in Nauvoo, the main character a sensitive woman married to a Mormon.

On This Star (Reynal, 1946). Describes the tightly knit insularity of the Mormon community and the religious conflicts of one woman.

WHIPPLE, MAURINE, 1904–

The Giant Joshua (Houghton, 1941). The story of the settlement of St. George, in southern Utah, as seen by the young third wife of an old Mormon leader. A substantial picture of the Mormon settlers versus Indians, hunger, United States agents, and their own personal problems.

WILSON, HARRY LEON, 1867–1940

The Lions of the Lord (1903). A rather sentimental treatment of the Mormons.

WILSON, MARGARET, 1882–

The Valiant Wife (Doubleday, 1933). Of a Quaker wife who crosses the ocean to live near Dartmoor prison, where her husband is imprisoned during the War of 1812. She is, of course, opposed to war.

WOODMAN, JEAN

Glory Spent (Carrick, 1940). A clumsily written first novel showing the smug emotional bleakness of a Utah Mormon town.

MINORITY ETHNIC GROUPS

Next in popularity to "Farm and Village Life" and "Industrial America" as themes for fiction writers comes "Minority Ethnic Groups." The peculiarities in dress, language, and folkways of the newly arrived immigrant and such other distinct groups as Negroes and Indians have been a constant invitation to comment, and the terrible social and psychological adjustments these minorities have had to make have been a challenge to observation and analysis. Since we are composed of so many ethnic fragments, any nationalistic or racial group represented here could be thought of as a minority ethnic group; but *America in Fiction* is concerned only with those books which in some way point out one or more groups as distinct. The British, because they formed the basic group for the nationality we now call American, have come in for very little of this separate treatment. Of the other groups, some have been treated extensively in fiction.

In the number of books written about him the Negro leads. We have noted more than twice as many novels about the Negro as about the Indian, who ranks second in our list. We have made a third group of the French, Spanish, Italians, and Latin Americans—since in many respects the books about these groups stress somewhat similar mores. Other ethnic groups, none of whom are represented so generously in American fiction as the foregoing, are lumped together in our Section 4.

1. THE NEGRO

The Negro is the largest and most distinct minority ethnic group in our population, since European nationalities, such as the German, which may actually outnumber the Negro in our total population, merge so completely with our basic pattern in a couple of generations that they are lost as a minority group. Several unique things are to be noted about the Negro group as compared to other minorities. First and foremost he is the most distinct minority, because of his color, and at the same time most like the great bulk of the American population in his folkways and his beliefs, because he has been here just as long as the "Puritans" of Massachusetts and the "Cavaliers" of Virginia and the "old-timers" of the West. He is "race problem" number one, for whom each state has a separate solution. Aside from fiction of the "Old South," listed elsewhere, the most noticeable subgrouping of fiction concerning him (were we to attempt division) would perhaps be into books about urban Northern Negroes and books about rural Southern Negroes. As with other subjects there has been a general progress from sentimental, romantic treatment in the nineteenth century to a realistic, analytical treatment in the twentieth century. Certain stereotyped misconceptions of Negro character have shown remarkable vitality. Like folklore, literature has been all too prone to think in terms of such types as the contented plantation darky, the amoral creature of joy, the arrogant brute of Reconstruction, the exploited proletarian. Sensational matters, including sex and lynching, have been overemphasized. The daily life of most Negroes, especially the psychological attitudes that result from segregation, have received proportionately meager treatment. So controversial is the whole "Negro question" that most stories dealing with it are partisan or propagandistic.

ADAMS, EDWARD C. L., 1876–
   Congaree Sketches (University of North Carolina, 1927). Forceful and effective stories of Negro life in South Carolina—of prayers, wakes, farming, chain gangs, etc. Some good, nonstereotyped Negro comedy.
   Nigger to Nigger (Scribner, 1928). Intimate folk humor but, even more, protest against the cruel ways of white folks.

APPEL, BENJAMIN, 1907–
   The Dark Stain (Dial, 1943). Told with detachment, an unencumbered account of the clash of white and black in Harlem. This tale of cop vs. Negro gone berserk sums up three centuries of "racial" conflict. "All the elements of a thriller and all the threat of a warning."

ATTAWAY, WILLIAM, 1911–
   *****Blood on the Forge** (Doubleday, 1941). A skillful depiction of what happens to three Negro boys who leave the Kentucky plantation to work among the slag heaps and Bessemers of Pennsylvania. Sharply-drawn picture of psychological effects on the Negro of the two ways of life.

BASSO, HAMILTON, 1904–
   Courthouse Square (Scribner, 1936). Shows the plight of a justice-loving liberal in a Southern town. Quietly demonstrates the cruel exploitation of the Negro.

BLAND, ALDEN, 1911–
   Behold a Cry (Scribner, 1947). About an urban Negro worker who has migrated from the South, and his personal and social tensions. Laid in Chicago during World War I and the early 1920's.

BODENHEIM, MAXWELL, 1893–1954
   Ninth Avenue (Liveright, 1930). A picture of the harsher aspect of Harlem dives.

BRADFORD, ROARK, 1896–1948
   This Side of Jordan (Harper, 1929). Pictures day-by-day life of Negroes on a plantation in the bayou country. Involves folkways and important happenings, such as an epidemic of syphilis and a Mississippi flood. Realistic.

*John Henry (Harper, 1931). One of the best versions of these tall tales of a superhuman Negro stevedore in the class with Paul Bunyan, Mike Fink, and Pecos Bill. More emphasis on philandering and other attributes commonly ascribed to Negroes.

Let the Band Play Dixie, and Other Stories (Harper, 1934). A collection of twelve short stories about the everyday life of the Southern Negroes. Presents also much of Negro psychology and an insight into Negro character, action, and motivation.

BROOKS, GWENDOLYN, 1917–

Maud Martha (Harper, 1953). Valid picture of colored people in Chicago through the eyes of a sensitive girl growing up and into marriage and motherhood. Written by a well-known poet.

CALDWELL, ERSKINE, 1903–

Kneel to the Rising Sun (Viking, 1935). The title story and others in the volume depict the Southern Negro as a member of the working class, crushed by the economic system.

CASPARY, VERA, 1899–

White Girl (Sears, 1929). Story of an ambitious girl from the South who comes to Chicago where she easily passes as a white. But throughout her new life and new experiences she is in constant fear lest she be discovered to be a Negro. Her love affair ends tragically. A good description of the lonely big city life and of the life of lower-class working girls.

CHESNUTT, CHARLES WADDELL, 1858–1932

The Conjure Woman (1899). Negro life as depicted by an old Negro telling stories to a white woman. Reminiscent of J. C. Harris.

The Wife of His Youth; and Other Stories of the Colour Line (1900). Studies of the character and racial feeling of half-breeds.

The House Behind the Cedars (1900). Concerned with the color line. A story involving an octoroon heroine and a mulatto suitor. By the first important Negro novelist.

The Marrow of Tradition (1901). A romantic story of the relationships between whites and blacks.

COHEN, OCTAVUS ROY, 1891–

Assorted Chocolates (Dodd, 1922). Included here to represent the many fatuous books that the professional funny men have turned out. Trite, stereotyped Negroes with absurd names, a vaudeville dialect, and a ridiculous psychology.

COLEMAN, RICHARD

Don't You Weep . . . . Don't You Moan (Macmillan, 1935). A tale of the sophisticated social life of certain Negroes in Charleston, South Carolina.

COOK, FANNIE, 1893–

Mrs. Palmer's Honey (Doubleday, 1946). About a St. Louis woman who evolves from being a "perfect servant" into a militant Negro leader. Covers the whole field of northern Negro thinking—attitudes toward world wars, intermarriage, education, segregation, labor unions. The characters are stock symbols of opposing forces rather than flesh-and-blood persons.

CULLEN, COUNTEE, 1903–1946

One Way to Heaven (Harper, 1932). Presents two aspects of Harlem life, the religious, hard-working underdogs and the intelligentsia with their assumed sophistication.

DuBois, WILLIAM E. B., 1868–

The Dark Princess (Harcourt, 1928). A romantic story of the welding together of all the dark races of the earth. The hero, an American Negro, loves an Indian princess from Asia. Realistic passages about such things as the life of a Pullman porter.

DUNBAR, PAUL LAURENCE, 1872–1906

The Best Stories of Paul Laurence Dunbar (edited by Benjamin Brawley) (Dodd, 1938). Selections from Dunbar's four collections of short stories: *Folks from Dixie,* 1898; *The Strength of Gideon,* 1900; *In Old Plantation Days,* 1903; *The Heart of Happy Hollow,* 1904. Entertaining sentimental stories of Negroes throughout the nineteenth century, ranging from broad comedy to serious treatment of labor strife and lynching.

FAULKNER, WILLIAM, 1897–

Intruder in the Dust (Random, 1948). Partly a propaganda piece on the subject of the Negro and lynching; partly an intense, vivid, macabre story involving violent Mississippi hill folk and a blood-hungry town.

FAUSET, JESSIE R.

There Is Confusion (Boni, 1924). Of present-day, wealthy Negroes, talented and descended from honored slave families. Tells of their struggle for self-expression and social betterment.

Plum Bun (Stokes, 1929). A love triangle involving a man, who is passing as white, and two sisters, one of whom is white. Clear contrasts of Negro and white life in New York City.

The Chinaberry Tree (Stokes, 1931). Pictures middle-class Negroes in a New Jersey town as living lives quite parallel to the lives of whites of similar economic and cultural status, including snobbery and social ostracism.

Comedy: American Style (Stokes, 1933). The story of a group of young near-white Negroes in Philadelphia. Shows the life of one family embittered because of the mother's determination to pass as a white person and to marry her children to white people.

FISHER, RUDOLPH, 1897–

The Walls of Jericho (Knopf, 1928). A picture of Harlem and of the Negro's thoughts and habits. A story of the tempestuous courtship of a large piano mover and a pretty housemaid.

FLANNAGAN, ROY C., 1897–1952

Amber Satyr (Doubleday, 1932). A condemnation of Southern lynch law. Shows a community killing a splendid mulatto who repulses the advances of a white woman.

FULLER, EDMUND, 1914–

A Star Pointed North (Harper, 1946). A novelized biography of Frederic Douglass, a slave who escaped north and became a leader in Abolitionism in the United States and abroad. Re-creates the days of slavery in the South and reform zeal in the North.

GORDON, ARTHUR

Reprisal (Simon, 1950). A lively story of a lynching in Georgia and the reprisal carried out by the Negro husband of one of the victims. A good action story, with overtones in regard to Southern custom and attitudes.

HARRIS, JOEL CHANDLER, 1848–1908

Uncle Remus (1881). Folk-stories in dialect as told by a "plantation Negro."

Nights with Uncle Remus (1883). More folk tales, told by Uncle Remus and others.

Free Joe and Other Georgian Sketches (1887). Contains two long stories of Negroes, old-fashioned "darkies."

HARRIS, MARK, 1922–

Trumpet to the World (Reynal, 1946). Of a Negro who is educated and loved by a white woman, and persecuted in Army and civilian life, and yet never loses his perspective. A clear-headed, constructive, unembittered book about individual and group relationships.

HEDDEN, MRS. WORTH TUTTLE

The Other Room (Crown, 1947). Of a young white Virginia woman who becomes a teacher in a Negro school in New Orleans and gradually loses most of her aversion for Negroes. Psychologically sound and satisfyingly dramatic.

HENDERSON, GEORGE W.

Ollie Miss (Stokes, 1935). An unusual story of a migratory Negro worker, a girl, who is a field hand for other Negroes. Interesting psychological study of simple-minded croppers.

Jule (Creative Age, 1946). Sequel to *Ollie Miss*. Of her son's boyhood in Alabama, his courtship, and his experiences in finding work and friendship in New York City.

HEWLETT, JOHN HENRY, 1905–

Cross on the Moon (Whittlesey, 1946). A study of bigotry, hypocrisy, and intolerance in the South, with the purpose of shocking the reader into a realization of the forces and conditions that lie behind the accounts of Southern racial violence.

HEYWARD, DuBOSE, 1885–

Porgy (Doubleday, 1925). Pathetic story of a crippled Negro in the swarming tenement quarter of Charleston.

Mamba's Daughters (Doubleday, 1929). Of three generations of Negro women and their struggles to amount to something.

HIMES, CHESTER B., 1909–

If He Hollers Let Him Go (Doubleday, 1945). Laid in the shipyards of wartime Los Angeles. A violent book about discrimination, torment, hate, and murder. Hardboiled in technique and bitter and protesting in spirit.

Lonely Crusade (Knopf, 1947). A story showing the psychological effects of fear on a union organizer in all his relationships with men and women. An angry, violent story of labor struggles, communist politics, race prejudice, and sexual aggression—among workers and employers in an aircraft plant.

HUGHES, LANGSTON, 1902–

Not Without Laughter (Knopf, 1930). A good, plain, realistic story of a Negro boy growing up in Kansas and Chicago. Autobiographic, seemingly. Pictures the struggles of an intelligent Negro family against discrimination and humiliation.

The Ways of White Folks (Knopf, 1934). A group of short stories told from a Negro's point of view about the relations between the Negro and white. Artistic and class-conscious.

HURSTON, ZORA NEALE, 1901–

Jonah's Gourd Vine (Lippincott, 1934). Pictures country life, including religion, in the far South, with abundant Negro dialect.

Mules and Men (Lippincott, 1935). An accurate recording of Negro folk tales of store porches and turpentine camps.

Their Eyes Were Watching God (Lippincott, 1937). A story of Florida Negroes, in particular of a handsome quadroon woman.

JOHNSON, JAMES WELDON, 1871–1938

*The Autobiography of an Ex-Colored Man (1912). A readable and important novel which discusses, either directly or by implication, snobbery within the Negro group, "passing," the attitude of the Southern white, and the artistic capacity of the Negro.

KELLEY, WELBOURN

Inchin' Along (Morrow, 1932). Of an Alabama Negro and his struggle for freedom and independence from white injustice and domination.

LARSEN, NELLA

Quicksand (Knopf, 1928). Of a woman, part Negro, part Dane, who belongs to two ethnic groups, yet not to either, and struggles for self-realization.

Passing (Knopf, 1929). Story of a fair-skinned, beautiful Negro who passed for "white" in society and marriage.

LEE, GEORGE W., 1894–

River George (Macaulay, 1937). Of an educated Tennessee Negro persecuted by whites for trying to aid his fellows.

LEWIS, BESSIE

To Save Their Souls (Christopher, 1939). A story running from 1810 to about 1870. Shows that the Negroes gained a great deal in being brought to America. Satirizes the Northerners for trying to "save their souls," and shows that the Southerner knows best.

LEWIS, SINCLAIR, 1885–1951

Kingsblood Royal (Random, 1947). A successful young man discovers that he is one-thirty-second Negro and is legally a Negro. Melodrama.

LUMPKIN, GRACE, 1898–

A Sign for Cain (Furman, 1935). Of the happenings in a small Southern town and of the organization of both Negro and white workers by a Negro Communist who returned from the North. Shows also the deterioration of the former ruling family of the town.

MCKAY, CLAUDE, 1890–

Home to Harlem (Harper, 1928). A tale of a returned soldier's search for a girl he met in a cabaret. A picture of the home and the night life of the Harlem Negro. Shows gay abandon in speak-easies and buffet flats.

MEADE, JULIAN R., 1909–1940

The Back Door (Longmans, 1938). A sympathetic novel of a Negro couple in the South, the girl a domestic helper for a white family, and her good-looking husband a factory worker.

MIERS, EARL SCHENCK, 1910–

Big Ben (Westminster Press, 1941). A fictionized biography of Paul Robeson. Clearly presents the problems of a gifted Negro in a society which demands that a Negro "know his place."

MOODY, MINNIE HITE, 1900–

Death Is a Little Man (Messner, 1936). The theme that the Negro is still downtrodden and above all a victim of his own ignorance, superstitions and folkways. Pictures the Negro communities fringing villages and cities in the South.

MOON, BUCKLIN, 1911–

The Darker Brother (Country Life Press, 1943). An excellent portrait of various believable Negro characters in New York today, particularly those migrating from Florida.

Without Magnolias (Doubleday, 1949). Story centering around the president of a Negro college in Florida, his secretary, and a member of his staff. Believable incidents and psychology.

NEARING, SCOTT, 1883–

Free Born (Urquhart, 1932). Subtitle: "An Unpublishable Novel." Of a class-conscious Negro. Contains gruesome details of lynching and physical maltreatment. "The first revolutionary novel of Negro life." More indignant than literary.

ODUM, HOWARD W., 1884–

Rainbow Round My Shoulder (Bobbs, 1928). An "Odyssey of a black Ulysses." A tale of a black man's wanderings through the Union, never more than a month in any one place. Tells of his odd jobs, his songs, his association with women, his religious conflict, superstition, and so on.

Cold Blue Moon (Bobbs, 1931). In the light of the "cold blue moon," "ha'ants" walk and Black Ulysses remembers all the great old stories of the white folks he served as a slave. Reminiscence and fancy. Artificial, but the language is quite realistic.

OWENS, WILLIAM A., 1905–

Walking on Borrowed Land (Bobbs, 1954). A good picture of a Negro principal of a school in Oklahoma. He meets personal tragedy, but keeps his dignity, makes friends among both Negro and white, and improves the lot of his community. Good, serious realism.

PAGE, THOMAS NELSON, 1853–1922

In Ole Virginia (1887). Pictures the old-fashioned darky. One of the important books "creating" the type who loved "ol' Marster," etc.

PEEPLES, EDWIN AUGUSTUS

Swing Low (Houghton, 1945). A story of a Negro, country bred and country loving, who is persuaded by his wife to move to Atlanta. Though he finds some friends and help there, ultimately he is defeated by prejudice and injustice, and returns to the country.

PETERKIN, JULIA M., 1880–

Black April (Bobbs, 1927). A popular novel doing much to help establish a twentieth-century folklore about the Negro. Emphasizes the widespread belief in his immoral sex habits, general looseness, superstition, etc.

Scarlet Sister Mary (Bobbs, 1928). Of a woman who had many illegitimate children. Part of the twentieth-century folklore.

Bright Skin (Bobbs, 1932). Modern Negro life on a Carolina sea-island plantation.

PETRY, ANN LANE, 1911–

The Street (Houghton, 1946). A realistic novel about the struggle of a young Negro woman to make a decent life for herself and her young son in the slums of Harlem. She is good and all the other adults are bad, although she grew up in the same environment. The book shows Harlem as a ghetto exploited by unscrupulous whites and Negro collaborators.

The Narrows (Houghton, 1953). See above, p. 32.

REDDING, JAY SAUNDERS, 1906–

Stranger and Alone (Harcourt, 1950). Fairly realistic story of a young man who works his way through college, and finally becomes a rather successful school administrator, double-crossing his racial group (Negro) in approved style.

REID, MAYNE, 1818–1883

The Quadroon (1856). A melodrama of "mixed blood." The basis for Dion Boucicault's sensational play, *The Octoroon*.

ROBERTS, ELIZABETH MADOX, 1885–1941

My Heart and My Flesh (Viking, 1927). A psychological study of the moods of a gently bred, white Kentucky girl who finds that some Negroes of the village are her half-sisters.

RYLEE, ROBERT, 1908–

Deep, Dark River (Farrar, 1935). Of a Negro who hopes to become a preacher but who kills another Negro and gets a sentence of life imprisonment. A symbolic title—the river typifies the stream of struggling blacks. The hero is happier in the penitentiary than he was outside.

Savoy, Willard W., 1916–
Alien Land (Dutton, 1949). Of the emotional problems of a boy who is part Negro. Tracing his life from the age of eleven to thirty-two, the author shows him passing for white for a time, but finally rejoining his father in the fight for all Negroes and identifying himself with them. Awkwardly written.

Saxon, Lyle, 1891–1946
Children of Strangers (Houghton, 1937). See above, p. 59.

Shelby, Gertrude (Singleton) Matthews, 1881–   , and Stoney, S. G.
Po' Buckra (Macmillan, 1930). Story of the penniless heiress to an unproductive plantation who marries a "po' buckra," who, unknown to her, has both Negro and Indian blood. The authors exploit the most extreme doctrine of racial inferiority, showing that one with Negro blood is certain to be indolent and vicious.

Smith, Lillian Eugenia, 1897–
*Strange Fruit (Reynal, 1944). Effective portrayal of how the Negro problem affects both white and Negro in the South, and how white discrimination affects everything a Negro says and does. Shows the ironic gap between religious theories and practices. Eloquent, yet artistically restrained.

Spivak, John, 1897–
Georgia Nigger (Harcourt, 1932). An exposure of the convict-lease system and the tortures and cruelties of chain-gang prisons.

Strauss, Theodore, 1912–
Night at Hogwallow (Little, 1937). Set in a shanty town in the South, a dramatic account of the lynching of an innocent Negro who is accused of rape.

Stribling, Thomas Sigismund, 1881–
Birthright (Century, 1922). Story of a Harvard graduate, a mulatto, who returns to his home in Tennessee, where he again is subjected to discrimination. His hopes for changing his native home dwindle as he becomes acquainted with the economic conditions.

Summer, Cid Ricketts, 1890–
Quality (Bobbs, 1946). A plea for moderation in the struggle for Negro rights, set forth in the experiences of a Southern nurse who has passed for white in the North.

Thurman, Wallace, 1902–1934
The Blacker the Berry (Macaulay, 1929). On the plight of the very dark Negro woman who encounters in some communities a double wall of color prejudice, within and without the race.

Toomer, Jean, 1894–
Cane (Boni, 1923). A collection of sketches and short stories dealing with emotional and sensual characteristics of the Southern Negro. Set in Georgia and the black belt of Washington, D.C.

TURPIN, WATERS E., 1910–

*These Low Grounds (Harper, 1937). Novel of four generations of Negroes from just before the Civil War until the present. Concentrates mostly on a young man who had a college education and whose plans were always for better education for his people.

O Canaan! (Doubleday, 1939). Story of one of the thousands of Negro families who came to Chicago from the South in 1916. The family prospers and becomes prominent in South Side social affairs.

VAN VECHTEN, CARL, 1880–

Nigger Heaven (Knopf, 1926). An early account of the abnormal conditions under which the Harlem Negro lives. A story of a graduate of the University of Pennsylvania who goes to Harlem, planning to write.

WARREN, ROBERT PENN, 1905–

Band of Angels (Random, 1955). Story of an almost purely white Negro girl, sold down the river just before the Civil War. The story deals with her psychology and her attempts to be "really free."

WHEATON, ELIZABETH LEE (FULTON), 1907–

Mr. George's Joint (Dutton, 1941). Overdrawn account of Negroes in a Texas seaport and their illegal activities, brawls, and sex life.

WHITE, WALTER F., 1893-1955

Fire in the Flint (Knopf, 1924). Of a well-educated Negro doctor who saves a sick white woman but is misunderstood by a Georgia mob.

Flight (Knopf, 1926). Describes a race riot in Atlanta and tells a tale of a New Orleans octoroon who could "pass." Shows a Negro choosing between Negro and white association.

WOOD, CLEMENT, 1888–

Nigger (1922). Pictures a Negro family from its origins in slavery to modern life in Birmingham. A careful, convincing sociological novel.

WRIGHT, RICHARD, 1908–

Uncle Tom's Children (Harper, 1938). A collection of four long short stories dealing with the Negro and white conflict in the present-day South and of the suppression of black by white. Wright tells in an artistic style that the children of Uncle Tom have just as much to fight today as they did in Tom's time.

*Native Son (Harper, 1940). Bigger Thomas, hemmed in by the restrictions of white-dominated Chicago, commits a series of crimes, finding in them the only positive self-expression of his life. An intense, realistic novel, the best yet written by an American Negro, which dramatizes the psychology of the Negro and the problem of giving the Negro the full rights due a native son.

YOUNG, ISADOR S.

Jadie Greenway (Crown, 1947). A sort of *Tree Grows in Brooklyn* for the colored people. An account, largely realistic and documentary, of a Brooklyn girl who slips into delinquency and then is saved and put on the right road.

2. THE INDIAN

In early fiction the Indian was either a misrepresented villain or an impossible nobleman. The white man's superior villainy was not mentioned. Now that he is on reservations, not a military foe, and generally not an economic competitor, the Indian is a subject of great interest, so much so that more fiction has been written about him in recent years than about any other ethnic group except the Negro. In many works of fiction he has been given central prominence, his cultural complex has been detailed, and much attention has been paid to his problems of adjusting himself to the dominating white civilization which surrounds him. Where once we had melodrama about the Indian with his bloody tomahawk, now we have clear-cut realism.

ARMER, LAURA ADAMS, 1874–

Waterless Mountain (Longmans, 1931). See above, p. 156.

Dark Circle of Branches (Longmans, 1933). Story of the removal of Navajos into exile in 1862, "the long walk."

ARNOLD, ELLIOTT, 1912–

Blood Brother (Duell, 1947). See above, p. 20.

AUSTIN, MARY, 1868–1934

One Smoke Stories (Houghton, 1934). Brief stories as told by the Indians around their campfires between their smokes of corn-husk cigarettes. Various tribes of the Southwest are represented.

BANDELIER, ADOLF F., 1840–1914

*The Delight Makers (1890). A remarkable re-creation of Indian life in the Southwest long before Columbus. Abundant details of the life of cliff- and pueblo-dwellers in El Rito de los Frijoles near Santa Fe, and of their relations with other tribes. By a noted anthropologist.

BUFFALO CHILD LONG LANCE, Blood Indian chief, d. 1932.

*Long Lance (Farrar, 1936). This fictionalized autobiography is excellent on life among the Blackfeet at the time white pressure to go on the reservation was growing severe.

CHATEAUBRIAND, FRANÇOIS RENÉ, VICOMTE DE, 1768–1848

Atala (1801). Indians pictured as having the freedom of savages, yet the knowledge and susceptibilities of Europeans. Of the Rousseau school, illustrating the theory of "nature's nobleman."

COOKE, JOHN E., 1830–1886

My Lady Pocahontas (1879). The life of a famous character who is both historical and legendary. Virginia in the seventeenth century.

COOLIDGE, DANE, 1876–1940

Silver Hat (Dutton, 1934). A romantic story of Silver Hat, a white man raised by the Navajos, involving fighting between the Navajos and Hopis.

CORLE, EDWIN, 1906–
   Fig Tree John (Liveright, 1935). Of an Apache Indian who left his tribe and settled on an isolated spot near Salton Sea with his wife and son. A picture of the adjustment of the Indian to the present world.
   *****People on the Earth** (Random, 1937). A modern realistic novel of Navajo life. Theme: the struggle of the young to adopt white ways and yet retain the good things of their own civilization.

DYK, WALTER, 1868–
   Son of Old Man Hat (Harcourt, 1938). A Navajo biography of Left-Handed as recorded by Walter Dyk.

FAST, HOWARD MELVIN, 1914–
   The Last Frontier (Duell, 1941). See above, p. 22.

FISHER, ANNE B., 1898–
   Cathedral in the Sun (Carlyle, 1940). Of three generations of California Indians and their connection with the California Missions between 1818 and 1882. Shows the Missions changing during the period.

FULLER, IOLA
   The Loon Feather (Harcourt, 1940). Perhaps the best novel yet written on the Great Lakes Indians. As told by Tecumseh's daughter, a tale of difficult adjustments as trappers and loggers come westward into Michigan.
   The Shining Trail (Duell, 1943). A story of Indians being pushed out of the Illinois country at the time of the Black Hawk War.

GARLAND, HAMLIN, 1860–1940
   The Captain of the Gray-Horse Troop (1902). An accurate presentation of life on a Montana reservation in the 1890's. Shows settlers and cowmen stupidly and cruelly abusing respectable Cheyenne Indians. A good story.
   The Book of the American Indian (Harper, 1923). Contains significant short stories dealing sympathetically with reservation Indians, Cheyennes, Teton, Sioux. A mixture of careful observation, oral record, and fictional interpretation. "The Silent Eaters" is a simple, forceful story of the life of Sitting Bull.

GREY, ZANE, 1875–1940
   The Vanishing American (Grosset, 1925). A sentimental story predicting the disappearance of the Red man. A story of the love of a white girl and an Indian.

JACKSON, HELEN HUNT, 1831–1885
   Ramona (1884). A popular presentation of the plight of the Mission Indians in California as land-hungry Anglo-Saxons swept over the state. The significance, however, is obscured by a sentimental love story that usurps the foreground.

LAFARGE, OLIVER, 1901–
   *****Laughing Boy** (Houghton, 1929). An excellent story of Navajos, their customs, their ideals, and their troubled relationships to whites. A moving

account of the plight of a minority misunderstood by the white man and forced into maladjustments.

All the Young Men (Houghton, 1935). A dozen effective short stories dealing largely with Indians—Apaches, Pahutahs, Navajos, and others.

*The Enemy Gods (Houghton, 1937). Of a Navajo boy's struggle with religious adjustment.

LAURITZEN, JONREED

Arrows Into the Sun (Knopf, 1943). Laid in pioneer times, the novel artistically describes Arizona scenery and a Mormon settlement. Penetrates into the mind of a Navajo half-breed torn between two ways of life, his American father's and his Indian mother's. A beautiful and spirited Mormon girl helps him find his white heritage.

LIGHTHALL, WILLIAM D., 1857–?

Master of Life (1908). An "aboriginal romance" of the prehistoric Hiawatha and his founding of the league of the Iroquois. Presents the chivalrous and reverent side of the Indian.

LINDERMAN, FRANK B., 1868–1938

Morning Light (Lige Mounts: Free Trapper) (Day, 1930). Fictionized biography, describing the fur trade on the upper Missouri a hundred years ago. Sincere and convincing. Story of a trapper who preferred Indian life to white.

Old Man Coyote (Day, 1931). Stories, sketches, and legends about the Montana Crow Indians, recorded by Linderman as he heard them from the Indian warriors whom he had known for forty years.

Red Mother (Day, 1932). The life of Pretty Shield. Presents the Indian from a woman's point of view. Interesting stories of the buffalo days, of the battle of Little Bighorn, and of the death of Custer.

McCLINCHEY, FLORENCE E.

Joe Pete (Holt, 1929). A story of present-day life of the Ojibway Indians of northern Michigan. As the author has lived with them for years, her material is quite authentic.

McNICHOLS, CHARLES L., 1895–

Crazy Weather (Macmillan, 1944). A good local-color story of western Arizona, in which two adolescent boys, one white, one Mojave, go through strenuous events during four days of terrible heat. Through the white boy's struggle to be either "white" or "Indian," various contrasts are built up between the two ways of life.

McNICKLE, D'ARCY, 1904–

The Surrounded (Dodd, 1936). Portrays a tribe of reservation Indians in western Montana. Shows the plight of the Indian—a conflict between traditions of the tribe and desire for a wider life.

MATHEWS, JOHN JOSEPH

Sundown (Longmans, 1934). Shows the Osage civilization destroyed by alien ideals and customs after the discovery of oil. Contrasts the potentialities of Indians with the decadence they have fallen into. Of an

Oklahoma Indian boy who tries to be a white man and ends up a man
without an ethnic group.

MILLER, JOAQUIN, 1841–1913

Life among the Modocs (1873). Enthusiastic eulogy of the Indian's
character. Stories and much prose poetry built around a small core of
fact.

MORROW, HONORÉ WILLSIE, 1880?–1940

Lydia of the Pines (1917). Interest centers about grafting politicians
confiscating Indian lands in Minnesota. In "Progressive Era" style the
young hero and heroine fight for the right.

OSKISON, JOHN M., 1874–

Black Jack Davy (Appleton, 1926). Life in Indian Territory and Oklahoma before and after the land rush of 1889.

REID, MAYNE, 1818–1883

The White Chief, a Legend of Northern Mexico (London, 1855).
A dramatic and satisfying adventure story of a white man who became
chief of an Indian tribe and underwent various experiences fighting
Spaniards who mistreated the Indians in what is now New Mexico.

RICHTER, CONRAD, 1890–

The Light in the Forest (Knopf, 1953). Story about a white boy
brought up by the Indians around the mid-eighteenth century. Contrasts
Indian and white ways of living and attitudes showing certain superiori-
ties in the Indian way of life.

RUESCH, HANS, 1913–

Top of the World (Harper, 1950). Simply-told story of an Eskimo
family, emphasizing the differences in custom and moral beliefs between
the Eskimo and the white man.

RYAN, DON

The Warrior's Path (Duckworth, 1937). An anthropological novel
about a captured Virginia boy who was adopted by the Lenape (Delaware
Indians) and became a white Indian, fighting with Pontiac and The
Prophet. Contains much reliable interpretation of social and religious life
among the Ohio Valley tribes during the days of bloody fights with Braddock, Bouquet, Armstrong, and other Tulhasaga (white men).

SHAFER, DONALD C., 1881–

Smokefires in Schoharie (Longmans, 1938). See above, p. 123.

SIMMS, WILLIAM GILMORE, 1806–1870

The Wigwam and the Cabin (1845). A volume of uneven short
stories, some realistic and some silly, including considerable humane
evaluation of Catawbas, Cherokees, and Choctaws.

SINGMASTER, ELSIE, 1879–

A High Wind Rising (Houghton, 1942). Of Pennsylvania, 1728–1755,
describing events on the frontier up to the beginning of the French and
Indian War.

SMITH, DAMA MARGARET

Hopi Girl (Stanford, 1931). A reliable and interesting story of changing customs in a Hopi village. Modern times.

SORENSEN, VIRGINIA (EGGERSTEN), 1912–

*****The Proper Gods** (Harcourt, 1951). A Yaqui brought up in Arizona returns as a veteran to his ancestral home in Mexico. Contrast of two cultures. An excellently-told story.

UNDERHILL, RUTH M., 1884–

Hawk over Whirlpools (J. J. Augustin, 1940). Of the desert Indians of Arizona and the changes in their community life because of contact with Americans. A story of the conflicts of a part-Mexican boy who wishes to gain white man's power.

WATERS, FRANK, 1902–

People of the Valley (Farrar, 1941). Of a valley high in the mountains of New Mexico and of its people—part French, part Spanish, part Irish, part Indian. The main character, Maria del Valle, is half-Indian.

The Man Who Killed the Deer (Farrar, 1942). Of a young Pueblo Indian, a nonconformist in his tribe, and how he finally returned to the blanket. A pathetic struggle, vividly presented.

3. THE FRENCH, THE SPANISH, THE ITALIANS, AND THE LATIN AMERICANS

The treatment of the French, the Spanish, and the Latin Americans varies from the highly romantic pictures of the old regime in California to the most drab picture of present-day living conditions in the slums of some of our Southwestern cities. Romance was made of the contrasts between Spanish and Yankee customs, of the peculiar customs and traditions of the Creoles of New Orleans and the Acadians of Central Louisiana, and of the explorations and settlements of the French throughout the Mississippi Valley. Recent stories have centered about the relation of the Latin American to the labor market, his living conditions in slums, and his religious superstitions and observances. Picaresque stories have been written about Mexican bandits of the Southwest, and pathetic stories about New Mexicans who are still a minority group meeting discrimination after three hundred years of life in our country. Among the newer immigrant groups, the Italians have rapidly become a special but integral part of the American pattern and are generously represented in recent fiction.

Owing to the color difference between many Latin Americans and the white North American, they are likely to remain a distinct minority for some time to come and hence receive separate treatment in fiction, as have the Negro and the North American Indian.

ARNOLD, ELLIOT, 1912–
The Time of the Gringo (Knopf, 1953). See above, p. 21.

ATHERTON, GERTRUDE F., 1857–1948
Los Cerritos: A Romance of Modern Times (1890). Poor whites and Mexicans settle on Los Cerritos, an abandoned ranch in Southern California. The owner attempts ejection.
The Californians (1898). The civilization of the old Spanish regime contrasted to the strenuous life of the Yankee.
The Splendid Idle Forties (1902). Romantic tales of early California. Interesting material on folkways, religious beliefs, etc. Accepts romantic notions of the chivalry of the Spanish (also their cruelty) and the barbarism and degradation of the Indian.
Rezánov (1906). A historical romance of Spanish California. Based on the courtship of Nicolai Petrovich Rezánov, of the Russian-American Company, and Doña Concha Argüello y Moraga, daughter of the Comandante of the Presidio in San Francisco. Once popular for its charming, sad love story.

BEALS, CARLETON, 1893–
*Black River (Lippincott, 1934). A picture of American oil companies in eastern Mexico. Contrasts the industrial pattern of the North American and the older Mexican pattern of life.

BRIGHT, ROBERT
The Life and Death of Little Joe (Doubleday, 1944). A sympathetic tale of a Spanish-American village in New Mexico. Pictures a poverty-stricken, dispossessed community, in which youth is torn between old and new ways. A revealing though often melodramatic account of the vanishing "native" culture in the Taos area.

CABLE, GEORGE WASHINGTON, 1844–1925
*Old Creole Days (1879). A famous collection of short stories about the Creoles of New Orleans. Realistic for its day.
The Grandissimes (1880). A long, involved romance of Creoles and others in the lower Mississippi Valley.
Dr. Sevier (1884). Of New Orleans before the Civil War. Much detail on Creole customs.
Bonaventure: A Prose Pastoral of Acadian Louisiana (1888). Good in detail of country homes, country schools, etc.

CAMPBELL, FRANCES
Men of the Enchantress (Bobbs, 1947). A story of present-day Mexico, centering in an American-owned silver mine worked by Mexican laborers. Skillfully paced and sensitive.

CATHER, WILLA SIBERT, 1876–1947
Death Comes for the Archbishop (Knopf, 1927). See above, p. 148.

CHOPIN, KATE, 1851–1904
Bayou Folk (1894). Artistic tales of Creoles, Negroes, and Cajuns along the lower Mississippi.

A Night in Acadie (1897). Additional dramatic tales of the Louisiana bayou country.

COOLIDGE, DANE, 1873–1940

Gringo Gold (Dutton, 1939). A melodramatic tale of the adventures of Joaquín Murieta, famous bandit in California Gold Rush days. Explains Murieta's motivation and sympathetically interprets the suppressed Mexican minority in California.

CRICHTON, KYLE, 1896–

The Proud People (Scribner, 1944). A Spanish-American family in Albuquerque in 1941—their relationship to the non-Spanish community.

D'AGOSTINO, GUIDO, 1906–

Olives on the Apple Tree (Doubleday, 1940). An understanding picture of the Italians in America, seen through the eyes of a young Italian-American character.

Hills Beyond Manhattan (Doubleday, 1942). Of the Americanization of a Frenchman—a struggle between New York villagers and rich interlopers from the city.

DE CAPITE, MICHAEL

Maria (Day, 1943). The setting is the "little Italy" of Cleveland, Ohio. Lifelike characters, especially Maria, who submits to an arranged marriage and cruelty from her husband, but tries to bring up her children to be Americans.

DE LA RUE, TREVINO, 1894–

Spanish Trails to California (Caxton, 1937). A romantic tale of an expedition from Spain to Old Mexico and on to California. Adds to the tradition of the dashing, romantic caballero.

DERLETH, AUGUST, 1909–

Shadow of Night (Scribner, 1943). One of the author's series of novels laid in and around Sac Prairie, Wisconsin, this shows how French and German immigrants to the Wisconsin Valley frontier slowly changed from being Europeans to being Americans.

DI DONATO, PIETRO, 1911–

*****Christ in Concrete** (Bobbs, 1939). Of a New York Italian family—its piety, its customs, its economic helplessness. Realistic portrayal of a slum district. Makes clear the immense importance of a job.

DUCHARME, JACQUES, 1910–

The Delusson Family (Funk, 1939). A simple, unexciting, but authentic story of French emigration from Canada to New England.

FANTE, JOHN, 1911–

Wait Until Spring, Bandini (Stackpole, 1938). Of an Italian-American family in the West. Good realism about the children's life.

Ask the Dust (Stackpole, 1939). Story of a young ambitious Italian, who comes to Los Angeles hoping to find fame as a writer but finds only hunger and discouragement.

FERGUSSON, HARVEY, 1890–
   The Conquest of Don Pedro (Morrow, 1954). See above, p. 15.

FORBES, HARRIE REBECCA PIPER (SMITH)
   Mission Tales in the Days of the Dons (1909). A collection of thirteen stories and poems of the Spaniards, Mexicans, and Indians of California before the North Americans came. Preserves some of the best legends.

FORGIONE, LOUIS
   Reamer Lou (Dutton, 1924). Of immigrant young men, Italian especially, and their personal adjustments, not all good for them and society, as they live and work on New York Harbor.
   The River Between (Dutton, 1928). Of a prosperous Italian immigrant family living in the Italian settlement on the Hudson Palisades.

FOSTER, JOSEPH O'KANE, 1898–
   *In the Night Did I Sing (Scribner, 1942). A psychological interpretation of Spanish-Americans in Taos Valley, New Mexico—their humor, religion, attitude toward Americans. A pathetic story in its realization of their present poor estate.

GARNER, CLAUD
   Wetback (Coward, 1947). Tells of a Mexican who swims the Rio Grande and struggles to become a happy citizen of the United States. He suffers from thieving fellow workers, unscrupulous bosses, and properly strict immigration officials but finally becomes an expert goat breeder and then a citrus rancher. Warm in human sympathy but too synoptic to be fully artistic.

GEROULD, KATHERINE F., 1879–1944
   Conquistador (Scribner, 1923). A story of an American (half-Mexican) who effected a reconciliation with his mother's alienated Mexican family, and himself became one of the conquistadores in spirit. A romantic tale hinging on the peculiar notions of the old high-caste Creole.

GILES, BARBARA
   The Gentle Bush (Harcourt, 1947). The chronicle of a Louisiana family from the post-Reconstruction period through the first decade of the twentieth century. Emphasis on Creole folkways and social cleavages along ethnic lines.

HEARN, LAFCADIO, 1850–1904
   *Creole Sketches (ed. by Charles Woodward Hutson) (Houghton, 1924). Sketches written, 1878–81, for *The Item*. Literary masterpieces about Creoles of his time.

HÉMON, LOUIS, 1880–1913
   *Maria Chapdelaine: A Tale of the Lake St. John Country (translated by W. H. Blake; Macmillan, 1921). A simple epic of French-Canadian pioneers in the early twentieth century. Dramatizes the role of church and family mores in a tender and convincing love story, with much poetical suggestion of scene and character.

HOBART, ALICE TISDALE (NOURSE), 1882–
The Cup and the Sword (Bobbs, 1942). See above, p. 67.

HUGGINS, CLELIE B.
Point Noir (Houghton, 1937). Morbid, melodramatic tale of a wealthy Creole family gone to seed.

JACKSON, HELEN HUNT, 1831–1885
*Ramona (1884). Intended to expose United States injustice to the Indian. Pictures the old-fashioned California rancho and the Mexican owners.

JESSEY, CORNELIA
Teach the Angry Spirit (Crown, 1949). Life in the Mexican quarter of Los Angeles. The time is during World War II, and the zoot-suit riots are the climax of the book. An appealing story of a brother and a sister caught between the two cultures.

KEYES, FRANCES PARKINSON (WHEELER), 1885–
Crescent Carnival (Messner, 1942). A story of New Orleans in which one of the themes is the relationship between the Creoles and the "Americans." See above, p. 97.

KING, GRACE E., 1851–1932
Balcony Stories (1893). Local-color tales of Negroes, Creoles, and others in Louisiana.

LIPSKY, ELEAZAR
Lincoln McKeever (Appleton, 1953). See above, p. 132.

MACLENNAN, HUGH, 1907–
Two Solitudes (Duell, 1945). A penetrating study of the conflict of English-speaking and French-speaking Canadians on the Island of Montreal in the period 1917–1939. Analyzes all the complications in Quebec society and the basic ethnic conflict.

MANGIONE, JERRE, 1909–
Mount Allegro (Houghton, 1943). Humorous, sympathetic sketches of Sicilian-Americans in Rochester, New York. Anecdotes depict religion, recreation, education, and so on, among a gay, bubbling people. A kind of Italian *Life with Father*.

MELLER, SIDNEY, 1906–
Home Is Here (Macmillan, 1941). Shows how Italian immigrants are slowly transformed into Americans on Telegraph Hill, San Francisco.

MOODY, ALAN B., 1900–1944
Sleep in the Sun (Houghton, 1945). Episodes in the lives of a group of poverty-stricken Mexican families living in a California canyon.

NORDHOFF, WALTER (ANTONIO DE FIERRO BLANCO, pseud.), 1858–1947
Journey of the Flame (Houghton, 1933). A likable account of the trip of a boy of twelve through the two Californias during Spanish days. True to the Mexican spirit and psychology.

NUNN, GUY, 1915–

White Shadows (Reynal, 1947). Effectively presents a Mexican family adjusting to the United States, from their arrival as immigrants until the children have grown up and received an education.

O'DONNELL, EDWIN P., 1895–

Green Margins (Houghton, 1936). A detailed picture of the daily life of the ethnic mixtures of inhabitants of the delta country below New Orleans—their food, clothing, customs, and picturesque language. Portrait of a subregion.

The Great Big Doorstep (Houghton, 1941). A rambling, rowdy tale of a Cajun family in the Mississippi delta.

PAGANO, JO, 1906–

The Paisanos (Little, 1940). Ten stories of Italians in Los Angeles. Mostly humorous and centering on folkways: eating, drinking, and talking.

Golden Wedding (Random, 1943). The story of an Italian family in a coal town in Colorado, in Denver, in Salt Lake City, and in Los Angeles.

PARSONS, VIVIAN

Not Without Honor (Dodd, 1941). Of a French-Canadian farm boy who migrates to a mining community on the Upper Peninsula of Michigan. Tells with vigor and realism of his exceptional success story and of his attempt to make all foreigners understand what the "promised land" meant to him.

PAZ, IRENCO, 1836–1924

Life and Adventures of the Celebrated Bandit Joaquín Murrieta (trans. by Frances P. Belle) (Powner, 1925). A spirited, fictionized biography of "the most famous bandit chief who has ever lived on this earth," his assistant, Jack Three Fingers, and his persistent pursuer, Captain Harry Love.

PEREZ, LUIS, 1904–

El Coyote the Rebel (Holt, 1947). Humorous, informal autobiography of a Mexican who was conscripted as a boy soldier in the Contreras Rebel Army in its fights with the Moralistas and Pancho Villa, and who finally escaped into the United States. There he obtained citizenship and worked his way through the public schools. Gives a gay version of the difficulties of an immigrant ignorant of the language.

ROBERTS, MARTA

*****Tumbleweeds** (Putnam, 1940). Traces the life of a Mexican family with six children living in California, with whom all was well until the father lost his job and the family had to go on relief. Shows the paradoxes and inadequacies of public relief.

ST. MARTIN, THADDEUS, 1886–

Madame Toussaint's Wedding Day (Little, 1936). A graphic local-color story of a Cajun community in Louisiana.

SHULMAN, IRVING

The Square Trap (Little, 1953). Interpretation of the home life and reactions of a Los Angeles Mexican family by a non-Mexican. The older son becomes a boxer—an exposé of the dead end at which a Mexican arrives in the fight game.

STEINBECK, JOHN, 1902–

Tortilla Flat (Viking, 1935). A pleasant fantasy about the Paisanos of Monterey. Emphasizes the carefree life of these descendants of the early inhabitants of Mexican Alta California. Humorous, with some realistic detail.

STILWELL, HART, 1902–

Border City (Doubleday, 1945). A story of racial intolerance and corrupt politics in a city on the border between Mexico and the United States. The hero is a newspaperman who first defends, then falls in love with, a Mexican girl.

STONE, ELINORE COWAN, 1884–

The Laughingest Lady (Appleton, 1940). A simple romantic story of a schoolma'am from the East who succeeds in capturing the "most eligible" male in a small New Mexican village. Much interesting detail about her third-grade Mexican-American class.

SUMMERS, RICHARD A., 1906–

Dark Madonna (Caxton, 1937). A story of present-day Tucson and its Mexican quarter. Emphasis on superstitions and amatory adventures. Realistic, but partly twentieth-century folklore.

The Devil's Highway (Nelson, 1937). Concerning the work of Padre Kino and the establishment of Mission San Xavier del Bac near Tucson. The main character is a Spanish boy soldier, detailed to watch over Father Kino. A dramatic story, with much on Spanish and Mexican folk beliefs.

TINKER, EDWARD LAROCQUE, 1861–

Toucoutou (Dodd, 1928). A tale of New Orleans of the 1850's, giving much of the local color of the time and showing the prevailing race prejudices.

TOMASI, MARI

Like Lesser Gods (Bruce, 1949). Well-told story of Italian workers in the granite quarries of Vermont. Good presentation of folkways and of the merging of two cultures.

WHITE, STEWART EDWARD, 1873–1946

Ranchero (Doubleday, 1933). Mexicans and Spanish in California in the 1840's. A contrast between the North American and the Spanish of California, in which the Yankee is captivated by Spanish ways. Neat **romance.**

4. OTHER ETHNIC GROUPS (INCLUDING THE IRISH, THE SCANDINAVIANS, THE GERMANS, AND THE POLES)

The Irish as well as other European nationalities appeared often as comic characters in fiction throughout the nineteenth century, but the present generation has made that ethnic group into serious subject matter for full-length treatment. The stream of books about Irish-Americans has steadily increased during the past three decades.

When the present vogue of writing about ethnic groups got under way, the Scandinavians were a group of immigrants new enough to be noticeably distinct and unique in customs and ideas. Hence they have been quite extensively used as subject matter. All the writers about them here included are of the present generation, and the setting of most of the stories is the Middle West.

There are almost as many stories about Germans as about Scandinavians, and many of them refer to the earlier periods of American history, since the Germans are one of our older immigrant strains. Other groups dealt with in fiction include Russians, Czechoslovaks, Poles, Japanese, Chinese, Armenians, Jugoslavs, Greeks and Dutch.

ADAMIC, LOUIS, 1899–1951

Grandsons (Harper, 1935). Concerns a Jugoslav family in which the three sons are completely a part of American life; one is a member of the I.W.W., one a gangster, and one a wounded war veteran.

ALGREN, NELSON, 1909–

Never Come Morning (Harper, 1942). Polacks in Chicago's Northwest Side—reminiscent of James T. Farrell's "Irish." Bruno Bicek (Lefty Biceps) is the "Studs Lonigan" of the story.

ALLEN, FRANCES N., 1865–

The Invaders (1913). Of the Poles and Celts who move into a New England village, and have prejudice to overcome.

ANGOFF, CHARLES, 1902–

Journey to the Dawn (Beechhurst, 1951). Volume one of a trilogy on a Russian family who migrated to America.

In the Morning Light (Beechhurst, 1952). Volume two of the saga of the Polonsky family who came to Boston in the early 1900's. Seemingly authentic picture of several Jewish families from Russia and Germany. Suffers from prolixity.

The Sun at Noon (Beechhurst, 1955). Continues the story of the Polonsky family. Centers upon a young son who attends Harvard.

ANTHONY, JOSEPH, 1897–

Golden Village (Bobbs, 1924). Of Rumanian immigrants seeking the golden village of their dreams only to find imperfect American towns that require great adjustments.

BAHR, JEROME

All Good Americans (Scribner, 1937). Thirteen short stories of the Jews, Poles, Germans, Irish, and Norwegians—all good Americans—who live in a small Wisconsin town.

BANCROFT, GRIFFING

The Interlopers: A Novel (1917). Presents material on the conflict between "native white" farmers in southern California and Japanese immigrants and their children. More interesting for theme than for style.

BELL, THOMAS, 1903–

Out of This Furnace (Little, 1941). See above, p. 72.

BENSON, RAMSEY, 1866–

Hill Country (Stokes, 1928). A biographical novel of James J. Hill, builder of the Great Northern Railway and, from one point of view, a potent influence in bettering the lives of early settlers in Minnesota. Presents the Swedish settlers as almost too clean and upright to be tolerated by their American neighbors.

BOJER, JOHAN, 1872–

*The Emigrants (Century, 1924). Written by a Norwegian about emigrants from Norway. Similar in theme to Rolvaag's Giants in the Earth. A good picture of the struggles of a pioneering Norwegian family.

BRINIG, MYRON, 1900–

May Flavin (Farrar, 1938). Story of an Irishwoman raising a family in the slums of New York.

BUDD, LILLIAN

Land of Strangers (Lippincott, 1953). Of the personal lives of two young Swedes, a man and a woman, their married life and the difficulties of adjustment in America.

CAHAN, ABRAHAM, 1860–

The Rise of David Levinsky (Harper, 1917). See above, p. 81.

CANNON, CORNELIA JAMES, 1876–

Red Rust (Little, 1928). See above, p. 42.

Heirs (Little, 1930). Of Polish immigrants supplanting "old stock" New Englanders in a New Hampshire village. Presents the problem of Americanization.

CASTLE, WILLIAM, and JOSEPH, ROBERT

Hero's Oak (Reader's Press, 1945). The setting is Vermont, the time, 1910 to 1936; the people, Polish immigrants through two generations of victory and defeat, in agriculture and the professions.

CATHER, WILLA SIBERT, 1876–1947

O Pioneers! (1913). Story of a capable Swedish-American girl running a big farm in Nebraska.

My Antonia (1918). A well-written story about a Bohemian family in Nebraska during the sod-house era.

Obscure Destinies (Knopf, 1932). Contains three short stories; notably "Neighbour Rosicky," which gives a mellow, optimistic picture of a Czech farmer in the prairie corn belt.

CHRISTOWE, STOYAN, 1898–

My American Pilgrimage (Little, 1947). Of a Macedonian who works in gangs building western railroads and catches a vision of America. A simple, eloquent testament of discovery and faith. Fictionalized autobiography.

CONWAY, BROOKE (pseud.)

The Loving Are the Daring (Prentice, 1947). Story of family life in a Midwestern German-American home, 1905–1920. The widow Kraemer and her six children are the leading figures. Similar to Forbes's *Mama's Bank Account.*

DEASY, MARY, 1874–

The Hour of Spring (Little, 1948). A lively story of several generations of a clannish Irish family in a Midwestern city.

DE JONG, DAVID CORNEL, 1905–

Belly Fulla Straw (Knopf, 1934). Of a Dutch family that disintegrates after settling in Michigan shortly before 1918.

DEMETRIOS, GEORGE, 1896–

When Greek Meets Greek (Houghton, 1947). Two dozen short stories, simply told, about Greeks in Macedonia or Greek immigrants in Boston.

DRISCOLL, CHARLES B., 1885–

Kansas Irish (Macmillan, 1943). See p. 42.

DUNNE, FINLEY PETER, 1867–1936

Mr. Dooley in Peace and in War (1898). See above, p. 131.
Mr. Dooley in the Hearts of His Countrymen (1899). See above, p. 131.
Mr. Dooley Says (1910). See above, p. 136.

EDMISTON, JAMES

Home Again (Doubleday, 1955). The story of one family of Japanese-American evacuees and their return to California. Good detail and good characterization.

FARRELL, JAMES T., 1904–

Gas House McGinty (Vanguard, 1933). See above, p. 83.
Can All This Grandeur Perish? (Vanguard, 1937). A collection of short stories.
*Studs Lonigan: A Trilogy (Vanguard, 1937). See above, p. 94.
Tommy Gallagher's Crusade (Vanguard, 1939). A study of the poisonous spirit and background of Tommy Gallagher, a representative of the young men who sell anti-Semitic literature on city street corners.
My Days of Anger (Vanguard, 1943). Fourth in the Danny O'Neill series, continuing *A World I Never Made* (1936), *No Star Is Lost*

(1938), and *Father and Son* (1940), this tells of Danny in the mid-1920's, when he attends the University of Chicago. With tough, turbulent Chicago as the background, this is essentially the tale of a sensitive young Irish-American, whose character is complex and full of apparent contradictions. Besides being vivid the story has the social value of showing what the Irish do to America and what America does to the Irish.

FREITAG, GEORGE H.

The Lost Land (COWARD, 1947). August Kreitzer, a German-American, marries an Irish-American girl. The story depicts the crosscurrents of the Old World and the New, and the efforts of August, who works in a steel mill, to develop a successful farm.

GLOCAR, EMILIAN, 1906–

Man from the Balkans (Dorrance, 1942). About a Serbian immigrant and his successful attempts to adjust himself to his new American environment.

GOLLOMB, JOSEPH, 1881–

Unquiet (Dodd, 1935). See above, p. 153.

HAGOPIAN, RICHARD, 1914–

The Dove Brings Peace (Farrar, 1944). A diverting series of sketches describing the life of an Armenian family in Massachusetts. Shows the attitude of older members and the bewilderment of the younger, as they try to adapt themselves to American ways.

HUMMEL, GEORGE F., 1882–

Heritage (Stokes, 1935). See above, p. 30.

HURLEY, DORAN, 1906–

Monsignor (Longmans, 1936). See above, p. 150.

The Old Parish (Longmans, 1938). See above, p. 150.

Herself: Mrs. Patrick Crowley (Longmans, 1939). A humorous though not realistic tale of Mrs. Patrick Crowley, who won an Irish sweepstake and so left Millington, Massachusetts, and went to spend her money and see great New York City.

HURST, FANNIE, 1889–

Lummox (Harper, 1923). Of a strong girl, half-Swede and half-Slav, and her lonely, hard life as a servant girl in New York City.

A President Is Born (Harper, 1928). A story of the first eighteen years of a boy born into a large Austrian family in the United States. Of a European family gradually being adjusted to American life.

IRWIN, WALLACE, 1875–

Letters of a Japanese Schoolboy (1909). Kindly humor which makes capital of the Oriental's difficulties with English idiom. Hashimura Togo comments on such things as political conventions, the third term, and the servant "problemb."

*Seed of the Sun (Doran, 1921). A story with a strong anti-Japanese bias. The author sees the Japanese in California as a menace, and their methods as devious, clever, and devilish. The facts that they want land, work hard, and raise children seem to him reprehensible.

JORDAN, MILDRED A. (MRS. J. LEE BAUSHER), 1901–

One Red Rose Forever (Knopf, 1941). A semifictional account of Heinrich Stiegel, a German who arrived in Pennsylvania in 1750 and later made beautiful glass. Lusty romance ill-paired with lively history.

Apple in the Attic: A Pennsylvania Legend (Knopf, 1942). A simply told story of the home life of a "Pennsylvania Dutch" family.

KEHOE, KARON

City in the Sun (Dodd, 1946). Of the tensions of Japanese-Americans in the Maricopa relocation center, Arizona. A story of the moral degeneration of an American boy.

LA PIERE, RICHARD TRACY, 1899–

Where the Living Strive (Harper, 1941). The story of the life of a Chinese immigrant in San Francisco, 1875 to the 1930's. Informative for insight into Chinese character.

LEBEDEFF, VERA

The Heart Returneth (Lippincott, 1943). Concerns a colony of White Russians in Detroit. Good on the social life and ideas of the group.

LESLIE, FRANK

There's a Spot in My Heart (Simon, 1947). Of a young Irish boy growing up in a "west side" New York house, living with his humorous grandfather and devout grandmother.

LEWIS, JANET, 1899–

Against a Darkening Sky (Doubleday, 1943). Of a Scotchwoman and her Swiss husband in Encina, California. Centers on the fine character of the woman.

LIN YU-TANG, 1895–

Chinatown Family (Day, 1948). A calm novel about the life and difficulties of a Chinese immigrant family in New York City. Full of sidelights on American civilization as seen through oriental eyes.

LINDBERG, WALTER

The Winding Road (Lutheran Literary Board, 1933). An autobiography in story form. The tale of an immigrant who runs into all manner of difficulties.

LION, HORTENSE, 1898–

The Grass Grows Green (Houghton, 1935). Of a Bavarian girl who comes to America determined to live a peaceful life and is finally greatly upset by World War I. Scene laid in New York's German colony.

MCLEAN, KATHRYN (ANDERSON), 1909–　　　(KATHRYN FORBES, pseud.)

Mama's Bank Account (Harcourt, 1943). Simple story of a Norwegian mother in San Francisco and how she took care of her family, in the words of one of her daughters. Ironic, sentimental, amusing, satisfying.

MCSORLEY, EDWARD, 1902–

Our Own Kind (Harper, 1946). A portrait of an Irish-American ironworker's family living in a Providence tenement a generation ago.

MARCHAND, MARGARET

Pilgrims on the Earth (Crowell, 1940). Of Irish-Americans in a steel town near Pittsburgh. Of labor strife, religious ideas, and folkways.

MEANS, FLORENCE CRANNELL, 1891–

The Moved Outers (Houghton, 1945). Story of a young Japanese-American girl and the year her family spent in a relocation camp before she went away to college.

MOBERG, VILHELM, 1898–

The Emigrants (tr. by Gustaf Lannestock. Simon, 1951). Based on research and first-hand experience. Laid in period of heavy Swedish emigration to America, 1840–1890. Book ends with family's arrival in New York City, 1850. Makes clear why Swedes left Europe. An earthy novel; artistic.

Unto a Good Land (Simon, 1954). See above, p. 6.

MULDER, ARNOLD, 1885–

Dominie of Harlem (McClurg, 1913). Dutch peasants in twentieth-century America trying to struggle against change or progress.

Bram of the Five Corners (McClurg, 1915). A story of Michigan Hollanders. The protagonist is a minister of high ideals who must solve his problem of being betrothed to a moron.

NICHOLS, EDWARD J., 1900–

Hunky Johnny (Houghton, 1945). About a second-generation Slovak-American, raised in Gary, who goes to Chicago and has to face the problems of the Depression and of love for a "white girl."

ORMONDE, CZENZI, 1913–

Laughter from Downstairs (Farrar, 1948). A series of sketches about a Bohemian family in a town in the Pacific Northwest. A happy picture of the melting-pot bubbling well from the very first generation on.

OSTENSO, MARTHA, 1900–

Wild Geese (Dodd, 1925). See above, p. 44.

PAPASHVILY, GEORGE, 1895–   , and PAPASHVILY, HELEN

Anything Can Happen (Harper, 1945). A pleasant, humorous autobiographical story of a Russian (from Georgia) who works at many jobs between Ellis Island and Hollywood.

PETERSON, ELMER T., 1884–

Trumpets West: An Epic of America (Sears, 1934). About a Swedish-American in the Middle West.

PINE, HESTER

The Waltz Is Over (Farrar, 1943). Careful presentation of "Germanic traits," in a picture of three generations of German-Americans from 1845 to 1942.

ROLVAAG, OLE E., 1876–1931

Giants in the Earth (Harper, 1927). See above, p. 12.

Peder Victorious (Harper, 1929). Sequel to *Giants in the Earth*. A son of the Norwegian family marries an Irish-Catholic girl. The melting-pot theme.

Their Father's God (Harper, 1931). See above, p. 151.

Boat of Longing (Harper, 1933). Seemingly autobiographic. An excellent portrait of a Norwegian immigrant, his homesickness, his struggles to get along in the United States, where he expected to gain wealth.

ROSTEN, LEO CALVIN (LEONARD Q. ROSS, pseud.), 1908–

The Education of Hyman Kaplan (Harcourt, 1937). An amusing story of an Americanization class in a New York City night school.

SAROYAN, WILLIAM, 1908–

My Name Is Aram (Harcourt, 1940). Tales of an American-born Armenian growing up in California. Boy's experiences set in an Armenian background and told with a combination of naïveté and cynicism.

SEIDE, MICHAEL, 1910–

The Common Thread (Harcourt, 1944). Ten stories about the adjustment of immigrants and the children of immigrants in Brooklyn. All men are bound by a common thread, the same hopes, the same capacity for joy and sorrow.

SHAW, HARRY, 1905–   , and DAVIS, RUTH, 1913–

Americans One and All (Harper, 1947). An anthology of twenty-three short stories, each about a different ethnic group. Among the authors are John Fante, Oliver La Farge, Nancy Hale, Ruth Suckow, Sinclair Lewis, Kathryn Forbes, and William Saroyan. Designed to show that "all people possess basic samenesses and essential differences," that all Americans have a common humanity.

SINCLAIR, UPTON B., 1878–

The Jungle (1906). The main characters are Lithuanian immigrants who work in the stockyards of Chicago and live in the slum district.

SPITZER, ANTOINETTE

These Are My Children (Macaulay, 1935). Thoughtful, sympathetic treatment of the familiar theme of three generations in America. The first generation is Austrian immigrants.

STONG, PHILIP DUFFIELD, 1899–

Iron Mountain (Farrar, 1942). A story of a Minnesota mining town and the various immigrant workers, showing American attitudes toward various minority groups.

SUCKOW, RUTH, 1892–

Country People (Knopf, 1924). A detailed record of the material advances of three generations of a German-American family on their Iowa farm.

SUHL, YURI, 1908–

*One Foot in America (Macmillan, 1950). This novel that reads like an autobiography deals with Polish Jews in the Williamsburg section of Brooklyn and a "greenhorn" who becomes a butcher's boy. Excellent for comedy and for contrasts of European background and American environment.

Cowboy on a Wooden Horse (Macmillan, 1953). Sequel to *One Foot in America*. In this story the main character becomes an upholsterer, a union member, and becomes engaged to an American Jewish girl. His "greenhorn" stupidities continue too long to be believable.

SYKES, HOPE WILLIAMS, 1901–

Second Hoeing (Putnam, 1935). Of a German-Russian family in the beet region of Colorado. Realistic.

The Joppa Door (Putnam, 1937). A quiet, understanding story of a German peasant woman transplanted to Utah.

THOMAS, NEWTON GEORGE

The Long Winter Ends (Macmillan, 1941). This faithfully represents the Cousin Jack—Cornishman—of the Michigan copper country on Keweenaw Peninsula. Competent writing, as in reproduction of the Cornish dialect, but more descriptive than narrative.

TOBENKIN, ELIAS, 1882–

Witte Arrives: A Novel (1916). Story of the Americanization of a Russian Jewish boy who works his way through high school and university, in Illinois, to become a Chicago reporter. He struggles in New York and finally marries a Gentile girl. A sincere, liberal account of the interaction of American and immigrant.

The House of Conrad (1918). Pictures a German immigrant family in New York through three generations. A story of European proletarians becoming Americanized.

TULLY, JIM, 1888–1947

Circus Parade (Boni, 1927). Dramatic episodes from the life of a roustabout in a small circus. Stark realism.

Shanty Irish (Boni, 1928). Tales of two families who came from Ireland in 1846—brawls, drinking contests, sentiment.

VARDOULAKIS, MARY

Gold in the Streets (Dodd, 1945). A good-humored presentation of immigrant peasants from Crete in a Massachusetts mill town. The author shows Greek customs and also the slow Americanization of the group.

WARD, LEO RICHARD, 1893–

Holding Up the Hills (Sheed and Ward, 1941). Sketches of Catholic Irish in Iowa who maintain old customs and phrases.

WEBER, LENORA (MATTINGLY), 1895–

Mr. Gold and Her Neighborhood House (Little, 1933). The story of a settlement house worker who points a way toward constructive work for democracy.

WHITE, GEORGIA (ATWOOD) (DASCOMB ATWOOD, pseud.), 1882–

Free as the Wind (Liveright, 1942). A chronicle novel of a Dutch family in Michigan from about 1850 to 1917.

WILLIAMS, WILLIAM CARLOS, 1883–

The Build-Up (Random, 1952). See above, p. 107.

WILLIAMSON, THAMES ROSS, 1894–

Hunky (Coward, 1929). A psychological study of a Slavonian laborer who is passive and unskilled, and a social study of his bewildered existence in a big American city.

WINTHER, SOPHUS K., 1895–

Take All to Nebraska (Macmillan, 1936). See above, p. 13.

Mortgage Your Heart (Macmillan, 1937). See above, p. 45.

YEZIERSKA, ANZIA, 1885–

Hungry Hearts (Houghton, 1920). Ten stories of the immigrant's struggles in the New York ghetto. Intense, vivid, and appealing.

Children of Loneliness: Stories of Immigrant Life in America (Funk, 1923). Full of feeling, of bread hunger, and hunger for people. Also full of protest, disillusion, affection, and desire to co-operate.

AUTHOR INDEX

DATE DUE

APR 20 '67			
GAYLORD			PRINTED IN U.S.A.